T0377374

Ultra-Brief Cognitive Behavioral Interventions

Ultra-Brief Cognitive Behavioral Interventions showcases a new practice model to address both physical and psychological health issues in mental health and integrated care settings, utilizing focused interventions in brief treatment formats.

This unique text offers a toolkit of effective interventions and methods – including cognitive behavioral therapy (CBT) methods that can be used in a very brief time frame of 10–20 minutes – that can be quickly and efficiently applied to ameliorate specific symptoms. The 20 most common interventions in short-term therapy practiced in mental health and integrated care settings are illustrated in session transcriptions of the full course of focused therapy, with common presentations such as depression, anxiety and acute distress, pain, sleep problems, and weight problems.

This book prepares emerging and experienced counselors and therapists to provide short-term therapy for their clients and equips them with the necessary skills to meet the challenges facing mental health care today and in the future.

Len Sperry, MD, PhD, is a professor at Florida Atlantic University with extensive experience in mental health and integrated care settings. His 1000+ publications include: *Behavioral Health* and *Treating Chronic Medical Conditions: Cognitive Behavioral Strategies and Integrative Protocols*.

Vassilia Binensztok, PhD, is an instructor at Florida Atlantic University who has trained and coached mental health professionals in case conceptualization and cognitive behavioral therapy (CBT) approaches, with an emphasis on ultra-brief cognitive behavioral interventions.

Ultra-Brief Cognitive Behavioral Interventions

A New Practice Model for Mental Health and Integrated Care

LEN SPERRY AND VASSILIA BINENSZTOK

NEW YORK AND LONDON

First published 2019
by Routledge
52 Vanderbilt Avenue, New York, NY 10017

and by Routledge
2 Park Square, Milton Park, Abingdon, Oxon, OX14 4RN

Routledge is an imprint of the Taylor & Francis Group, an informa business

© 2019 Taylor & Francis

The right of Len Sperry and Vassilia Binensztok to be identified as authors of this work has been asserted by them in accordance with sections 77 and 78 of the Copyright, Designs and Patents Act 1988.

All rights reserved. No part of this book may be reprinted or reproduced or utilised in any form or by any electronic, mechanical, or other means, now known or hereafter invented, including photocopying and recording, or in any information storage or retrieval system, without permission in writing from the publishers.

Trademark notice: Product or corporate names may be trademarks or registered trademarks, and are used only for identification and explanation without intent to infringe.

Library of Congress Cataloging-in-Publication Data
Names: Sperry, Len, author. | Binensztok, Vassilia, author.
Title: Ultra-brief cognitive behavioral interventions : a new practice model for mental health and integrated care / Len Sperry and Vassilia Binensztok.
Description: New York, NY : Routledge, 2019. |
Includes bibliographical references and index.
Identifiers: LCCN 2018061587 (print) | LCCN 2019000431 (ebook) |
ISBN 9781351202473 (E-book) | ISBN 9780815384939 (hbk) |
ISBN 9780815385066 (pbk.) | ISBN 9781351202473 (ebk)
Subjects: | MESH: Cognitive Behavioral Therapy–methods |
Psychotherapy, Brief–methods | Mental Disorders–therapy
Classification: LCC RC489.C63 (ebook) |
LCC RC489.C63 (print) | NLM WM 425.5.C6 |
DDC 616.89/1425–dc23
LC record available at https://lccn.loc.gov/2018061587

ISBN: 978-0-8153-8493-9 (hbk)
ISBN: 978-0-8153-8506-6 (pbk)
ISBN: 978-1-351-20247-3 (ebk)

Typeset in Dante and Avenir
by Newgen Publishing UK

Printed in the United Kingdom
by Henry Ling Limited

Contents

Foreword	*vii*
Introduction	1

Part I   Ultra-Brief Interventions and the Cutting Edge of Clinical Practice — **5**

1 Ultra-Brief Interventions in Mental Health and Integrated Care Practice	7
2 20 Key Ultra-Brief Interventions in Mental Health and Integrated Care Practice	22
3 Brief Assessment in Mental Health and Integrated Care Practice	73
4 Pattern-Focused Therapy in Mental Health and Integrated Care Practice	100

Part II   Application of Ultra-Brief Interventions — **123**

5 Ultra-Brief Interventions with Depression	125
6 Ultra-Brief Interventions with Anxiety and Trauma	152
7 Ultra-Brief Interventions with Chronic Pain and Medication Misuse	184

vi Contents

8 Ultra-Brief Interventions with Sleep Problems 211

9 Ultra-Brief Interventions for Weight Problems 235

10 Ultra-Brief Interventions with Diabetes 261

Appendix A: Screening Instruments 293
Appendix B: Treatment Handouts 308
Index 330

Foreword

The rapid proliferation of integrated behavioral health, the systematic, team-based approach to prevention and treatment of medical, behavioral, and life-style problems, is a welcome change in our health care system. New positions for integrated behavioral health clinicians (BHC) in primary care and other medical settings presents an exciting new area of opportunity in the field. However, the demand for BHC positions exceeds the supply of adequately trained clinicians. Traditional psychotherapy programs leave clinicians woefully underprepared to meet the demands of integrated behavioral health delivery: physician consultations, team "huddles", brief patient assessment, and brief treatment. Clinicians must adapt to the emerging trends in health care delivery like the Patient-Centered Medical home, population health, value-based care, and also be able to incorporate behavioral health technologies into clinical practice to succeed in this new frontier.

Enter Len Sperry and Vassilia Binensztok's new book, *Ultra-Brief Cognitive Behavioral Interventions: A New Practice Model for Mental Health and Integrated Care*. This book expertly describes how mental health clinicians will effectively adapt to this changing health care landscape. The authors call it a "new practice model" that transforms nearly every aspect of traditional mental health practice – who, where, what, and how long therapeutic encounters will last – to meet the challenges of integrated behavioral health care delivery. They offer a resource for Evidence-Based Practice in primary care and related settings that will benefit newbies and seasoned clinicians.

The foundation of their approach lies in Evidence-Based Practice, which requires clinicians to keep abreast of best practices for common medical

viii Foreword

conditions such as diabetes, behavioral conditions such as depression and anxiety, and lifestyle behaviors such as nutrition and physical activity that underlie obesity and chronic, non-communicable disease. The beauty of this book is the way it combines guidelines, tools, and case studies to meet this daunting task. Pattern-focused therapy is a model that the clinician applies to identify the unique patterns of maladaptive behavior that drive the patient presenting problem. Case conceptualization includes a functional analysis based on screening tools consistent with population health and a clinical interview to home in on the presenting problem. Shared decision-making ensures effective patient engagement and optimal choice of treatment from the patient perspective. The book contains treatment guidelines for the most common conditions encountered in mental health and primary care settings such as depression and anxiety, pain and medication misuse, insomnia, and diabetes. Case studies with detailed clinician-patient transcripts illustrate the use of pattern-focused therapy for each specific condition.

The authors are attuned to the need to apply population health to identify and engage those at risk of poor clinical and cost outcomes that are common in value-based contracting. First, the authors incorporate patient feedback on progress and alignment with the treatment plan using simple but effective rating scales each session. Second, the importance of documenting patient progress with a focus on tracking treatment targets over time allows the clinician to be alert to lack of progress and return to the assessment phase. Third, the authors encourage them to incorporate emerging health technologies such as smartphone apps for behavior change, remote monitoring, and wearables, into the treatment plan. Health technologies feed additional data to the clinician on patient health status, from the number of steps walked per day to sleep duration, from self-reported depression to body mass index and blood pressure.

The purpose of this book is to provide the clinician with a recipe for effective and efficient assessment, a road map to initiating and evaluating treatment progress, and tools such as treatment handouts and screening measures to assist on the journey. "Ultra-brief" interventions will only be effective when based on a comprehensive approach that combines theory and practice. By utilizing this book, clinicians can gain competency in the many performance facets inherent in integrated behavioral health care delivery. As important, it will aid them in applying the model to other conditions and patient problems not covered in the book. This book will be an excellent addition to the supplemental readings for graduate courses on integrated behavioral health practice. Clinicians and students will find this book a practical approach to a new practice model that will develop or enhance their competencies on brief interventions. This brings us full circle back to Evidence-Based Practice, a key for professional success in the field through life-long learning.

Ronald O'Donnell, Ph.D., Clinical Professor,
Integrated Behavioral Health Program, Arizona State University

Introduction

Health care and mental health care are rapidly changing. These changes are rooted in the culture of accountability that pervades healthcare reform. Several challenges follow from these changes. Arguably, the primary challenge facing mental health professionals today is demonstrating competence in providing evidence-based interventions that are effective and tailored to client need and value.

A second challenge involves the significant shifts in the practice patterns and environments of psychotherapy practice in specialized mental health settings. The hallowed "50-minute hour" that has long characterized the practice of psychotherapy has been eliminated by a recent policy change. New billing codes for reimbursement now are based on 15-minute billing units, making the "45-minute hour," or less, the new norm. At the same time, it is predicted that within five years increasing numbers of mental health providers will be relocated to integrated primary care settings. This means that a very large percentage of clinic- and agency-based counselors and therapists will increasingly practice in health care settings as funding shifts to integrated care settings. Specialized mental health services will still continue but in fewer clinics and private practice settings. Still, amidst these daunting changes will be unique opportunities for therapists to succeed and thrive.

A third challenge is that some 70% of those seeking medical care have related psychological conditions such as generalized anxiety disorder, panic disorder, depression, bipolar disorder, and chronic pain, as well as troublesome health behaviors like sleep problems, nicotine use, sexual problems, and weight issues (Hunter, Goodie, Oordt, & Dobmeyer, 2009). These disorders and health behaviors are important since they can trigger, exacerbate, or

2 Introduction

perpetuate medical symptoms and impaired functioning. These same problematic health behaviors are also present in those seeking conventional psychotherapy. In the past, most psychotherapists simply ignored such health behaviors even though these complicate the client's psychological condition.

Research-based policy will inevitably "disallow" this common psychotherapist response. A recently published national study of the 40 million Americans insured by Blue Cross Blue Shield provides very compelling evidence for the new direction health and mental health care reform must take (Blue Cross Blue Shield Association, 2017). The study found that mental and substance use disorders significantly impact not only the physical health and well-being of Americans but also their longevity and productivity. Collectively, depression, anxiety and mood disorders, and substance disorders have the greatest impact on Americans' health compared to any health condition, followed by hypertension, diabetes, and high cholesterol.

A new kind of practice model is needed that addresses both physical and psychological health whether in specialized mental health or integrated settings. Reimbursement and employment will increasingly depend on mental health professionals, particularly therapists and counselors, having the requisite training and competence for this new practice model. Competence in utilizing focused interventions in brief treatment formats will predictably be a key component of this new model irrespective of whether services are provided in a mental health or integrated care setting. Presently, this training is virtually nonexistent in graduate and postgraduate counseling and psychotherapy programs.

This book is intended to equip both emerging and experienced counselors and therapists with the necessary skills to meet the challenges facing health/mental healthcare today and in the future. It focuses on several such interventions and how they can be incorporated in any practice setting irrespective of the therapist's therapeutic orientation, and the number and duration of sessions.

Unique to this book is a clinically useful description of what the new practice model and practice patterns will look like in specialized mental health and integrated care settings. It describes and illustrates 20 most common ultra-brief interventions: with descriptions, typical indications, treatment protocol, and case illustration of the intervention. To illustrate the changes in practice patterns, particularly in integrated care settings, there are session transcriptions of the full course of focused therapy that incorporates ultra-brief interventions with specific symptomatic presentation like depression, anxiety and acute distress, pain, sleep problems, and weight problems. An appendix includes a listing of the ten most commonly used brief screeners for functional assessment and monitoring of treatment, as well as 24 treatment handouts.

This book will be of most value to three audiences. The first is students and trainees in techniques courses in psychology, mental health counseling, and marital and family therapy programs who are preparing to meet the challenges of the changing health care landscape. The second is practicing therapists, whether psychologists, social workers, clinical mental health counselors, or marital and family therapists, who are or will soon be expected to practice in different ways and in different settings. A third audience is nurses, advanced nurse practitioners, physicians and medical students in primary care settings who wish to increase their understanding and competence in dealing with the behavioral health components of their patients' medical issues.

References

Blue Cross Blue Shield Association (2017). *Blue Cross Blue Shield Association report finds link between a population's health and a growing economy, higher incomes and lower unemployment* (March 29). Retrieved from www.bcbs.com/news/press-releases/blue-cross-blue-shield-association-report-finds-link-between-populations-health

Hunter, C.L., Goodie, J.L., Oordt, M.S., & Dobmeyer, A.C. (2009). *Integrated behavioral health in primary care: Step-by-step guidance for assessment and intervention.* Washington, DC: American Psychological Association.

Part I

Ultra-Brief Interventions and the Cutting Edge of Clinical Practice

Ultra-Brief Interventions in Mental Health and Integrated Care Practice

1

Today, mental health and behavioral health clinicians face several challenges brought on by the pervasive changes in health care and the need for a new practice model. As noted in the Introduction, these challenges include: (1) significant shifts in the current practice patterns and the demise of the "50-minute hour;" (2) that the majority of those seeking medical care have related psychological conditions that trigger, exacerbate, or perpetuate their medical conditions. If these patients were to seek conventional psychotherapy, such conditions would likely be ignored by therapists, which might complicate their psychological or medical conditions or both; and (3) that reimbursement and even employment is increasingly dependent on mental health clinicians, particularly psychotherapists, having the requisite training and competence for this new practice model. To meet these challenges, this book advocates for a new model of practice that addresses both the physical and psychological health of clients in both mental health and integrated care settings. Consistent with this new model is short-term therapy consisting of very brief sessions that necessitate the use of focused interventions, which we call ultra-brief interventions.

This chapter begins by describing published predictions for the future of mental health practice in mental health settings. Next, it introduces integrated care settings as a viable practice option for mental health clinicians. Since this option is not well known, a typical day in the life of such clinicians, as a member of the health care team, is described. Then evidence-based practice is described, along with ethical considerations. Finally, it describes ultra-brief interventions and their role in both mental health and integrated care settings.

8 Ultra-Brief Interventions

A New Model of Mental Health Practice in Mental Health Settings

Several predictions have been published about the future of mental health and psychotherapy practice that suggest a new model of mental health practice is emerging in mental health settings. This section discusses three sets of predictions and briefly addresses a key feature of the new model: treatment and session duration.

The first set of predictions is an empirically-based group of prognostications (Norcross, Pfund, & Prochaska, 2013). Norcross and associates have been conducting Delphi polls on future trends in psychotherapy every ten years for the past three decades. Most notable has been the uncanny accuracy and specificity of their predictions. In 2012 they empaneled 70 psychotherapy experts to forecast psychotherapy trends in the next decade. The polling focused on five areas: theoretical orientations, therapeutic interventions, psychotherapist background, therapy formats, and forecast scenarios (Norcross et al., 2013).

In terms of theoretical orientations, they predicted that mindfulness, cognitive behavioral, integrative, and multicultural approaches would increase the most, while Jungian therapy, classical psychoanalysis, and transactional analysis were expected to decline the most. That prediction for transactional analysis has already been borne out in the USA. With regard to therapeutic interventions, they forecasted that technological, self-change, skill-building, and relationship-fostering interventions would be most utilized. In terms of psychotherapist background, they expected that master's degree practitioners would be the dominant providers of therapy services. Regarding therapy formats, they predicted that internet programs and telephone therapy would increase dramatically. Forecast scenarios with the highest likelihood centered on expansion of telepsychology, evidence-based practice, and psychopharmacotherapy. Finally, they concluded that four themes were responsible for driving these trends: technology, economy, evidence-based treatment, and innovative ideas and practices (Norcross, et al, 2013).

In a nutshell, here is their overall prediction of the future of psychotherapy:

> In 2022, we expect briefer episodes of individual, group, and couple treatments increasingly conducted by master's-level professionals involving evidence-based methods and relationships; theoretical formulations and clinical methods more associated with the cognitive, integrative, multicultural, and mindfulness orientations; and progressively more on the Internet, smart phones, and social networking. (Norcross et al., 2013, p. 369)

That same year, Wade Silverman, then editor of the journal, *Psychotherapy*, predicted four trends in psychotherapy's future. He described the first trend as the "new diversity." By this he meant that therapy would be identified by levels of technological sophistication in both providers and clients rather than by race, ethnicity, or sexual orientation. The second trend he foresaw was the expanding use of the technology itself, encompassing social networking and other online communication platforms. The third trend would be the development of new forms of health care service delivery that would reward successful efforts in disease treatment and prevention, be evidence-based, require documentation of clinical outcomes, and focus research on discovering successful treatments. His fourth trend is the emerging markets for consumers interested in performance enhancement and quality of life (Silverman, 2013).

Three years before, Thomason (2010) identified evidence-based practice and empirically supported treatments as the main trend influencing the future of psychotherapy practice. He made several specific predictions about evidence-based psychotherapy practice. Most notable were that evidence-based practice and non-evidence-based psychotherapy would diverge. Eventually, only evidence-based practice would be reimbursed and covered by liability insurance, while other forms would not. He also predicted that psychotherapy would become briefer and more integrated into primary care practice (Thomason, 2010).

Common to all three sets of predictions is that the practice of psychotherapy and mental health would be briefer, evidence-based, and account for health issues or be integrated in health care settings. Accordingly, this chapter reflects these three common predictions. In fact, this entire book elaborates clinical practice consistent with these predictions.

Treatment and Session Duration

The Current Procedural Terminology (CPT) codes for billing insurers for mental health services including Medicare and Medicaid took effect on January 1, 2013. Before then the CPT code 90807 was used to bill for the 50-minute hour. There is no longer a code for 50-minute sessions. Instead, there is the CPT code 90834 for coding 45-minute sessions. Reportedly, the Centers for Medicare and Medicaid Services made these code changes to more accurately represent the way clinicians provided services. However, clinicians feared that reducing session length would reduce treatment effectiveness and that insurers would use the changes to justify reducing reimbursement rates (Miller, 2012). While research has not borne out the loss of treatment effectiveness, reimbursement has been reduced.

10 Ultra-Brief Interventions

Table 1.1 Treatment Duration

long-term therapy	longer than 20 sessions
short-term therapy	5–12 sessions
very short-term therapy	1–3 sessions

Table 1.2 Session Duration

conventional therapy sessions	50 minutes
brief sessions with focused interventions	30 minutes
brief sessions with ultra-brief interventions	10–20 minutes

Besides the CPT code changes, other previously mentioned factors have contributed to the demise of the 50-minute hour, and expectations to integrate physical and psychological health concerns in mental health settings. The result is that a new model of mental health practice in mental health settings is emerging. Some of the more telling indicators of this new model involve treatment duration and session duration. Instead of the usual 12–20 psychotherapy sessions as the norm, the expected duration of treatment will more likely be four to six therapeutic encounters. Instead of 50-minute sessions, the length of the therapeutic encounter will last for 15–30 minutes. These changes were predicted by Nicholas Cummings (Cummings & O'Donahue, 2008). Over the past 30 years, Cummings and others have advocated that psychotherapists should be able to assess, diagnose, and begin treatment with clients within 15 minutes, just like physicians (Thomason, 2010). We would add that ultra-brief interventions can be delivered in 10–20 minutes.

These durations are surprisingly similar to those from the Delphi polling results. The consensus among the 70 experts polled was that by 2022, treatment duration will no longer be unlimited sessions or even 20 sessions. The expectation is that short-term therapy (5–12 sessions) and very short-term therapy (1–3 sessions) will increase, while long-term therapy (longer than 20 sessions) will significantly decline (Norcross, Pfund, & Prochaska, 2013 p. 367).

Table 1.1 and Table 1.2 provide summaries of these various projections.

Outcomes Assessment and Technology

Incorporating clinical outcome measures is an essential component of the new practice model (Meier, 2015). The challenge will be for clinicians to not only utilize clinical outcome measures and progress monitoring, but to incorporate the feedback from these measures to modify treatment. A related challenge will be to document and report such clinical outcomes. Without measurable outcomes, psychotherapy can deteriorate to a friendly interchange between clinician and client that is costly, ineffective, inappropriate, and likely unethical.

Another component of the new model is the use of alternate formats, i.e., technology, for the delivery of mental health services in mental health settings. For instance, a meta-analysis of several internet studies supported the adoption of online psychological interventions as a legitimate therapeutic activity. In fact, no differences were found between face-to-face and internet interventions (Barak, Hen, Boniel-Nissim, & Shapira, 2008). Even with these promising findings, internet interventions will require further research (Cottone, 2015). Because of the press of time, client need, and the availability of alternate delivery formats, ultra-brief interventions will inevitably be incorporated in both face-to-face and alternate delivery formats in mental health settings and possibly in integrated care settings.

A New Model of Mental Health Practice in Integrated Care Settings

Probably the most significant change predicted for mental health practice is that much of it is likely to occur in integrated primary care settings. Here, the mental health provider will function as part of a team that includes, at a minimum, a physician, a nurse, and a mental health provider in the role of behavioral health consultant. At first, being such a team member may seem alien to mental health clinicians, but there are several advantages. For some, a major advantage will be the focus on prevention and not just pathology. For others, there is little or no need to seek authorization for treatment or provide extensive documentation for mental health services provided. For many, working as a salaried member of a team beats competing with other mental health professionals for Health Maintenance Organization (HMO) panels and insurance reimbursement. When practice in mental health settings is compared to practice in integrated care settings, a therapist can expect less paperwork and less stress than in mental health settings, as well as more variety and increased knowledge, especially about health and medical conditions (Noonan, 2018).

However, the starting point for our discussion about the new model of integrated care begins with the increasing need for mental health services in primary care. This section begins with such statistics. Next, is a brief overview of integrated care and health care teams. Then, the behavioral health

12   Ultra-Brief Interventions

consultants' (BHC) job and role functions are briefly described. Finally, the unique way in which they practice is illustrated in a typical work day.

Need for Integrated Care

Health care expenditure data shows that 5 percent of the population is responsible for nearly half of all health care spending (National Institute for Health Care Management, 2012). These are individuals who suffer from multiple, chronic medical conditions such as diabetes, hypertension, and heart failure. Unfortunately, many become depressed and anxious because of their health problems, which exacerbates their medical conditions and leads to more health care expenditure.

The reality is that there is no shortage of mental health needs among patients in primary care settings. Table 1.3 summarizes this reality. Fortunately, the addition of behavioral health providers – also referred to as behavioral health consultants and behavioral health clinicians in this book – on the integrated care team can effectively address both mental health conditions as well as the common behavioral component of medical conditions called treatment nonadherence, i.e., failure to take medication or follow a lifestyle change prescription, such as lose weight, increase exercise, or reduce salt intake, which worsens or complicates the medical conditions.

Table 1.3   Need for Mental Health Services in Primary Care Settings*

70% of primary care visits are because of patients' psychological problems : anxiety, panic, depression, or stress

80% of patients with medically unexplained symptoms receive psychological treatment by a primary care physician

50% of all primary care visits involve chronic medical conditions for which there is nearly always a behavioral component

10% will follow up on a primary care referral to a mental health provider if it is co-located (in the same building); the rest will not

70% of patients' clinical depression remains undetected by a primary care physician

90% of individuals who die by suicide had a mental disorder

40% had a primary care visit in the month before their suicide

*Adapted from APA Center for Psychology and Health (2014).

The Integrated Care Team

Primary care providers (PCP) are usually a physician, MD or DO, although they may also be advanced practice nurses (APRN). In the standard primary care model, the PCP provides treatment that is supported by nurses and medical assistants (MA). In the "new" primary care model, called integrated primary care, the health care team provides treatment. This team consists of the PCP, RNs, MAs, and a BHC. A dietician or nutritionist may be another member of the team.

The goal of providing mental health services in primary care settings is threefold: (1) increase the patient's health care experience, including quality and satisfaction, (2) improve the health of the overall population by prevention, and (3) reduce health care costs. Providing mental health services in integrated settings results in decreased cost, largely because of reduced emergency room and hospital admission expenses. Because it also identifies undiagnosed conditions and concerns, patients in integrated care settings are more likely to receive necessary mental health services.

Continuum of Integrated Primary Care Services

Health policy analysts describe a continuum of integration of mental health services, which range from partially integrated to fully integrated. It consists of three basic models. In the Coordinated Model, the BHC is an externally employed and housed professional who partners with a specific primary care practice. In the Co-Located Model, the BHC is onsite and provides mental health services to selected patients utilizing the conventional psychotherapy model. In the Fully Integrated Model, the BHC is a full-time provider within an integrated health team in a primary care practice. The first two models are also known as partially fully integrated, in contrast to the third which is fully integrated.

Job Description and Intervention Competencies

BHCs are critical to the integrated care team because of their expertise in effectively providing a broad spectrum of services with the aim of early identification and quick resolution based on brief diagnostic evaluations, functional assessments, and risk assessments. They regularly provide brief behavioral and cognitive behavioral interventions for patients. They also are responsible for

14 Ultra-Brief Interventions

triaging patients with severe or high-risk behavioral health problems and referring them to community resources or specialty mental health services. BHCs also provide consults with PCPs and other team members. It is common for integrated clinics to employ at least two BHCs. One primarily provides brief mental health care to patients while the other provides direct consultation to PCPs, other team members, and patients typically in psychoeducation groups, as well as meetings with family members to better support the patient's treatment plan and compliance.

In our graduate program at Florida Atlantic University, we teach trainees to practice in the "very brief" time frames of integrated care. At a minimum, students are expected to master or achieve competence with 12 ultra-brief therapeutic interventions in the course of a semester. These interventions include:

(1) Assertive communication is a method of expressing emotions, opinions, and needs clearly and appropriately.

(2) Behavioral activation is a method for breaking cycles of inactivity and avoidance by substituting activating behaviors. Used with depression and other avoidance conditions.

(3) Behavioral self-analysis is a model for analyzing a situation in ABC terms: A is the antecedent or activating event that precedes behavior, B, and is followed by a consequence, C, or effect.

(4) Controlled breathing is a method to slow breathing and restore regulated breathing rhythms to reduce stress-related symptoms.

(5) Emotional first aid is a method to treat emotional wounds as they arise, without the direct aid of a mental health professional.

(6) Habit reversal is a method to reduce tics, stuttering, hair-pulling, and skin-picking by engaging in a competing response that suppresses the unwanted behavior.

(7) Mindfulness is a method of focusing on the present without judgment, which results in reduced stress, anxiety, mood symptoms, and mindless action.

(8) Motivational interviewing is a method of resolving ambivalent feelings and insecurities in order to find the internal motivation needed to change one's behavior.

(9) Self-monitoring is a method of recording one's behavior as the basis for changing or regulating it.

(10) Stimulus control is a method for identifying factors (stimuli) that precede a behavior to be changed and then taking steps to alter the factors to bring about the desired result.

(11) Strategies for improving treatment adherence include motivational interviewing, self-monitoring, and behavioral self-analysis.

(12) Thought stopping is a method to interrupt and replace distressing, ruminative thoughts.

A Day in the Life of a Mental Health Clinician in an Integrated Care Setting

Julia is a graduate of a master's program in clinical mental health counseling during which she completed a supervised internship in an integrated care setting. She has been licensed for the past year and employed as a BHC in a fully integrated primary care clinic. Its clientele includes a wide range of adult patients, many of whom experience one or more chronic medical conditions. She is the clinic's only BHC and provides both direct therapy services and consultation. Julia finds her position to be both challenging and rewarding. Here is how she spent a typical day contributing her expertise, including ultra-brief interventions, to her health team at the clinic.

Morning

The day begins with a "huddle" (team members standing in a circle) in which the team reviews scheduled appointments, especially high-risk patients. After that she follows up with two scheduled BHC appointments. The first patient is a 67-year-old married male with a long-standing diagnosis of chronic obstructive pulmonary disease and depression. Julia reviews the behavioral activation ultra-brief intervention she imitated with the patient at their last appointment week and engages the patient in a discussion of his activity level over the past week. The second is a new patient, a 44-year-old divorced female with a cardiac arrhythmia and panic symptoms, who is seen together with the PCP. Julia instructs the patient in controlled breathing so that she can better control her anxiety. After that, one of the nurses asks her for help with a hypertensive (high blood pressure) patient with medication and diet noncompliance issues. Next, the PCP gives her a "warm hand-off" (in-person referral). The PCP briefly introduces Julia to a 51-year-old male patient with diabetes who continually ruminates about becoming blind as a complication of his medical condition. Julia conducts a brief diagnostic evaluation, teaches the patient thought stopping, and sets up a follow-up appointment in three days with him for short-term therapy. Next, she sees

16 Ultra-Brief Interventions

a patient for a 30-minute therapy session who is struggling with severe neck pain, insomnia, and posttraumatic stress symptoms following a traffic accident two months ago. While they have made some progress, Julia decides she will present the patient in the team's case conference on Wednesday and make the recommendation that the patient be referred for specialty mental health treatment. Just before lunch she has a curbside consult (quick meeting in the hall) with the PCP about a diagnostic issue.

Afternoon

Her first scheduled BHC appointment is at 1:30 p.m. This is her fifth follow-up meeting with a cardiac patient with moderate anxiety symptoms. Julia finds that the patient is now nearly symptom-free because of the successful use of stimulus control and assertive communication in the context of very short-term therapy. After that is a warm hand-off from the PCP for a brief diagnostic and risk assessment. Julia sees another two BHC scheduled patients and does a curbside consult with the PCP. Her last consult for the day is with the nurse practitioner who wants Julia to help her with a patient with a chronic pulmonary condition who is noncompliant with medication and physical therapy appointments. In the process she engages the patient in increasing change talk using motivational interviewing. Afterwards, Julia and the nurse discuss a follow-up plan.

Evidence-based Practice in Mental Health and Integrated Care Practice

The stated goal of nearly all graduate mental health programs is for trainees to inform clinical decisions with research. Unfortunately, relatively few programs can claim that they achieve this goal. The reality is that while many programs require one or more research course, seldom are trainees taught the requisite skills for using research clinically. Statistics and research method courses are necessary conditions for informing clinical practice, however, they are not sufficient conditions for change. Specific training is needed in the requisite skills of critical thinking in using research as a basis for clinical decisions, i.e., the capacity to effectively "translate" research into clinical practice. Developments in the past two decades have culminated in what has come to be called evidence-based practice (EBP) to address such transactional issues. This section focuses on evidence-based treatment and EBP, which are core features of the new practice model.

Essentially, EBP is the integration of three elements: (1) interventions proven to have a high degree of evidence such as research support; (2) that are individualized to client need, expectations and values; and (3) are expertly planned and implemented by a trained clinician. When these three elements are present, evidence informs clinical decision-making and practice (Williams, Patterson, & Edwards, 2014).

EBP was originated by Sackett and colleagues (1996), formally defined by the Institute of Medicine in 2001 and then adopted by the American Psychological Association (2006). The basic intent of EBP is to provide the best individualized treatment that is both effective and accountable, i.e., measurable and reportable. It should be noted that the terms "evidence-based treatments" and "empirically supported treatments" are commonly confused with EBP. While both of these have some or much research support, they are not individualized to a specific client, nor are they necessarily applied expertly by a clinician.

Because Division 12 of the American Psychological Association promotes and provides a list of empirically supported treatments, some clinicians mistakenly assume that the "evidence" element of EBP "requires" the use of such empirically supported treatments. That was never the intention of the originators of EBP (Sackett, et al, 1996). In fact, they delineated two kinds of evidence: *external evidence*, which is quality empirical research, and *internal evidence* or clinical expertise, which involves gathering information from the client or couple and then tailoring the external evidence to a specific client or couple. Thus, an empirically supported treatment may be chosen, but it is "the ethical responsibility of all clinicians regardless of orientation to be guided by current empirical research as well as their own specific areas of competence, experience, and limitations when making treatment recommendations" (Sookman, 2015, p. 1295).

Is ethics really involved in EBP? Actually, there is an inseparable link between EBP and professional ethics. To many, practicing ethically means insuring confidentiality and informed consent while avoiding conflicts of interest. While important, these considerations are secondary to the core ethical values of beneficence and non-maleficence which are essential considerations in clinical decision-making. Accordingly, ethically-sensitive clinical decisions are based on whether a treatment is safe, effective, and appropriate for a given individual with a specified concern or need (Sperry, 2018).

Historically, it was common for clinicians to make treatment decisions based on their espoused orientation and experience rather than on evidence

18 Ultra-Brief Interventions

that the treatment provided would be safe, effective, and appropriate. That began to change in the early 1990s with the appearance of evidence-based practice (Margolin et al., 2015). As originally described, evidence-based practice is a process of inquiry whose purpose is to help therapists and their clients make important decisions about treatment. It is a process whereby clinicians decide which interventions to provide by considering research evidence, their clinical experience and expertise, client preferences and values, professional ethics, situational circumstances, and the availability of resources (Gambrill, 2011).

Today, only a limited number of therapeutic approaches report empirical support. One practical implication is that some of these approaches will lose eligibility for third-party reimbursement given the increasing demand for utilizing evidence-based interventions. Another implication is that only a few of these approaches would provide sufficient external evidence to warrant being incorporated in clinical decision-making.

Despite increasing expectation by third-party payers for EBP, there remains an anti-empirical research bias and antipathy towards EBP among some practicing clinicians (Lilienfeld et al., 2013). Fortunately, a new generation of therapy trainees is emerging that is eager for scientifically informed treatment interventions. More than ever before, trainees are asking: "'What does the research say about that treatment approach or intervention approach in addressing problem X?' Their assumption is that there should be research to support what we do" (Williams, Patterson, & Edwards, 2014, p. 206). Furthermore, trainees are "most motivated to learn EBP when the EBP skills help them with their own clients" (Williams et al., 2014, p. 236).

Whether experienced or emerging, clinicians who succeed in either specialized mental health or integrated care settings are the ones who embrace EBP as well as ultra-brief interventions.

Ultra-Brief Interventions in Mental Health and Integrated Care Practice

Irrespective of how therapists think about or conceptualize a case and therapeutically respond, clinicians will need a new set of effective interventions or methods that can be quickly and effectively applied to ameliorate specific symptoms. Ultra-brief interventions are such methods. These interventions include specific cognitive behavioral methods that can be utilized in a very brief, i.e., ultra-brief, time frame of 10–20 minutes. They include behavioral activation, exposure, breath retraining, cognitive replacement, and more.

Chapter 2 provides detailed instruction on 20 of these interventions. These ultra-brief interventions are already being successfully taught in some university programs to prepare their mental health students and interns for working in both mental health and integrative care settings.

The professional literature distinguishes "ultra-brief treatment protocols" from "ultra-brief interventions." The designation "ultra-brief treatment protocols" (Otto & Hofmann, 2010) refers to the number of sessions of treatment, which we have called session duration. Ultra-brief treatment protocols are typically five sessions as compared to the customary delivery of psychotherapies like CBT that can range from 12–20 sessions (Otto et al., 2012). In primary care settings, short-term therapy is often delivered in six to eight individual or group sessions, instead of 16–18 individual or group sessions in conventional mental health settings. Of note is that this such short-term therapy is more suitable for primary care settings and more acceptable for patients (Schene et al., 2014). In contrast, "ultra-brief interventions" refer to the use of very brief (10–20 minutes or less) interventions within a specific session.

Most of the ultra-brief interventions as described in this book have their origins in Behavior Therapy or in CBT. Some are rooted in Cognitive Therapy, Adlerian Therapy, or other approaches. Whatever their origins, these interventions can easily be incorporated in clinical practice, irrespective of the clinician's theoretical orientation, and whether or not the clinician provides long-term or very short-term therapy.

Concluding Note

This chapter began with predictions about the future of mental health practice, and the emergence of a new practice model. Then it described the two settings in which this model is and will be practiced, for which ultra-brief interventions are well suited. Whether in specialized mental health settings when the number of sessions is limited, and time frames are shorter, or in primary care settings, these interventions can be easily incorporated with any therapeutic orientation to achieve effective therapeutic outcomes.

Subsequent chapters in Part I include Chapter 2, which describes and illustrates the application of 20 key ultra-brief interventions. Chapter 3 overviews the assessment process in the new practice model. It incorporates personality assessment, diagnostic assessment, and functional assessment. Chapter 4 overviews Pattern-Focused Therapy, an approach that is compatible with the new practice model and the need for briefer sessions of short-term

20 Ultra-Brief Interventions

and very short-term therapy. It provides an effective therapeutic context for the delivery of ultra-brief interventions.

References

American Psychological Association. (2006). Evidence-based practice in psychology: APA presidential task force on evidence-based practice. *American Psychologist*, 61(4), 271–285.

APA Center for Psychology and Health (2014). *Briefing Series on the Role of Psychology in Health Care*: Primary Care. January. Retrieved from www.apa.org/health/briefs/primary-care.pdf

Barak, A., Hen, L., Boniel-Nissim, M., & Shapira, N.A. (2008). A comprehensive review and a meta-analysis of the effectiveness of internet-based psychotherapeutic interventions. *Journal of Technology in Human Services*, 26(2–4), 109–160.

Cottone, R. (2015). The end of counseling as we know it. *Counseling Today*, 57(10), 49–53.

Cummings, N.A., & O'Donahue, W.T. (2008). *Eleven blunders that cripple psychotherapy in America*. New York, NY: Routledge.

Curtis, R., & Christian, E. (2012). *Integrated care: Applying theory to practice*. New York, NY: Routledge.

Gambrill, E. (2011). Evidence-based practice and the ethics of discretion. *Journal of Social Work*, 11(1), 26–48.

Lilienfeld, S.O., Ritschel, L.A., Lynn, S.J., Cautin, R.L., & Latzman, R.D. (2013). Why many clinical psychologists are resistant to evidence-based practice: Root causes and constructive remedies. *Clinical Psychology Review*, 33, 883–900.

Margolin, G., Shapiro, L.S., & Miller, K. (2015). Ethics in couple and family psychotherapy. In J. Sadler, B. Fulford, & C. Van Staden (Ed.), *Oxford handbook of psychiatric ethics, Vol. 2.* (pp. 1306–1314). New York, NY: Oxford University Press.

Meier, S. (2015). *Incorporating progress monitoring and outcome measures into counseling and psychotherapy: A primer*. New York, NY: Oxford.

Miller, D. (2012). The end of the 50-minute hour?: Will the new CPT codes change mental health practices? *Psychology Today*. December 2, 2012. Retrieved from www.psychologytoday.com/us/blog/shrink-rap-today/201212/the-end-the-50-minute-hour

National Institute for Health Care Management Research and Educational Foundation (2012 July). *The Concentration of Health Care Spending NIHCM Foundation Data Brief.* Retrieved from www.nihcm.org/pdf/DataBrief3%20Final.pdf

Noonan, D. (2018). Integrated care: Perspectives from a behavioral health consultant. *Psychiatric News*, 53(15). https://doi.org/10.1176/appi.pn.2018.8b11

Norcross, J.C., Pfund, R.A., & Prochaska, J.O. (2013). Psychotherapy in 2022: A Delphi poll on its future. *Professional Psychology: Research and Practice*, 44(5), 363–370.

Otto, M., Tolin, D.F., Nations, K.R., Utschig, A.C., Rothbaum, B.O., Hofmann, S.G., & Smits, J.A. (2012). Five sessions and counting: Considering ultra-brief treatment for panic disorder. *Depression and Anxiety*, 29(6), 465–470.

Otto, W., & Hofmann, S.G. (2010). *Avoiding treatment failures in the anxiety disorders.* New York, NY: Springer.

Sackett, D., Richardson, W., Rosenberg, W., Haynes, R., & Brian, S. (1996). Evidence based medicine: What it is and what it isn't. *British Medical Journal, 312,* 71–72.

Schene, A.H., Baas, K.D., Koeter, M., Lucassen, P., Bockting, C.L.H., Wittkampf, K. F., … & Huyser, J. (2014). Brief cognitive behavioural therapy compared to optimised general practitioners? Care for depression: A randomised trial. *Journal of Depression and Anxiety,* S2(1), 1–9. doi:10.4172/2167-1044.S2-001

Silverman, W.H. (2013). The future of psychotherapy: One editor's perspective. *Psychotherapy,* 50(4), 484–489.

Sookman, D. (2015). Ethical practice of cognitive behavior therapy. In J. Sadler, B. Fulford, & C. Van Staden (Ed.), *Oxford handbook of psychiatric ethics, Vol. 2.* (pp. 1293–1305). New York, NY: Oxford University Press.

Sperry, L. (2018). Mindfulness, soulfulness, and spiritual development in spiritually oriented psychotherapy. *Spirituality in Clinical Practice,* 5(4), 225–230.

Williams, L., Patterson, J., & Edwards, T.M. (2014). *Clinician's guide to research methods in family therapy: Foundations of evidence-based practice.* New York, NY: Guilford.

Thomason, T.C. (2010). The trend toward evidence-based practice and the future of psychotherapy. *American Journal of Psychotherapy,* 64(1), 29–38.

20 Key Ultra-Brief Interventions in Mental Health and Integrated Care Practice

2

This chapter focuses on 20 common ultra-brief interventions that we have found to be useful – and even essential – in everyday counseling practice. We describe and illustrate each of these interventions in sufficient detail so that you can try them in your practice. As we indicated in Chapter 1, these can rather easily be incorporated in a counselor's practice irrespective of the counselor's preferred theoretical orientation.

The chapter begins with a brief overview of these 20 ultra-brief interventions that are effective in everyday clinical practice. Definitions and indications are briefly described in Tables 2.1 and 2.2. Then, each is described and illustrated. A common format is followed in each of these interventions. It includes the following six elements:

Defining It: The entry begins with a definition of the intervention.

How It Works: The intervention is described in terms of its origins and mechanism of change.

When to Use It: The common uses or indications for which it is likely to be successful as well as uses when it is unlikely to be successful.

How to Use It: The step-by-step protocol for applying the intervention.

Example of How to Use It: A case example illustrating the use of this protocol in everyday counseling practice.

Learning More About It: Some key resources.

Table 2.1   List of Interventions and Definitions

Intervention	Definition
Assertive Communication	A behavioral intervention for teaching individuals to express emotions, opinions, and needs clearly and appropriately.
Behavioral Activation	A behavioral intervention to help individuals break cycles of inactivity and avoidance by substituting activating behaviors.
Behavioral Experiments	A behavioral intervention to help individuals test a belief or prediction using planned activities in a real-world setting.
Behavioral Rehearsal	A behavioral intervention to help individuals identify and practice behaviors that can be useful and appropriate in social settings.
Behavioral Self-Analysis	A model for teaching individuals to analyze behaviors and situations in ABC terms: (A) is the antecedent or activating event that precedes behavior (B) and is followed by a consequence (C) or effect.
Controlled Breathing	A behavioral intervention used to slow an individual's breathing and restore regulated breathing rhythms to reduce stress-related symptoms.
Cognitive Defusion	A mindfulness-based method for distancing oneself from troublesome thoughts, rather than disputing or restructuring them.
Cognitive Disputation	A cognitive behavioral intervention that uses logic to help individuals identify the irrationality of their maladaptive thoughts.
Distress Tolerance Training	A cognitive behavioral technique that teaches individuals the ability to tolerate distressing and painful emotions without attempting to change or stop them.
Emotional First Aid	A behavioral intervention that teaches individuals to treat their emotional wounds as they arise, without the direct aid of a mental health professional.

(*continued*)

Table 2.1   (*Cont.*)

Intervention	Definition
Goal Setting	A social-cognitive intervention used to help clients improve self-management skills and build self-efficacy by setting realistic goals.
Habit Reversal	A behavioral intervention used to reduce tics, stuttering, hair-pulling, and skin-picking by engaging in a competing response that suppresses the unwanted behavior.
Harm Reduction	A model that focuses on decreasing adverse health, social, and lifestyle consequences without requiring abstinence from substances.
Mindfulness	A technique used, either as a meditative practice or as a component of another therapeutic intervention focusing on the present without judgment, which results in reduced stress, anxiety, mood symptoms, and mindless action.
Problem-Solving Training	A behavioral intervention used to teach individuals skills needed to cope with distressing situations.
Push-Button Technique	An Adlerian intervention that helps individuals alleviate negative feeling states by replacing them with more positive feelings.
Relapse Prevention	A technique that teaches individuals to maintain sobriety while coping with everyday stressors and temptations.
Relaxation Training	A behavioral intervention that uses different techniques to help individuals to induce relaxation and alleviate stress.
Stimulus Control	A behavioral intervention for identifying factors (stimuli) that precede a behavior to be changed and then taking steps to alter the factors to bring about the desired result.
Thought Stopping	A behavioral intervention used to interrupt and replace distressing, ruminative thoughts.

Table 2.2 When to Use Interventions

Intervention	Indications
Assertive Communication	Stress, bullying, anxiety, depression, eating disorders, substance abuse, self-esteem, and autism spectrum disorders.
Behavioral Activation	Depression and avoidance conditions.
Behavioral Experiments	Depression, anxiety, and limiting thoughts and beliefs.
Behavioral Rehearsal	Rehearsal of skills including assertive communication, social skills, etc.
Behavioral Self-Analysis	Depression, anxiety, medical conditions.
Controlled Breathing	Panic, stress, anxiety, chronic pain, insomnia, and headaches.
Cognitive Defusion	Depression, anxiety, substance abuse, eating disorders, and impulse control disorders.
Cognitive Disputation	Depression, anxiety, eating disorders, substance abuse, and marital distress.
Distress Tolerance Training	Personality disorders, substance use disorders, depression, anxiety disorders, and eating disorders.
Emotional First Aid	Negative emotional states from difficulties and setbacks including rejection, loneliness, failure, loss, guilt, rumination, and crises.
Goal Setting	Weight loss, medication management, adherence to treatment plans, exercise, smoking cessation, etc.
Habit Reversal	Tic disorders, hair-pulling disorder, skin-picking disorder, stuttering, and habits like nail biting, teeth grinding, scratching, and oral-digital habits.
Harm Reduction	Substance use.
Mindfulness	Chronic pain, medical problems, anxiety disorders, mood disorders, eating disorders, substance abuse, and personality disorders.
Problem-Solving Training	Impulsivity, aggression, relational problems, anger, antisocial behaviors, depression, anxiety, and social anxiety.
Push-Button Technique	Depression.
Relapse Prevention	Substance use, eating disorders, overeating, smoking, and self-harm.
Relaxation Training	Anxiety, hyperactivity, phobias, insomnia, asthma attacks, migraine headaches, and chronic pain.
Stimulus Control	Health-related behaviors, sleep disorders.
Thought Stopping	Depression, panic, generalized anxiety, tobacco use, drug and alcohol use, and body dysmorphic disorder.

26 Ultra-Brief Interventions

Assertive Communication

Defining It

Assertive communication is a behavioral intervention for teaching individuals to express their emotions, opinions, and needs both clearly and appropriately.

How It Works

Being assertive in communication means that an individual knows the difference between four types of communication: assertive, aggressive, passive aggressive, and passive. It is also the capacity to say no, to make requests, and to respond and give feedback with a reasonable degree of confidence. Assertive communication teaches individuals how to speak to others in a manner that is calm and appropriate to the situation, while remaining firm and communicating their needs. Clients are taught the four types of communication and their impact. By learning how to express their needs using assertive verbal and nonverbal social skills, and practicing through therapeutic role-play, clients become better equipped to build healthier relationships and improve their self-esteem.

When to Use It

Assertive communication can be used alone or as an adjunct to other interventions. It is useful for clients presenting with stress, bullying, anxiety, depression, eating disorders, substance abuse, and autism spectrum disorders. Additionally, it is useful in increasing self-esteem in sexual-abuse survivors and improving interpersonal skills in clients with disabilities. Assertiveness communication is not recommended for clients whose difficulty communicating arises from a mood state. In that case, the mood state should be treated. Providers should also be aware of views of assertiveness in non-Western cultures. Some clients may warrant adjunct techniques to assertiveness training, such as cognitive restructuring or motivational interviewing.

How to Use It

1. The provider begins by assessing the client's existing assertiveness skills, and any obstacles that may hinder the client's communication patterns. Obstacles may include significant others, social isolation, and the client's personality style. The provider completes this assessment by asking questions about times the client has difficulty communicating or fails to get a desired response from others. The provider then asks questions to clarify how long the client has had difficulty communicating, and with which people or situations this difficulty is most common. Factors that enable or inhibit communication should also be explored as well as thoughts associated with communication difficulty and any physical sensations that may arise. The provider then uses the information gathered to tailor the intervention to the specific client.
2. Next, the provider summarizes and reflects what the client has expressed and asks if the client would like to learn to communicate more effectively.
3. If the client agrees to practice more effective communication styles, the provider provides the client with psychoeducation on assertive communication. This can be in the form of handouts. The provider teaches the client how to use "I" statements like, "when you do _____, I feel _____." The provider teaches the client different words to use for different emotions. A feelings chart may be used. The provider teaches the client a formula for assertive statements that includes calmly expressing thoughts about a person's behavior, expressing the client's feelings, and identifying a behavior that the client would like to see from the other person.
4. The provider teaches the client nonverbal communication strategies like posture, using a calm tone of voice, and making eye contact. The provider may model this behavior and/or show the client a video demonstrating these skills.
5. The client and provider then practice the communication through behavioral rehearsal and therapeutic role-play. The provider gives the client appropriate feedback and positive reinforcement during the behavioral rehearsal.
6. The provider assigns the client homework to practice the new assertiveness skills in a real-life context. The provider explains that the goal is to appropriately express oneself and that the client cannot control the other person's response.

28 Ultra-Brief Interventions

Example of How to Use It

Jasmine is a 28-year-old female graduate student who self-refers to therapy, stating she feels "frazzled and run down." She states she is "always doing everything for everyone," and recently her grades have started suffering. She reports that in one week she had to drive an hour each way to her mother's house to help with grocery shopping and chores, pick her friend up at the airport, and cover her coworker's shift, leaving her no time to do her homework. Jasmine says she is angry but doesn't know how to say 'no.'

The provider assesses Jasmine's current level of assertiveness skills and finds she has difficulty saying 'no,' setting boundaries, and communicating her needs. The provider finds Jasmine's most concerning situation is the one with her mother and that her guilt is a major obstacle. The provider uses a handout to teach Jasmine the difference between assertive, aggressive, passive, and passive-aggressive communication. The provider then helps Jasmine identify her feelings on a chart and gives her a handout explaining how to use "I" statements. Jasmine identifies that she feels frustrated when her mother asks her to do copious amounts of chores. The provider then demonstrates the "I" statement – "when you ask me to do a lot of chores when I am already busy, I feel frustrated." The provider then helps Jasmine identify which behavior she would prefer to see from her mother. Jasmine states she would prefer if her mother asked her what her schedule is like before making requests. The provider demonstrates how to make this statement in a calm tone of voice and points out how an open posture and eye contact can help.

Jasmine and the provider then practice the assertive statement in a role-play, in which the provider plays Jasmine's mother. Jasmine states, "Mom, when you ask me to do a lot of chores when I am already busy, I feel frustrated. I feel overwhelmed that I cannot get it all done and then feel more stressed out. I would prefer if you could ask me about my schedule first and consider that before asking me for help with your chores." The provider praises Jasmine's statement and her good eye contact but points out that Jasmine had her arms crossed. Jasmine practices the statement again with a more open posture.

For her homework assignment, Jasmine expresses her thoughts to her mother. She continues practicing assertiveness skills and completes homework assignments in which she writes a script of an interaction between her and her mother where she responds assertively. Jasmine is able to build up to refusing some of her mother's requests while effectively communicating her needs and boundaries.

Learning More About It

Alberti, R. (2008). *Your perfect right: Assertiveness and equality in your life and relationships* (9th ed.). San Luis Obispo, CA: Impact Publications.

Michelli, D. (2013). *The assertiveness workbook: A teach yourself guide.* New York, NY: McGraw-Hill.

Behavioral Activation

Defining It

Behavioral activation is a behavioral intervention to help individuals break cycles of inactivity and avoidance by substituting activating behaviors.

How it Works

This technique aims to break the self-perpetuating cycle of inactivity often accompanying depression and avoidance conditions. As individuals reduce pleasurable activities, they receive less positive reinforcement, leading to worsened depression and further reduction of activities. Similarly, individuals who avoid necessary tasks may be left with a sense of defeat that worsens their mood symptoms. Behavioral activation emphasizes the role of environmental factors over internal causes in depression and avoidance conditions. The focus is on increasing activity, rather than analyzing cognitions. By scheduling both pleasant and necessary activities weekly, the individual increases pleasure, motivation, and self-efficacy. Small changes reinforce the individual and help lead to increasingly challenging activities.

When to Use It

Behavioral activation was initially used with depression but is also helpful with avoidance conditions. This technique can be particularly helpful for individuals that have difficulty analyzing their cognitions.

30 Ultra-Brief Interventions

How to Use It

1. The provider teaches the client about cycles of inactivity and explains how the client's avoidant behavior reinforces his/her symptoms. The provider and client discuss how the client's current inactivity and avoidant behavior has been contributing to his/her symptoms. The intervention and its rationale is then explained.

2. Next, the provider helps the client make three lists – one of the activities the client currently engages in, one of necessary tasks the client needs to perform but has been avoiding, and one of pleasurable activities the client can potentially engage in. The provider may give the client a handout of possible activities to choose from.

3. For the first week, the client chooses one to two activities that take no longer than 15–20 minutes each to complete. It is important that the client begins by setting small goals and not taking on too much at once. The chosen activities should include both pleasurable and necessary tasks. When beginning, the client should choose easier activities. This can also be achieved by breaking down a larger task into several small tasks.

4. The provider helps the client schedule the activities for the week, choosing a specific day and time for each. Backup activities should also be identified to increase the likelihood that activities will be completed.

5. The provider gives the client a handout to track the completion of tasks. The client is asked to rate each activity on a scale from 0–10 for level of completion and amount of pleasure derived.

6. The client brings the activity log to the next session, in which the activities are reviewed. The provider reviews each activity separately and asks the client to explain his/her ratings for completion and pleasure. The provider asks what was good and what was not good about each activity.

7. Over the next few sessions, the client increases the number of activities completed each week, as well as the duration and complexity of activities.

Example of How to Use It

David is a 38-year-old Caucasian male diagnosed with Major Depressive Disorder. David reports low mood, fatigue, and loss of pleasure. The provider evaluates David's current repertoire of behaviors and finds he avoids daily tasks and limits his engagement in pleasurable activities. David reports he has been avoiding cleaning out his garage and car, and both serve as a daily reminder of his fatigue and lack of motivation. David feels guilty and defeated by his inability to complete these tasks. He reports that he watches television and falls asleep on the couch every night.

The provider explains that David's pattern of inactivity serves to reinforce his depression. The provider illustrates how the client's feelings of defeat and thoughts of helplessness are related to his avoidance of cleaning out the garage, fueling his cycle of depression. The provider explains how completing even some small tasks can break this cycle of inactivity. David agrees to try behavioral activation despite his fatigue and lack of motivation.

The provider helps David write a list of his current behaviors, which include watching television, avoiding phone calls, and falling asleep on the couch. Additionally, they write a list of tasks David needs to complete but has been avoiding, which include cleaning out the garage and car. Finally, they write a list of pleasurable activities David would like to engage in, which include spending time with friends, running, and kayaking. The provider helps schedule two activities for David to complete, instructing David to keep track of the activities he completes and rate each on a scale from 0–10 for both completion and enjoyment. The provider helps David identify backup activities in case he is unable to complete the ones he scheduled.

For the first week, David completes two scheduled tasks – cleaning out his car's trunk and running around the block twice. The provider reviews the activity and inquires about David's ratings, asking what was good and not so good about each activity. Two more activities are scheduled for the following week. In the following weeks, David reports he has cleaned up most of his garage, increased his running time, and gone kayaking with friends. He states that he finds more pleasure in these activities than he did initially and finds his mood generally improved.

Learning More About It

Martell, C.R., Addis, M.E., & Jacobson, N.S. (2001). *Depression in context: Strategies for guided action*. New York, NY: Norton.

Veale, D., & Willson, R. (2007). *Manage your mood. A self-help guide using behavioural activation*. London: Constable & Robinson.

32 Ultra-Brief Interventions

Behavioral Experiments

Defining It

A behavioral intervention to help individuals test a belief or prediction using planned activities in a real-world setting.

How It Works

Individuals may have deeply held beliefs about themselves, others, or specific situations. These are often accompanied by negative predictions about the potential outcomes of their behaviors. As a result, individuals may avoid certain situations and, thus, not have the opportunity to test their beliefs. Individuals may also engage in safety-seeking behaviors, intended to prevent uncomfortable experiences. This behavior reinforces avoidance as clients learn they can manage discomfort this way (Salkovskis, 1996). Behavioral experiments help individuals use planned experiences to test the accuracy of their beliefs and predictions so they can form more realistic appraisals of themselves and situations. The provider helps the client identify these beliefs, and design and schedule the experiment. Once the behavioral experiment is completed, the provider helps the client reevaluate the targeted belief.

When to Use It

Behavioral experiments are useful for individuals with thoughts and beliefs that keep them from engaging in certain activities. It is a valuable intervention on its own or in conjunction with automatic thought records (Bennet-Levy, 2003).

How to Use It

1. The provider helps the client identify negative beliefs and the avoidance behaviors associated with those beliefs.
2. The provider explains the purpose of behavioral experiments and how they are completed.
3. The client and provider collaborate to plan an experiential activity in which a particular belief can be tested. The activity should be appropriate

and attainable. The provider asks the client to predict the outcome of the experiment. The provider and client discuss how the client will test his/her prediction.

4. The client carries out the experiment as homework and logs his/her thoughts, feelings, and behaviors during the experiment.
5. The provider helps the client evaluate the outcome of the experiment. Evidence for and against the original prediction is discussed. The client is encouraged to explore what he/she learned from the experiment.
6. The original prediction is reexamined and the client rates how strongly the belief is held after completing the experiment.

Example of How to Use It

Joseph is a 29-year-old male who presents to therapy with social anxiety. He reports he has been limiting his activities because of fears he will be ridiculed in public. He states a particularly troubling recent event involves him having to go to the library to ask the information desk to help him with research for an assignment. The provider helps Joseph identify his beliefs about what would happen in this situation. Joseph states he believes the library staff will laugh at him and think he is stupid. Joseph states he has been avoiding going to the library for a month even though the deadline for his assignment is approaching.

The provider explains the purpose of the behavioral experiment. Together, Joseph and the provider decide he will go to the library help desk and ask for information on how to research his particular topic. They select a day and time for Joseph to complete the experiment. The provider asks for Joseph's prediction about the outcome of the experiment. Joseph's prediction is that the staff will laugh at him and he will freeze up and not be able to speak. He decides he will test this prediction by asking for help and seeing what happens. The provider instructs Joseph to write down his thoughts, feelings, and behaviors during and after the experiment.

Joseph completes the experiment and asks for help at the library. He states he was able to get the help he needed and no one ridiculed him. He also did not freeze up and engaged in a conversation with the librarian. In his log, Joseph wrote that he felt scared before the experiment and his thought was, "I am going to fail and be a laughing stock." After the experiment, however, he wrote that he felt relieved and thought, "that was not so bad. They were very friendly." Joseph states he gained evidence that disproves his initial prediction because the actual outcome was different

34 Ultra-Brief Interventions

from his prediction. He states he no longer supports his initial prediction because it turned out to not be accurate.

Learning More About It

Bennet-Levy, J. (2003). Mechanisms of change in cognitive therapy: The case of automatic thought records and behavioural experiments. *Behavioural and Cognitive Psychotherapy*, 31(3), 261–277.

Salkovskis, P.M. (1996). The cognitive approach to anxiety: Threat beliefs, safety-seeking behaviour, and the special case of health anxiety and obsessions. In P.M. Salkovskis (Ed.), *Frontiers of cognitive therapy* (pp. 48–74). New York, NY: Guilford.

Behavioral Rehearsal

Defining It

A behavioral intervention to help individuals identify and practice behaviors that can be useful and appropriate in social settings.

How It Works

Behavioral rehearsal helps individuals build appropriate social skills through modeling, practice, and feedback. The individual identifies social skill deficits and the provider helps generate behaviors that would be more effective in social settings. The provider models appropriate verbal and nonverbal behaviors for the client to learn. The client is encouraged to be an active participant, giving the provider feedback and suggestions. The provider then role-plays a situation, allowing the client to practice the new social skills. Skills should be easy to learn and implement. The provider uses praise and constructive feedback to help the client improve the new skills.

When to Use It

Behavioral rehearsal can be used with clients of varying ages and developmental levels. It is useful as an adjunct technique to help clients practice the new techniques and skills they learn in therapy before implementing them in real-world settings. Providers should take cultural and contextual factors into account before teaching and modeling targeted behaviors.

How to Use It

1. The provider helps the client identify the social skill deficit to be targeted. The client may identify a specific situation in which he/she is unsure of behaviors to implement.
2. The provider explains the process and benefits of behavioral rehearsal and elicits the client's permission to engage in the intervention.
3. The provider describes and then models appropriate social skills for the targeted situation. The provider asks the client for feedback and suggestions and modifies the modeling accordingly.
4. The provider then role-plays the situation with the client, allowing the client to practice the new skills.
5. After the role-play, the provider praises the client for his/her efforts and provides constructive feedback. The role-play may be repeated incorporating this feedback.

Example of How to Use It

Maryanne is a 31-year-old female who reports she is having difficulty communicating with her mother. She states her mother often demands they spend time together, even if Maryanne is busy. Maryanne usually responds by either agreeing to see her mother when she does not want to, or by avoiding her phone calls. The provider asks Maryanne how she would ideally like to respond. Maryanne states she would like to be able to tell her mother when she is busy. The provider explains that it is often helpful to rehearse behaviors so the person can figure out what to say and become more comfortable with the behaviors prior to implementing them. Maryanne agrees to the behavioral rehearsal.

The provider asks Maryanne how her mother would typically approach her. Maryanne responds that her mother would call and announce she is five minutes away and is stopping by the house. The provider responds by saying, "I would love to see you, Mom, but I am very busy right now. It is not a good time." The provider asks for feedback and further suggestions. Maryanne adds that it might be a good idea to schedule a time to see her mother that would work.

36 Ultra-Brief Interventions

The provider then sets up the role-play and plays the role of Maryanne's mother, saying, "I am five minutes away from your house. I'm stopping by." Maryanne responds, "I would love to see you but this is not a good time for me. I am very busy. Maybe we can do it another time." The provider praises Maryanne for her calm tone and statement but suggests she schedule a time that works for her. Maryanne repeats the role-play and this time says, "I would love to see you but this is not a good time for me. I am very busy. I am free on Friday night if you would like to have dinner then." The provider praises Maryanne's efforts.

Learning More About It

Wolpe, J., & Lazarus, A.A. (1966). *Behavior therapy techniques: A guide to the treatment of neuroses*. New York: Pergamon Press.

Behavioral Self-Analysis

Defining It

A model for teaching individuals to analyze behaviors and situations in ABC terms: (A) is the antecedent or activating event that precedes behavior (B) and is followed by a consequence (C) or effect.

How It Works

Behavioral self-analysis teaches individuals a model to analyze their behaviors and the contexts in which those behaviors occur. The ABC model states that an activating event (A) triggers an individual's behavior (B). The consequence to that behavior (C) then serves to either increase or decrease the likelihood that the individual will repeat the behavior in the future. This is based on the principles of punishment and reinforcement from operant conditioning. Clients are taught to keep a log of their activating events, behaviors, and consequences. In this way, clients become aware of their reflexive behaviors as well as the environmental factors that either increase or decrease those behaviors. Another way to use the ABC method is to analyze beliefs (B) and their emotional consequences (C) in relation to activating events (A). Here, clients are taught how their beliefs influence their responses to activating events.

When to Use It

Behavioral self-analysis is useful for depression, anxiety, and medical conditions.

How to Use It

1. The provider first explains the intervention and rationale. The explanation includes the components of ABC and how consequences reinforce behaviors or how beliefs lead to consequences.
2. The provider then asks the client to think of examples of situations the client has experienced, where the ABC model can be applied.
3. The client is asked to identify the A, B, and C component in each situation.
4. The provider instructs the client to keep a log of activating events and their associated behaviors, or beliefs, and resulting consequences.

Example of How to Use It

Sandra is a 38-year-old mother of two who presents to counseling because of stress in her family life. She reports she feels frustrated and angry and often at her wit's end. This has led her to increase her drinking as she finds it is the only way to calm down after her children go to sleep.

The provider introduces Sandra to the ABC model and teaches her the concept of how activating events (A), behaviors or beliefs (B), and consequences (C) are related. Sandra is asked to think of a recent situation to analyze using the ABC model. She presents a situation in which she asked her husband to help her with the dishes while she was putting the children to bed. She reports she asked her husband several times and then began yelling at him. Only then did he agree to do the dishes. The provider helps Sandra see how her husband refusing to comply (A) triggered her yelling (B), and how her yelling was actually reinforced because the consequence was her husband agreeing to do the dishes (C).

Sandra presents a second situation in which she became angry and found herself wanting to drink more after a phone conversation with her mother-in-law. Sandra states her mother-in-law gave her advice that was "completely wrong" and that Sandra became angry and ended the call in a hurry. The provider helps Sandra ascertain what she was thinking about her mother-in-law's statement (A). Sandra states her belief was "she thinks I'm stupid. She thinks

I'm a bad mom no matter how hard I try" (B). The provider explains to Sandra how her thoughts about the situation led to her feeling angry (C).

Sandra then keeps a log of her ABCs, including both beliefs and behaviors. She finds that when she displays anger, her family members are more likely to comply with her demands immediately, reinforcing her anger. Sandra also comes to realize that she is most angry after conversations and interactions in which she believes she is being criticized.

Learning More About It

Ellis, A., & MacLaren, C. (1998). *Rational emotive behavior therapy: A provider's guide*. San Luis Obispo, CA: Impact.

Hunter, C.L., Goodie, J.L., Oordt, M.S., & Dobmeyer, A.C. (2017). *Integrated behavioral health in primary care: Step-by-step guidance for assessment and intervention* (2nd ed.). Washington, DC: American Psychological Association.

Controlled Breathing

Defining It

A behavioral intervention used to slow an individual's breathing and restore regulated breathing rhythms to reduce stress-related symptoms.

How It Works

Controlled breathing is used to train individuals to regulate their breathing rate. Shallow or rapid breathing patterns can increase stress and panic, while regulated deeper breathing patterns can lead to a more relaxed state by calming the parasympathetic nervous system response. Purposely engaging in controlled breathing can also interrupt negative thought patterns and give an individual a sense of control over symptoms. Diaphragmatic breathing is the primary method of teaching individuals how to take slow, deep inhales and exhales from the abdominal area, rather than the chest. Diaphragmatic breathing should slow respiration to about half of the typical rate – about six to eight breaths per minute. The individual may place a hand on the stomach in order to gain feedback on the depth of the breaths. Paced respiration is another technique for controlling breathing. With this method, the individual inhales and exhales at a paced rate, often by counting or by using a pacing instrument like a metronome. The individual may be instructed to position his/her lips in a way that facilitates slowed breathing, e.g., pretending to blow on a spoonful of soup.

When to Use It

This technique can be used with individuals suffering from symptoms associated with panic, stress, anxiety, chronic pain, insomnia, and headaches, among other concerns. It is useful for children, adolescents, and adults. Controlled breathing is often combined with other techniques like progressive muscle relaxation, guided imagery, or cognitive restructuring.

How to Use It

1. First, the provider asks the client to breathe normally and observes the client's normal breathing pattern.
2. The provider then explains the role of breathing in the client's presenting symptoms. The provider explains how controlled breathing can help alleviate symptoms.
3. The provider teaches the client to take slow, smooth, deep breaths that originate in the abdomen. The provider may model the diaphragmatic breath for the client. The provider can instruct the client to position his/her lips in such a way that breathing is slower and smoother. The provider can use examples like, "imagine you are blowing bubbles or blowing on a spoonful of hot soup."
4. The provider instructs the client to take six to eight breaths per minute. Inhales and exhales can be paced by counting.
5. The provider instructs the client to practice the breathing technique between sessions and when symptoms arise.

Example of How to Use It

Donna is a 26-year-old graduate student who reports stress and anxiety related to pressure from school and a separation from her boyfriend. She reports that when she begins to feel stressed out, her symptoms often escalate quickly and she begins feeling panicked, shaky, and light-headed.

40 Ultra-Brief Interventions

The provider explains how stress and panic can increase the pace of breathing and how quick, shallow breaths can exacerbate panic symptoms. The provider also explains how controlled breathing can alleviate these symptoms and that it is an easy-to-implement tool that can give Donna more control over her stress. Donna agrees to try controlled breathing.

The provider asks Donna to breathe normally while concentrating on a stressful event in order to observe Donna's breathing pattern. The provider observes that Donna takes short, shallow breaths and reports this to her. The provider instructs Donna to take slow, smooth, deep, abdominal breaths and models these breaths for her. She shows Donna how she can purse her lips, as though she is breathing through a straw, to help control the breaths. The provider has Donna practice the breaths, with a hand on her diaphragm to provide feedback on the depth of her inhales and exhales. The provider helps Donna count rhythmically to eight on each inhale and exhale so she can pace herself. The provider instructs Donna to continue practicing controlled breathing between sessions and when she finds herself feeling stress and panic symptoms coming on.

Learning More About It

Lehrer, P.M., Woolfolk, R.L., & Sime, W.E. (2007). *Principles and practice of stress management* (3rd ed.). New York, NY: Guilford Press.

Mirgain, S., Singles, J., & Hampton, A. (n.d.). The power of breath: Diaphragmatic breathing clinical tool. Retrieved from http://projects.hsl.wisc.edu/SERVICE/modules/12/M12_CT_The_Power_of_Breath_Diaphragmatic_Breathing.pdf

Cognitive Disputation

Defining It

A cognitive behavioral intervention that uses logic to help individuals identify the irrationality of their maladaptive thoughts.

How It Works

Cognitive disputation is based on the understanding that cognitions lead to feelings and behaviors and focuses on challenging individuals' maladaptive beliefs. The provider disputes the client's irrational beliefs by using logic, with the goal of teaching the client to challenge his/her own thoughts without the help of a provider. Thoughts can be disputed using Socratic questioning, an approach based on Aaron Beck's cognitive therapy, focusing on logical errors or cognitive distortions, i.e., catastrophizing, all-or-nothing thinking. The provider can also directly dispute the thoughts, an approach based on Albert Ellis' Rational Emotive Behavior Therapy (REBT), focusing on an individual's belief that things "should" be a certain way and that situations are unbearable. Both approaches encourage the client to test their thoughts against reality, with Beck's method encouraging clients to view their thoughts as testable hypotheses rather than facts. Clients learn to become aware of their thoughts by recording them, as well as events that may later help dispute irrational thoughts.

When to Use It

Cognitive disputation is useful for treating depression, anxiety, eating disorders, substance abuse, and marital distress. Cognitive disputation is contraindicated for individuals who have limited cognitive capacity, including those with intellectual disability, borderline intellectual functioning, dementia, and psychosis.

How to Use It

1. The provider first helps the client identify maladaptive thoughts. Thoughts may be specific to a situation or more generalized. The client may be asked to document thoughts as homework.
2. The provider explains the rationale for cognitive disputation and explains how thoughts influence feelings and behaviors.
3. The provider disputes the client's maladaptive thoughts, using logic to demonstrate how the thoughts are irrational. The provider may use Socratic questioning or directly try to convince the client that the thoughts are irrational. The provider may ask the client to view the thought as a hypothesis and test it against reality.
4. The provider asks the client how much he/she believes the thought on a scale from 0–10. After gathering evidence for and against the belief, the provider asks the client to again rate how much he/she believes the thought on the same scale.

42 Ultra-Brief Interventions

5. The client is given homework to continue to identify maladaptive thoughts as they arise. The provider asks the client to journal about daily occurrences to provide a basis for disputing other beliefs.
6. The client then practices disputing his/her own thoughts both in and out of session.

Example of How to Use It

Jordan is an 18-year-old Caucasian male in his first year of college. He reports feelings of loneliness and intermittent depression and expresses a desire to make friends. "I just don't feel like I belong here or like anyone here wants to hang out with me," he states during the intake session with the provider. The provider asks for an example of Jordan's predicament, and Jordan describes attending a party he was invited to, at which he didn't speak to anyone and spent the entire time by himself before leaving early.

The provider helps Jordan identify what he was thinking during the party. Jordan identified two thoughts, "no one wants me here anyway," and "no one wants to talk to me." The provider asks how much Jordan believes those thoughts. Jordan reports he believes them at an 8 on a 1–10 scale. The provider illustrates to Jordan how these thoughts are maladaptive and are linked to his feelings and behavior. Jordan begins to understand how his thoughts contribute to his loneliness and keep him from actually trying to interact with others, ensuring he does not make friends.

The provider invites Jordan to view his identified thoughts as hypotheses and ask himself if they are rational. The provider points out the logical errors (all-or-nothing thinking, and selective abstraction) in his thinking. The provider probes Jordan for more details about the event that might help him test his thoughts against reality. Jordan states a classmate invited him to a party, proving that his first thought, "no one wants me here," is irrational. Jordan then realizes that several people attempted to interact with him at the party but he did not engage with them because of his feelings of inadequacy. Jordan understands that his second thought, "no one wants to talk to me," is irrational as well and his own belief prevented him from engaging with others. Jordan now states he believes his thoughts at a 2 on the 0–10 scale.

The provider gives Jordan homework to keep track of his thoughts and daily activities. In the following session, Jordan reports one of his thoughts was, "I'm not likeable." When reading through his list of activities from the previous week, Jordan mentions he was invited to work on a group project in his Romance Literature class. The provider uses this occurrence as evidence to dispute Jordan's global belief, "I'm not likeable." Jordan is encouraged to practice cognitive disputation outside of sessions.

Learning More About It

Beck, A.T. (1979). *Cognitive therapy of depression*. New York, NY: Guilford Press.
Ellis, A., & MacLaren, C. (1998). *Rational emotive behavior therapy: A provider's guide*. San Luis Obispo, CA: Impact.

Cognitive Defusion

Defining It

A mindfulness-based method for distancing oneself from troublesome thoughts, rather than disputing or restructuring them.

How It Works

Cognitive defusion is based on the idea that individuals "fuse" with negative thoughts and judgments, leading to distressing feelings. Cognitive defusion is used to help the client accept distressing thoughts instead of disputing them, which may serve to reinforce these thoughts. This technique teaches individuals to treat thoughts as just thoughts and not attach feelings or judgments to the thoughts. The individual is encouraged to see himself/ herself as not comprised of his/her thoughts but that thoughts are a separate entity from the person. The individual is also encouraged to change the language used to address the thoughts. Language can be used to separate oneself from the distressing thoughts. For example, the person can say, "I am having an anxious thought," rather than, "I am anxious," or "I can't stand it." The individual can repeat distressing thoughts over and over again until they lose their meaning, thus changing the person's perspective on the thoughts. One or more of these methods can be used with the goal of the individual not fusing with the thoughts, thus weakening their hold on the individual.

44 Ultra-Brief Interventions

When to Use It

Cognitive defusion can be used to treat depression, anxiety, substance abuse, eating disorders, and impulse control disorders.

How to Use It

1. The provider first helps the client identify a problematic situation and the client's thoughts associated with the problem.
2. The provider helps the client understand the nature of thoughts and how they tend to come and go and do not comprise who the person is. The provider explains how language influences thoughts and the way the individual defines his/her experiences accordingly. The provider can use metaphors to explain this. The provider explains how language reinforces thoughts and behaviors.
3. The provider helps the client defuse from thoughts by teaching the client to notice them without judgment and label them differently.
4. The client practices cognitive defusion by labeling thoughts without judgment and interaction.

Example of How to Use It

Jane is a 19-year-old college student who presents to counseling with anxiety triggered by stress from school. Jane reports that she has to give an oral presentation in her economics class and she is so worried about this prospect she is considering dropping the class. The provider helps Jane identify her thoughts associated with giving the presentation. Jane states she thinks, "I'm going to embarrass myself," and, "everyone is doing better than me." The provider explains to Jane that thoughts are transient and they come and go without necessarily having meaning and explains how Jane gives her thoughts power with the language she uses. The provider explains how Jane can learn to let her thoughts pass and minimize their effect on her emotions and behaviors. Jane learns to notice her thoughts and label them as they pass through her mind. When she has the thoughts, "I'm going to embarrass myself," and, "everyone is doing better than me," Jane says out loud, "I am having those thoughts again," and "thoughts about public speaking are passing through." The provider also has Jane pick one of these thoughts and say it over and over again in a funny voice. Jane repeats the thought "everyone is doing better than me" in a funny voice ten times until it seems comical and loses its meaning. The provider helps Jane continue to practice cognitive defusion so her thoughts are just thoughts and do not comprise her reality.

Learning More About It

Hayes, S., & Smith, S. (2005). *Get out of your mind and into your life: The new acceptance and commitment therapy*. Oakland, CA: New Harbinger.

Distress Tolerance Training

Defining It

A cognitive behavioral technique that teaches individuals the ability to tolerate distressing and painful emotions without attempting to change or stop them.

How It Works

Distress tolerance training helps individuals develop the skills needed to survive and tolerate crises and difficult experiences, by accepting these moments as they come. The individual learns to manage his/her responses to the environment without trying to change his/her emotional state or the environment. The individual learns to observe and accept his/her thoughts and emotions, as well as how to self-soothe and distract oneself from distressing thoughts. Distress tolerance reduces the likelihood of the individual engaging in self-destructive behaviors. Distraction techniques can include engaging in another activity (listening to music, taking a walk, making a phone call), thought stopping, or inducing physical sensations by holding ice cubes or flicking a rubber band on the wrist. Distraction techniques are intended to interrupt painful thoughts and emotions. Self-soothing skills can include controlled breathing, listening to soothing music, and relaxation techniques. Radical acceptance skills help the individual completely and willingly accept reality without attempting to change it.

When to Use It

Distress tolerance training is useful for individuals with personality disorders, substance use disorders, depression, anxiety disorders, and eating disorders.

How to Use It

1. The provider assesses the client's ability to distract himself/herself from disturbing and painful thoughts and feelings, as well as the ability to self-soothe.
2. The provider teaches the client skills for acceptance, distraction self-soothing based on the deficits observed during the assessment.
3. The client can practice these skills within the session, for example concentrating on an unpleasant thought while holding ice cubes.

Example of How to Use It

Kevin is a 35-year-old Caucasian male diagnosed with moderate Alcohol Use Disorder. Kevin reported he had maintained two years of sobriety but relapsed when his coworker was fired and Kevin was forced to do more work. He stated that using alcohol is the only thing that helps him "really calm down and take my mind off work."

The provider asks Kevin how he copes with his urges to use alcohol and Kevin replies that he often acts on the impulse without thinking about it. He states that he often feels so stressed from work and his other responsibilities that he "can't stand it" and turns to alcohol to soothe himself.

The provider teaches Kevin radical acceptance and how to accept that he feels distressed and has distressing thoughts without trying to change them. The provider then has Kevin concentrate on these thoughts in the therapy session and snap a rubber band on his wrist to distract himself from the thoughts. Kevin practices concentrating on the thoughts and distracting himself with the sensation of snapping the rubber band. The provider helps Kevin brainstorm other ideas for distracting himself from distressing thoughts. Kevin decides he will either call a friend or listen to music. Finally, the provider teaches Kevin skills to soothe himself. Kevin decides he will listen to a meditation CD and practice deep breathing.

Learning More About It

Linehan, M. (1993). *Skills training manual for treating borderline personality disorder*. New York, NY: Guilford Press.

Emotional First Aid

Defining It

A behavioral intervention that teaches individuals to treat their emotional wounds as they arise, without the direct aid of a mental health professional.

How It Works

Emotional first aid draws similarities between physical and emotional injuries, treating these emotional injuries so they do not worsen. The intent is for individuals to master emotional first-aid techniques so they can apply them without the aid of a provider. The provider teaches the individual how to recognize the need to administer emotional first aid by becoming familiar with states of emotional pain, whether through emotional or physical symptoms. The individual is instructed to practice self-compassion through positive self-talk, disputing negative beliefs, or writing encouraging notes to himself/herself. For individuals who ruminate, distraction is a common first-aid technique. Distraction can be accomplished through an activity that requires concentration, like a crossword puzzle, or through physical activities. The individual is also taught to reframe failures and losses as opportunities to grow or find meaning. The goal is to become more emotionally resilient, the more one pays attention to emotional states and practices emotional first aid.

When to Use It

Emotional first aid can be applied to treat negative emotional states from life's common difficulties and setbacks including rejection, loneliness, failure, loss, guilt, and rumination. It is also useful in crises.

48 Ultra-Brief Interventions

How to Use It

1. The provider assesses the client's needs and situations when emotional first aid could be useful. The provider explains how addressing emotional distress can be beneficial.
2. The provider helps the client recognize emotional distress so the client learns which emotional and/or physical symptoms are signs of distress.
3. The provider then helps the client identify methods for relieving negative emotions. These may include journal writing, hobbies, speaking to a loved one, etc.
4. The provider addresses self-defeating behaviors by helping the client identify harmful behaviors, such as rumination and negative self-talk, and identifying activities to distract from these behaviors, like exercise, crossword puzzles, etc.
5. The provider helps the client learn to reframe negative thoughts by disputing irrational beliefs and teaching the client to see the opportunities within failure and the meaning within losses.
6. The provider helps the client generate a list of factors within the client's control, so the client feels less helpless. The client might also be encouraged to build a social network that can be turned to for support.

Example of How to Use It

Jeffrey is a 37-year-old African-American market analyst who was recently laid off from his job of 10 years. Jeffrey presents to therapy stating he has been isolating himself since he lost his job and all he can think about is how he is "too old to find a job as good as the one I had." Jeffrey admits he has been ruminating about why his company chose to lay him off and believes the layoff is a reflection on his competence and his self-esteem has suffered as a result.

Jeffrey agrees he needs better ways to tend to his own emotional wounds. Jeffrey does some journaling and finds it cathartic. He also reaches out to some friends and is delighted that they are understanding and supportive. He makes plans to meet with friends once a week and reports feeling less isolated.

The provider helps Jeffrey find ways to distract himself from rumination through exercise, and art. Jeffrey engages in running and painting, two activities he once used to enjoy regularly. The provider also helps Jeffrey dispute his irrational beliefs and Jeffrey realizes he is not too old to find a new job, and admits he was feeling stagnant at his old job. Jeffrey finds being laid off may have been the push he needed to find a new and exciting job that would allow him to grow. He places notes around his house that say things like, "you're awesome!" and "you got this!" to encourage himself.

Learning More About It

Winch, G. (2013). *Emotional first aid: Healing rejection, guilt, failure, and other everyday hurts.* New York, NY: Hudson Street Press.

Goal Setting

Defining It

A social-cognitive intervention used to help clients improve self-management skills and build self-efficacy by setting realistic goals.

How It Works

Goal setting is an intervention in which providers help clients identify specific, measurable goals. When setting goals, the provider first elicits goals from the client. The client may already have specific goals or may have only a vague idea. Asking the client what he/she would like to change is the first step in identifying general goals. Once this is done, the provider helps further define the client's goals. Goals should be challenging but attainable. They should be realistic and within the client's control. For example, a goal of having another person behave differently around the client would not be reasonable. Goals should also be specific. Sometimes, general goals (e.g., being a better employee) need to be phrased in terms of specific behaviors (e.g., arriving to work on time). Large goals may be broken up into several sub-goals, making them more attainable. Goals should be defined as to whether they are long-term or short-term goals and must be prioritized, with more urgent goals coming first. The provider then helps the client explore the reason for his/her goals. Goals that are personally significant to the client are more likely to be attained than those imposed by someone else in the client's life. Next, the provider and client agree on goals and set a time frame for each one. Goals can be set by the individual, assigned by a physician or provider, or collaborative. Regardless of which type of goal is set, the client must agree and commit to each one (Shilts, Horowitz, & Townsend, 2004). Finally, as the client progresses towards each

50 Ultra-Brief Interventions

goal, the provider should give consistent feedback and can set up a schedule for rewards, which can be either internal (sense of pride) or external (material reward). Regular feedback has been shown to greatly help clients attain goals (Shilts, Horowitz, & Townsend, 2004).

When to Use It

Goal setting is useful for weight loss, medication management, adherence to treatment plans, exercise, smoking cessation, and other goals related to health, mental health, and relationships.

How to Use It

1. The provider elicits the client's goals. The provider asks questions about what the client would like to see change in his/her life, what would be a marker of successful therapy, etc., in order to begin identifying goals.
2. The provider helps the client define specific goals. Goals are explored in the following terms:
   a. Challenge – goals should be challenging but attainable.
   b. Control – goals should be realistic and within the client's control.
   c. Specific – goals should be specific. This might require breaking down goals into sub-goals and/or specifying specific behaviors.
   d. Priority – the client determines if goals are long-term or short-term and which are the greatest priority.
   e. Reason – the provider helps the client determine the reason for his/her goals.
3. Once goals are specified, the client should agree on them and commit to achieving each goal. A time frame is set for goal attainment.
4. The provider monitors the client's progress and provides regular feedback and reinforcement. The provider helps the client identify rewards for goal attainment.

Example of How to Use It

David is a 32-year-old male presenting to counseling in an integrated care setting. He states his doctor advised him he needs to lose about 20 pounds. The provider begins by asking what David would like to change in order to begin losing weight. David states he would like to exercise more. He states this would be a difficult thing for him to do as he has a sedentary lifestyle and has not exercised in a long time. The provider asks David about specific ways he would like to exercise more. David says he would like to start by taking walks. The provider helps David decide he would like to walk in his community for 20 minutes, three times per week with the ultimate long-term goal of walking for 50 minutes three times per week. David states his reason for this goal is because he is tired of being sedentary and he hopes walking will give him more energy and help him lose weight. The time frame for David's long-term goal of walking for 50 minutes is eight weeks and he commits to begin walking for 20 minutes, three times per week right away. With the provider's help, David decides he will reward himself after two weeks of walking with a date night at the movies. As David progresses towards his goal, the provider gives him regular feedback and praise.

Learning More About It

Hunter, C.L., Goodie, J.L., Oordt, M.S., & Dobmeyer, A.C. (2017). *Integrated behavioral health in primary care: Step-by-step guidance for assessment and intervention* (2nd ed.). Washington, DC: American Psychological Association.

Shilts, M.K., Horowitz, M., & Townsend, M.S. (2004 November/December). Goal setting as a strategy for dietary and physical activity behavior change: A review of the literature. *American Journal of Health Promotion*, 19(2), 81–93.

Habit Reversal

Defining It

A behavioral intervention used to reduce tics, stuttering, hair-pulling, and skin-picking by engaging in a competing response that suppresses the unwanted behavior.

How It Works

Habit reversal is intended to reduce the occurrence of compulsive behaviors like hair-pulling by replacing those behaviors with inconspicuous, opposing behaviors. Habit reversal therapy is comprised of four stages: building

52 Ultra-Brief Interventions

awareness, developing a competing response, increasing motivation, and skill generalization. In the awareness stage, the client increases awareness of the behavior by describing it or performing it in a mirror, as well as identifying situations in which the behavior frequently occurs. In the competing response stage, the client learns a behavior that is incompatible with the unwanted behavior. The competing response should be the opposite of the unwanted behavior and inconspicuously performed in social situations. The competing behavior should also induce isometric tension of the muscles involved in the unwanted behavior and be practiced for several minutes at a time. In the motivation stage, the client explores reasons to discontinue the unwanted behavior, including times when the behavior has proved embarrassing or inconvenient. The client's friends and family are asked to encourage the client's reduction of the unwanted behavior and the client controls the unwanted behavior in front of trusted people. Finally, in the generalization phase, the client rehearses the competing behavior in other situations.

When to Use It

Habit reversal is useful in treating tic disorders, hair-pulling disorder, skin-picking disorder, stuttering, and other habits like nail biting, teeth grinding, scratching, and oral-digital habits. It can be used with children, adolescents, and adults. Habit reversal is not indicated for clients with borderline intellectual functioning or intellectual disability.

How to Use It

1. The provider helps the client become aware of the unwanted behaviors. The client either describes the behavior in detail or observes himself/herself performing the behavior while looking in a mirror. The provider can also point out when the behavior occurs during sessions until the client becomes more aware of the behavior.
2. The provider helps the client identify warning signs for the oncoming behavior like urges, physical sensations, or thoughts. Situations in which the behavior is most likely to occur are also identified.
3. The provider helps the client identify a competing behavior that is opposite to the unwanted behavior and is inconspicuous in public. The behavior may involve putting one's hands in one's pockets or pinching one's forearm.

20 Key Ultra-Brief Interventions   **53**

4. The client practices the competing behavior for several minutes at a time.
5. The provider works with the client to write a list of problems, inconveniences, and embarrassments caused by the unwanted behavior.
6. The client enlists family and friends for support and demonstrates suppression of the unwanted behavior in front of them. Loved ones are enlisted to praise the person for control of the behavior.
7. The provider helps the client symbolically rehearse performing the competing behavior in different areas of the client's life.
8. The client practices the competing behavior in different contexts.

Example of How to Use It

Maria is a 21-year-old Hispanic female who presents for counseling with Trichotillomania – Hair-Pulling Disorder. Maria reports pulling her hair out, particularly when experiencing stress, since she was 19 years old. She arrives at intake wearing a hat but when she removes it, it is evident she has bald spots at the crown of her head and right temple. Her eyebrows also appear sparse. Maria states she feels intense urges to pull her hair associated with stress and anxiety. Although she is embarrassed by her areas of missing hair, she feels she cannot control pulling her hair. Maria's embarrassment has led her to spend most of her time at home with her family where she can spend up to three hours at a time pulling her hair. Maria states she would like to control this behavior and move on with her life, stating her goals are to obtain a job and date.

The provider helps Maria become aware of when she pulls her hair and the situations that trigger her hair-pulling. Maria identifies that anxiety about her future and about social interactions trigger her hair-pulling. The provider also points out instances in session, while talking about stressful subjects, when Maria's hand drifts up to her eyebrows. Maria identifies strong physical urges to pull her hair. The provider then helps Maria decide on a competing behavior that she can do without being noticed in public. Maria decides she will put her hands in her pockets or sit on her hands when she feels the urge to pull her hair. Maria practices this competing behavior in and out of session, for at least three minutes at a time.

In a following session, the provider helps Maria write a list of times she has been inconvenienced or embarrassed by her hair-pulling. Maria identifies being embarrassed seen with bald spots, and a time a friend noticed the hair missing on her temple and eyebrows. Maria's parents praise her effort

54 Ultra-Brief Interventions

to reduce hair-pulling and notice she hasn't pulled her hair for the last week. Maria spends an entire evening watching a movie with her family and does not pull her hair.

Finally, Maria's provider helps her symbolically rehearse not pulling her hair when she is alone in her room, when she is with her family, and when she sees her friends. Maria slowly starts resisting the urge to pull her hair when she is alone and with others, putting her hands in her pockets until the urge passes.

Learning More About It

Azrin, N.H., & Peterson, A.L. (1988). Habit reversal for the treatment of Tourette syndrome. *Behaviour Research and Therapy, 26*(4), 347–351. doi:10.1016/0005-7967(88)90089-7

Woods, D.W., & Miltenberger, R.G. (1995). Habit reversal: A review of applications and variations. *Journal of Behavior Therapy and Experimental Psychiatry, 26*(2), 123–131. doi:10.1016/0005-7916(95)00009-O

Harm Reduction

Defining It

A model that focuses on decreasing adverse health, social, and lifestyle consequences without requiring abstinence from substances.

How It Works

Harm reduction is a humanistic model that views substance use on a continuum. Some users are compulsive and have physiological addictions while others are more casual users who can make informed decisions about whether and when to use. Those that can make decisions about when to use are seen as voluntaristic and can use a rational thought process. Harm reduction proponents describe views of substance users as a societal construction largely fueled by parties who benefit from this manufactured paradigm. Harm reduction proposes a humanistic view of substance use, focusing on problematic consequences rather than pathologizing users, and views substance use problems within their environmental context. The harm reduction model neither opposes nor promotes abstinence, with the primary goal being minimization of adverse consequences. The model acknowledges that abstinence may be necessary for some but that most abstinent individuals will relapse at some point as well. Providers who practice harm reduction must be nonjudgmental and non-dogmatic, and refrain from coercing the client into any course of action. Because the model is individualized, there is no universal treatment formula, viewing any change that decreases harm as an improvement. Harm reduction efforts can range from decreasing use, to using in a safe environment, to needle exchange programs. Treatment plans are collaborative and empowering, focusing on client strengths and setting achievable goals. The provider's role should be patient and supportive.

When to Use It

Harm reduction can be implemented through individual therapy, community programs, and changes in policy. Harm reduction is not indicated for clients with severe physiological addictions who would revert to compulsive drug use without complete abstinence.

How to Use It

1. The provider first evaluates the client's level of use, contributing social and environmental factors, and consequences of use. This information helps the provider tailor the approach to the client.
2. The provider and client collaborate to set small, achievable, intermediate goals that will minimize harm to the client. Goals may include not using during the week, or not driving after drinking.
3. The provider is supportive, does not propose any particular course of action, and does not give ultimatums regarding ceasing drug use.
4. The provider recognizes small steps the client makes, does not chastise the client for relapses, and continues to support and encourage the client.

Example of How to Use It

Kevin is a 35-year-old Caucasian male diagnosed with moderate Alcohol Use Disorder. Kevin reported he had maintained two years of sobriety but relapsed when his coworker was fired and Kevin was forced to do more work. He stated that using alcohol is the only thing that helps him "really calm down and take

56 Ultra-Brief Interventions

my mind off work." Kevin's recent relapse led to him drinking so heavily after work that he began coming to work late, hungover, or still under the influence.

The provider speaks to Kevin about his drinking and the adverse consequences it has on his life. Kevin expresses he is motivated to keep his job and admits he feels terrible physically and emotionally after a night of heavy drinking. The provider understands Kevin's drinking within the context of his stress, loneliness, and poor coping mechanisms. The provider collaborates with Kevin to create a suitable treatment plan, emphasizing that Kevin is the primary agent of change. Kevin decides he will decrease his drinking to two beers a night during the week and four beers on weekends. He decides he will abstain from drinking for two nights every week. Kevin and the provider agree that he will not drive after he has been drinking.

The provider applauds Kevin when he reports he has been sticking to his plan to cut down his drinking. Together, they discuss coping mechanisms and Kevin starts spending more time with friends. He reports that his loneliness has decreased and he feels the need to drink even less than he imagined he would. After four weeks in treatment, Kevin reports he drank excessively after a very stressful day and called in sick to work the next day. The provider does not scold Kevin for the lapse and acknowledges that Kevin did not decide to show up to work inebriated.

Learning More About It

Marlatt, G.A. (1998). *Harm reduction: Pragmatic strategies for managing high-risk behaviors.* New York, NY: Guilford Press.

Tatarsky, A. (2002). *Harm reduction psychotherapy: A new treatment for drug and alcohol problems.* Northvale, NJ: Jason Aronson.

Mindfulness

Defining It

A technique used, either as a meditative practice or as a component of another therapeutic intervention focusing on the present without judgment, which results in reduced stress, anxiety, mood symptoms, and mindless action.

How It Works

Mindfulness originates in Buddhist meditative practice and is used to mediate physical, emotional, and behavioral symptoms. Mindfulness helps individuals build awareness and observation of thoughts, sensations, and mood states without active engagement with or judgment of them. The individual becomes aware of bodily sensations, emotional states, thoughts, and mental images, while practicing remaining fully present in the moment. Instead of attempting to escape these sensations, the individual views them as objective facts. For example, one might observe physical symptoms of anxiety and describe, "my throat feels tight right now." Observation of thoughts and feeling states should be nonjudgmental and the participant should bring all attention to the current experience. Individuals are encouraged to cultivate mindful attention in daily activities. As mindfulness practice evolves, individuals habituate to unpleasant sensations and thoughts. Mindfulness is thought to relieve distressing thoughts, improve self-management, and allow individuals to recognize impending relapse or mood symptoms so they can implement coping skills to manage these occurrences.

When to Use It

Mindfulness can be used for chronic pain, medical problems, anxiety disorders, mood disorders, eating disorders, substance abuse, and personality disorders. This intervention can be applied as a skills training, as a meditative technique, or as a component of other interventions. Though typically taught in a group setting, mindfulness instruction may take place in a one-on-one format.

How to Use It

1. First, the provider teaches the client to observe his/her thoughts without labeling or describing them. The provider assigns homework for the client to continue observing thoughts, feelings, and sensations.
2. The provider teaches the client to observe sensations without judgment through an activity like mindful eating, in which he/she focuses on the smells, texture, temperature, and physical sensations during the experience. The client is asked to describe thoughts and sensations as they arise, e.g., "the tomato is watery," without making judgments, e.g., "I don't like

58 Ultra-Brief Interventions

it." The provider helps the client practice making a running commentary on events and experiences without judgment.

3. The provider assigns homework for the client to practice giving full attention to experiences, either in daily meditation or during everyday activities.

Example of How to Use It

Paula is a 26-year-old graduate student who reports stress and anxiety related to pressure from school and a separation from her boyfriend. She reports frequent headaches, insomnia, and tension in her neck and shoulders, also stating that her increased stress makes it difficult for her to concentrate on her schoolwork. Paula states she would like some practical tools for managing her stress during her busy schedule.

The provider explains the concepts of mindfulness to Paula and has her practice the technique of observing without judgment. In the session, Paula practices observing her thoughts and labeling them without engaging with them. The provider gives Paula homework to observe her feelings and sensations without judgment. As part of the homework, she practices mindfully eating a slice of apple, noticing the cool sensation, the crunching texture and sound, and the subtle sweetness without attributing meaning to the observations.

During the second week, the provider has Paula recount an incident at work by specifying only facts and not making judgments. Paula reports her coworker "told a story" instead of saying she "tried to waste everyone's time," a judgment she would normally make. Paula practices these observations daily for the next two weeks.

Finally, the provider instructs Paula to practice remaining in the present and giving her complete attention to any current task. Paula continues to practice daily and eventually notices she is slower to react and feels a decrease in stress.

Learning More About It

Crane, R. (2009). *Mindfulness-based cognitive therapy: Distinctive features*. New York, NY: Routledge.

Forsyth, J.P., & Eifert, G.H. (2007). *The mindfulness and acceptance workbook for anxiety*. Oakland, CA: New Harbinger Publications.

Problem-Solving Training

Defining It

Problem-solving training is a behavioral intervention used to teach individuals skills needed to cope with distressing situations.

How It Works

Problem-solving training helps individuals learn adaptive skills to help decrease negative emotional and behavioral symptoms. Individuals are taught to identify and systematically solve problems and ameliorate distressing responses. The provider works with the client to determine the client's existing problem-solving skills, problem orientation (beliefs and attitudes about problems), and problem-solving style. Problem orientation is seen as a determining factor in how the individual will cope with problems. Individuals with positive problem orientations view problems as challenges and are optimistic about the probability of solving them, leading to increased self-efficacy. Problem-solving style refers to an individual's cognitions and behaviors when facing a problem. A rational problem-solving style involves understanding a problem and systematically searching for and applying solutions, as opposed to impulsive or avoidant styles. Problem-solving training involves four stages: (1) identification of problematic situations; (2) generation of alternatives; (3) decision-making; and (4) implementation.

First, the provider helps the client define the problem and contributing factors and set attainable goals. The provider helps the client view the problem from different angles, identify associated feelings, and distinguish between facts and assumptions about the problem. The provider may have to use cognitive restructuring to help the client correct distorted beliefs. The client then generates a wide range of possible solutions while the provider takes a non-judgmental stance, helping the client think about the problem in a more flexible way. All possible solutions are then considered in terms of their short-term and long-term consequences and the likelihood that the solutions will help the client achieve his/her goal. Role-playing and skills training can be used to help the client implement the chosen course of action. The client is encouraged to reward himself/herself for implementing the selected course of action. If the chosen solution does not work, the process is repeated and another solution chosen. The provider and client act as a team when choosing solutions with the provider offering feedback, encouragement, and modeling.

60 Ultra-Brief Interventions

When to Use It

Problem-solving training can be used with children, adolescents, and adults in individual, couple, or group settings. It is useful for externalizing disorders that include impulsivity, aggression, relational problems, anger, and antisocial behaviors, as well as for internalizing disorders including depression, anxiety, and social anxiety.

How to Use It

1. The provider first assesses the client's current problem-solving skills related to problem identification, goal setting, generating alternatives, decision-making, and implementation.
2. The provider then works with the client to process a specific, current problem. The client describes the problem in detail and the provider asks questions to help the client identify emotions associated with the problem.
3. The provider asks questions to encourage the client to see the problem from different perspectives.
4. Next, the provider helps the client generate a list of alternatives. The provider maintains a nonjudgmental stance and encourages the client to brainstorm possible solutions.
5. The client then evaluates each of the alternatives in terms of their potential consequences. After this evaluation, the client chooses a course of action.
6. If the chosen course of action requires a skill the client does not possess, skills training can be implemented. If necessary, the provider can help the client role-play the solution and provide feedback.
7. The client then implements the chosen course of action. If the problem is still not solved, the provider helps the client choose another alternative from the list.

Example of How to Use It

Darneshia is a 28-year-old female graduate student who self-refers to therapy, stating she feels "frazzled and run down." She states she is "always doing everything for everyone," and recently her grades have started suffering. She reports that in one week she had to drive an hour each way to her mother's house to help with grocery shopping and chores, pick her friend up at the airport, and cover her coworker's shift, leaving her no time to do her homework.

Darneshia says she is angry but doesn't know how to say 'no.' She states she feels overwhelmed because her friend asked her to help plant the community garden the weekend before Darneshia has a big paper due.

The provider assesses Darneshia's current problem-solving skills related to problem identification, goal setting, generating alternatives, decision-making, and implementation. The provider finds that Darneshia is able to identify her problems but has difficulty setting goals, generating and deciding on alternatives. The provider then has Darneshia describe her problem and Darneshia reports that her friend asked her to help plant the community garden the weekend before Darneshia has a big paper due. The provider has her expand on the details and describe her feelings of being overwhelmed, frustrated, and angry.

Darneshia then generates ten alternatives for her problem and weighs the potential consequences of each. She decides to implement the alternative of telling her friend she cannot help with the garden this weekend and identifying another time that would work for her. Darneshia and the provider role-play informing the friend. Darneshia implements the alternative and finds her friend is understanding and now she has ample time to finish her paper.

Learning More About It

D'Zurilla, T.J., & Nezu, A.M. (2007). *Problem-solving therapy: A positive approach to clinical intervention* (3rd ed.). New York, NY: Springer.

Haley, J. (1987). *Problem-solving therapy* (2nd ed.). San Francisco, CA: Jossey-Bass.

Push-Button Technique

Defining It

The push-button technique is a cognitive intervention that helps individuals alleviate negative feeling states by replacing them with more positive feelings.

How It Works

The push-button technique is an Adlerian intervention designed for treating depression. The technique requires a client to practice concentrating on a pleasant experience or memory and the feelings it provokes, alternating with

62 Ultra-Brief Interventions

an unpleasant experience and its associated feelings. By alternating between the pleasant and unpleasant memories, the individual learns that he/she is able to take control of his/her emotional states. The individual imagines pushing a button to replace negative emotions. The provider does not have to focus on restructuring or disputing the client's cognitions as the client practices replacing feeling states.

When to Use It

The push-button technique is useful for depression and other negative feeling states.

How to Use It

1. The provider introduces the technique and explains the rationale behind it.
2. The provider asks the client to close his/her eyes and concentrate on a memory of an unpleasant experience. The provider asks the client to describe the memory and the feelings associated with it.
3. Next, the provider asks the client to concentrate on a memory of a pleasant experience. The provider asks the client to describe the memory and the feelings associated with it.
4. The client and provider discuss the client's experience of being able to change mood states with "the push of a button." The client can imagine pushing a button while doing the exercise.
5. The client is instructed to practice the technique between sessions and continue to generate additional pleasant memories.

Example of How to Use It

Sam is a 43-year-old female who reports sadness accompanied by distressing thoughts and feelings of guilt. She states she feels helpless during times when she feels especially sad and guilty. She says she hopes these emotional states will pass but they can last for most of the day. Sam states the most effective coping mechanism she has for these negative emotional states is taking naps.

The provider explains that there is a useful technique for changing emotional states that can work quickly once it is learned. Sam agrees to try the technique. The provider has Sam close her eyes and think of an unpleasant memory. Sam describes when she found out her husband was leaving her and her two children. She states she feels sad and tearful when she thinks of this memory. The provider then has Sam concentrate on a pleasant memory. Sam describes when her first child was born and states she feels joy and excitement when thinking of this memory.

The provider asks Sam what her experience was like with the exercise. Sam says she was surprised that she was able to actually feel different when concentrating on the two experiences. The provider teaches her that she can be in control of her negative emotional states by pushing a button to switch between emotional states. The provider has Sam practice the exercise again and imagine pressing a button to move from the negative to positive emotional state. Sam is told to practice the exercise outside of the session and think of more positive experiences to use for reference.

Learning More About It

Mosak, H.H., & Maniacci, M. (1998). *Tactics in counseling and psychotherapy*. Itasca, IL: F. E. Peacock.

Relapse Prevention

Defining It

Relapse prevention is a technique that teaches individuals to maintain sobriety while coping with everyday stressors and temptations.

How It Works

After completing treatment for substance use issues, individuals are tasked with maintaining sobriety while facing stressors and obstacles. Individuals may find it challenging to avoid relapsing if their judgment is still affected by years of use. Relapse prevention helps clients build coping skills, cognitive behavioral skills, and self-efficacy. The approach is based on the idea that when facing a stressful event, an individual's coping skills are the main determining factor between relapse and maintained sobriety. Employing effective coping mechanisms in the face of distressing events leads to

64 Ultra-Brief Interventions

increased self-efficacy and a decreased risk of relapse. Relapse prevention utilizes relapse education, which teaches individuals to identify warning signs and high-risk situations, learn effective coping skills, challenge irrational beliefs, form more realistic expectations, and create a toolkit that includes social support, self-care, and avoidance of relapse triggers.

When to Use It

Relapse prevention is useful for individuals in recovery for substance abuse, as well as other addictive behaviors like eating disorders, overeating, smoking, and self-harm.

How to Use It

1. The provider assesses the client's patterns of use or behavior, coping skills, self-efficacy, expectations, and readiness for change.
2. The provider then educates the client on relapse and the benefits of a relapse prevention plan.
3. The provider helps the client make a list of the client's high-risk situations, and stressful events that can potentially trigger the unwanted behavior. The client and provider discuss the high-risk situations and how they lead to use.
4. The provider then helps the client identify and challenge irrational beliefs about use. The client may have irrational beliefs that use will provide emotional relief in difficult situations.
5. The client and provider make an inventory of relapse warning signs, including major stressors as well as a culmination of small stressors. The client is taught to address initial small stressors rather than waiting to reach his/her breaking point. The client is encouraged to keep a log of warning signs.
6. The client and provider make a plan for a toolkit of supportive factors that can include continued therapy, attending 12-step meetings, a list of supportive people to call, a list of people and places to avoid, the use of a sponsor, and improved self-care.
7. The client commits to a lifestyle change that supports his/her recovery, including caring for his/her health, exercise, positive social interactions, etc.

Example of How to Use It

Kevin is a 35-year-old Caucasian male currently completing inpatient treatment for moderate Alcohol Use Disorder. Kevin reported he had maintained two years of sobriety but relapsed when his coworker was fired and Kevin was forced to do more work. He stated that using alcohol is the only thing that helps him "really calm down and take my mind off work." Kevin's recent relapse led to him drinking so heavily after work that he began coming to work late, hungover, or still under the influence. Kevin stated his weekly schedule consists of work and then drinking until he passes out. He does not exercise, spend time with friends, or engage in any other hobbies.

The provider assesses Kevin's patterns of use, coping skills, self-efficacy, expectations, and readiness. The provider finds Kevin uses alcohol as his primary coping mechanism and his use is triggered by stress. Kevin appears highly motivated to stop using as he is concerned about his job but expresses uncertainty about his ability to maintain sobriety and expects he will probably fail. The provider and Kevin make a list of high-risk situations and Kevin identifies stress at work, loneliness, and financial stress as his high-risk stressors.

The provider educates Kevin on relapse prevention and together they trace back his recent relapse as a culmination of spending more time at work, feeling he could not speak up to his boss, and cutting positive lifestyle choices such as exercise from his life. The provider helps Kevin see the irrationality of his belief that alcohol is the only way to find emotional relief as Kevin identifies he previously maintained his sobriety through yoga, time with friends, and attending 12 step meetings.

Learning More About It

Gorski, T., & Miller, M. (1986). *Staying sober: A guide for relapse prevention*. Aspen, CO: Independence Press.

Marlatt, G.A., & Donovan, D. (2005). *Relapse prevention, second edition: Maintenance strategies in the treatment of addictive behaviors*. New York, NY: The Guilford Press.

Relaxation Training

Defining It

Relaxation training is a behavioral intervention that uses different techniques to help individuals to induce relaxation and alleviate stress.

66 Ultra-Brief Interventions

How It Works

Relaxation training helps individuals relieve stress-related emotional and behavioral symptoms by employing different techniques, including progressive muscle relaxation and imagery-based relaxation techniques. Progressive muscle relaxation helps individuals relax by helping them focus on their muscle sensations when they are relaxed vs. tense. To practice, the provider instructs the client to tense and then relax individual muscle groups including those in the face, legs, hands, arms, feet, shoulders, abdominals, and eyes. The client schedules practice of progressive muscle relaxation in between sessions. Imagery-based relaxation techniques utilize either guided or emotive imagery. Using guided imagery, the provider has the client imagine taking a journey through a peaceful landscape, e.g., a beach, prompting the client to imagine visual, auditory, and olfactory sensations. Using emotive imagery, the client is instructed to imagine a scene or image that evokes positive feelings. Both imagery-based techniques must be practiced out of session as well as applied during times of stress.

When to Use It

Relaxation training can be used with children and adults to alleviate both psychological and somatic symptoms including anxiety, hyperactivity, phobias, insomnia, asthma attacks, migraine headaches, and chronic pain. It can be used as a stand-alone technique or as an adjunct to other interventions.

How to Use It

1. For progressive muscle relaxation, the provider first explains the purpose of the technique and the difference between tense and relaxed muscle states.
2. The provider instructs the client to sit in a relaxed position, preferably with eyes closed. The provider guides the client to systematically tense and relax individual muscle groups. The provider can model the tense-relax procedure, if necessary. Deep breathing techniques may be employed to increase relaxation.

3. The provider instructs the client to practice progressive muscle relaxation at least twice a day. An audio recording or worksheet may be provided to guide the client.
4. For guided imagery, the provider instructs the client to imagine a peaceful place such as a beach or forest. The provider guides the client to journey through the landscape and the client can take creative liberty, imagining him/herself flying through the scene or as an animal within it.
5. The provider instructs the client to practice the guided imagery between sessions. An audio recording or worksheet may be provided to guide the client.
6. For emotive imagery, the provider instructs the client to imagine an image that evokes positive feelings like happiness, courage, and excitement.
7. Next, the provider instructs the client to imagine regular or stressful events in the client's life and visualize the positive image accompanying the client through these events.
8. The provider instructs the client to practice the emotive imagery between sessions. An audio recording or worksheet may be provided to guide the client.

Example of How to Use It

Paula is a 26-year-old graduate student who reports stress and anxiety related to pressure from school and a separation from her boyfriend. She reports frequent headaches, insomnia, and tension in her neck and shoulders, also stating that her increased stress makes it difficult for her to concentrate on her schoolwork. Paula states she would like some practical tools for managing her stress during her busy schedule.

The provider introduces progressive muscle relaxation and explains the difference between tense and relaxed muscle states. The provider then has Paula close her eyes and get comfortable in the chair. The provider guides Paula through systematically tensing then relaxing muscles in her body starting with her toes and leading up to her face. For example, the provider instructs Paula to scrunch her toes tightly and then release them, noticing the difference between the tense and relaxed sensation.

After completing the exercise in session, Paula practices progressive muscle relaxation in a quiet space at home, once in the morning and once at night. The provider gives her a checklist of muscle groups to guide her through her practice.

68 Ultra-Brief Interventions

Learning More About It

Bernstein, D.A., Borkovec, T.D., & Hazlett-Stevens, H. (2000). *New directions in progressive relaxation training: A guidebook for helping professionals.* Westport, CT: Praeger.

McCallie, M.S., Blum, C.M., & Hood, C.J. (2006). Progressive muscle relaxation. *Journal of Human Behavior in the Social Environment,* 13(3), 51–66. doi:10.1300/J137v13n03_04

Stimulus Control

Defining It

A behavioral intervention for identifying factors (stimuli) that precede a behavior to be changed and then taking steps to alter the factors to bring about the desired result.

How It Works

Stimulus control works by using an individual's ability to associate a stimulus with a consequence. The stimulus then works to control the individual's behaviors. A stimulus can be an object, activity, image, or place. Stimulus control can be achieved when a stimulus is paired with either a pleasant or unpleasant experience, or when a behavior is reinforced or punished in the presence of a stimulus. For example, a person who gets food poisoning after eating chicken may then avoid chicken entirely, with the dish serving as the stimulus and its consumption as the behavior being controlled. The stimulus then serves as a trigger for a specific behavior or response.

The client is taught how stimuli become triggers when they are associated with certain behaviors. The provider helps the client list factors that trigger the undesired behavior. These can include thoughts, feelings, behaviors, and environmental factors. The client is encouraged to become more aware of possible triggers by monitoring the targeted behavior. For example, an individual with insomnia may find he cannot fall asleep on days when he answers work emails before bed. Once the client identifies triggers and agrees he/she would like to control them, the provider helps the client identify ways to control each trigger. For example, the client can plan to stop answering work emails at a specific time each day.

When to Use It

Stimulus control can be used to increase any desired behavior and decrease any undesired behavior.

How to Use It

1. The provider helps the client identify a targeted behavior that the client would like to either increase or decrease.
2. The provider then explains how stimuli become behavioral triggers and how stimulus control can be used to modify behaviors.
3. The client explores possible triggers to the targeted behavior as the provider asks about contributing thoughts, feelings, behaviors, and environmental factors, including other people.
4. The client monitors his/her target behavior and keeps a log of occurrences to identify all possible triggers.
5. The client and provider review triggers and agree on which triggers will be controlled.
6. The provider helps the client make a plan for controlling each specific trigger.

Example of How to Use It

Tyra is a 43-year-old woman seeking help controlling her eating. She states she is trying to lose weight but finds herself often overeating. The provider asks Tyra about her eating behaviors and finds that she is eating healthy meals but often overindulges in snacks and junk food. The provider explains how stimuli can become associated with certain behaviors and then become triggers to those behaviors. The provider uses an example of someone trying to quit smoking who smokes to relieve stress from his boss. The boss then becomes a trigger for smoking. The provider explains how stimuli can be identified and controlled and Tyra agrees to try the stimulus control intervention. The provider asks Tyra about thoughts, feelings, behaviors, sensations, people, and other environmental factors associated with her eating snacks. Tyra identifies she is triggered to eat when she feels stressed out and when she thinks about how busy she is at home and at work. The provider gives Tyra a log to fill out as she monitors her eating behavior over the next week. Tyra subsequently discovers she is also triggered when she walks through the cookie and snack aisle at the grocery store and when she sees advertisements for unhealthy foods. The provider helps Tyra come up with a plan to control each stimulus as follows: trigger (a) feeling stressed out – do a deep breathing exercise or go for a run; trigger (b) thinking about how busy she is – write down what she needs to do and distract herself by listening to music; trigger (c) walking down the snack aisle – avoid that aisle; trigger (d) seeing ads for junk food – avoid TV ads by not watching commercials, distract herself, eat a healthy snack.

Learning More About It

Bootzin, R.R. (1972). A stimulus control treatment for insomnia. *Proceedings of the American Psychological Association, 7*, 395–396.

Hunter, C.L., Goodie, J.L., Oordt, M.S., & Dobmeyer, A.C. (2017). *Integrated behavioral health in primary care: Step-by-step guidance for assessment and intervention* (2nd ed.). Washington, DC: American Psychological Association.

Thought Stopping

Defining It

A behavioral intervention used to interrupt and replace distressing, ruminative thoughts.

How It Works

Thought stopping is a therapeutic technique that aims to interrupt, remove, and replace distressing thoughts. Originally designed for use with obsessive thoughts, thought stopping assumes that interruption of obsessive thoughts will decrease their frequency and the anxiety they produce. Before application of the thought stopping technique, the provider helps the client generate a list of his/her common distressing thoughts. The provider then introduces an inhibitory behavior, typically a "Stop!" command, as the client focuses on a distressing thought. The "Stop!" command is intended to distract the individual from the distressing thought. Practicing thought stopping should give the individual a sense of control over unwanted thoughts. Alternatives to the

"Stop!" command include snapping a rubber band on the wrist, using a word other than "stop," or picturing a stop sign.

When to Use It

Thought stopping can be used for obsessive thoughts associated with depression, panic, generalized anxiety, tobacco use, drug and alcohol use, and body dysmorphic disorder. It can be used as either a stand-alone or auxiliary treatment. It is not indicated for obsessive-compulsive disorder as suppression of these thoughts has been shown to increase their severity.

How to Use It

1. First, the provider assesses the client's symptoms and behaviors. The client and provider generate a list of the client's common distressing thoughts. The distressing thoughts are discussed as well as the reason for suppressing them.
2. The thoughts are ranked in a hierarchy from least to most distressing. Thought stopping practice will progress from the least to the most distressing thought.
3. The client is asked to close his/her eyes and focus on the distressing thought. The client raises a finger when he/she is focused on the thought. When the client raises a finger, the provider loudly says, "Stop!" This command startles the client. The procedure is repeated for about ten minutes or 20 repetitions.
4. The client then practices the technique by saying the "Stop!" command out loud or in his/her head when a disturbing thought manifests. The client may modify the procedure by replacing the "Stop!" command with a word other than "stop," snapping a rubber band on the wrist, or picturing a stop sign. The client is instructed to practice the technique between sessions.

Example of How to Use It

Monica is a 41-year-old African-American woman who self-refers to counseling because of anxiety. She reports having distressing thoughts that seem to spiral out of control and leave her feeling immobilized with overwhelming

72 Ultra-Brief Interventions

anxiety. She expresses worry that there is something wrong with her because of the disturbing nature of her thoughts.

The provider assesses Monica and assures her that disturbing thoughts are common and most people experience them at some point in their lives. Monica is relieved and states she would like to rid herself of the upsetting thoughts. The provider helps Monica write a hierarchy of her disturbing thoughts from least to most distressing. She lists (1) she will be fired from her job, (2) she will become ill leaving no one to care for her children, (3) her children will die in a house fire.

The provider instructs Monica to close her eyes and focus on her first distressing thought: she will be fired from her job. As instructed, Monica raises a finger when she is focused on the thought. The provider yells, "Stop!" The command startles Monica and the provider explains that she cannot focus on two thoughts at once – both the distressing thought and the "Stop!" command. The provider repeats this procedure with Monica 19 more times until she reports feeling more comfortable with the technique. The provider helps her think of a more pleasant thought to focus on each time she suppresses the unwanted thought.

Monica then practices the "Stop!" command outside of sessions when she experiences the distressing thought. She imagines herself hugging her children during a happy memory every time she suppresses her disturbing thought. She and the provider eventually repeat the same procedure for each of her targeted disturbing thoughts.

Learning More About It

Wolpe, J., & Lazarus, A.A. (1966). *Behavior therapy techniques: A guide to the treatment of neuroses* (1st ed.). New York, NY: Pergamon Press.

Wolpe, J. (1958). *Psychotherapy by reciprocal inhibition*. Stanford, CA: Stanford University Press.

Concluding Note

This chapter describes the 20 ultra-brief interventions most useful in integrated care settings. Each intervention is designed to produce changes in behaviors and presenting symptoms in a short time frame, using easy-to-implement strategies. Chapters 5 through 10 will illustrate use of these interventions in various case examples.

Brief Assessment in Mental Health and Integrated Care Practice

3

An adequate assessment of the client's presenting problem facilitates treatment planning and leads to more successful outcomes. While an accurate assessment is important in all treatment settings, it is particularly important in settings that deliver ultra-brief interventions. Providers, whether mental health providers or behavioral health providers, must choose and implement targeted interventions in a short amount of time. In this and subsequent chapters, the designation "provider" is used unless treatment is specified as occurring in a mental health setting or integrated care setting, in which case the designations mental health provider or behavioral health provider is used.

Assessment directs the provider to select the interventions that will be most useful most quickly. A thorough assessment rules in or out any mental health disorders, identifies the client's pattern or personality style, determines the impact the presenting problem has had on the client's level of functioning, and screens for potential risk to self or others. Completing this specific type of assessment in 20–30 minutes is the challenge in mental health and integrated care settings. While assessment in mental health settings might extend to a follow-up session, in integrated care settings the behavioral health provider is expected to collect all pertinent information in a single session. This chapter provides an overview of the diagnostic and various types of functional and risk assessments that are the basis for planning and implementing treatment. Strategies for completing the assessment in an effective and timely manner are outlined, and a case example illustrates the assessment process.

74 Ultra-Brief Interventions

Forms of Assessment

Assessment in integrated care and mental health care settings can vary, and depends largely on the client's presenting problem. For example, a client referred for depression and a client referred for medical treatment noncompliance will likely warrant two different kinds of assessments. The latter might not require a diagnostic evaluation while the former requires a diagnostic evaluation for major depression as well as a risk assessment. The behavioral health provider must determine what to assess for each individual client. The different forms of assessment used in integrated mental health care settings include functional assessment, diagnostic evaluation, pattern identification, assessment of treatment compliance, risk assessment, medication misuse assessment, and cultural assessment. The focused format of behavioral health sessions in these settings requires clients to set short, measurable goals, so an assessment of goals should be part of the process for each client. After the initial assessment, the focus will be on ongoing assessment and progress monitoring. Following, is a description of each type of assessment.

Functional Assessment

Regardless of whether or not a diagnostic evaluation is warranted, the behavioral health provider should complete a functional assessment for each client. A functional assessment gathers information about how the problem affects the client's daily life. The presenting problem can affect the client's vocational and/or educational functioning, social functioning, ability to maintain intimate relationships, and ability to maintain self-care and household tasks. Clients may find themselves worried about their financial situation, responsibility for caring for dependents, or another significantly stressful context. Emotions and cognitions are also often affected by the presenting problem. For example, a client presenting with insomnia may find himself more irritable, more self-critical, and less focused. The functional assessment determines not only the nature of the problem, but the real-time effect it has had on the client, which can often be a cascade of issues. This gives the provider information as to whether a diagnostic evaluation is also warranted.

Individuals react to problems differently, depending on personality, environment, and related factors. Therefore, it is necessary to determine how the client has adjusted to the presenting problem. For example, two people with chronic pain can react in completely opposing ways, with one choosing to take up a healthier lifestyle by losing weight and incorporating daily exercise, and the other becoming sedentary and limiting daily activities. The client who became sedentary will likely experience more pain, leading to increased use of medical care, possible reliance on opiates, and increased possibility of depression and suicide risk. The client who adopted a healthier, more active lifestyle in response to pain is likely to avoid these negative consequences. Understanding how the client lives with the problem reveals client strengths as well as areas that need improvement or further attention.

Structure of the Assessment. The provider first clarifies the reason for the referral in order to assess the purpose of the counseling visit and the client's understanding of the problem. The client may have a different understanding of the problem than the referring physician, or may want to discuss more issues than those he or she was initially referred for. Some clients may be resistant to treatment and disagree with the physician's referral for sessions with the behavioral health provider. The provider assesses the duration of the problem, any triggering events, as well as the problem's frequency and intensity. A client experiencing chronic pain may not feel the pain every day or pain may fluctuate in intensity depending on the context. The behavioral health provider should determine how the problem presents for that specific client.

The functional assessment should also determine what makes the problem either better or worse. Factors that can either improve or worsen symptoms can be either physical, environmental, social, emotional, cognitive, or behavioral. Physical factors can include poor sleep or physical discomfort. Environmental factors can include a setting or situation. Social factors can include family or friends. Emotional factors can include anger or loneliness. Finally, cognitive and behavioral factors refer to the client's own unhelpful thoughts and behaviors.

Next, the provider should assess how the problem has affected the person in different common settings and activities. Areas to explore include social relationships, household duties, work function, and engagement in hobbies, exercise, or enjoyable activities. The provider should assess any other symptoms that might be attributable to the presenting problem, such as low mood, decrease in appetite, sleep disturbance, or fatigue. For clients presenting with low mood and other relevant symptoms, an assessment of suicidal and homicidal ideation may be necessary and should be determined by the provider. This is covered further in the section on risk assessment.

The provider can inquire about prescribed and over-the-counter medications and supplements and may inquire about alcohol, tobacco, or caffeine use, if it is relevant to the problem. For example, Monica is a 43-year-old working mother of two. She presents to counseling with complaints of not being able to fall asleep. She states she is constantly feeling stressed out and finds it difficult

76 Ultra-Brief Interventions

to fall asleep most nights. On an average night, Monica can get four hours of sleep until she is awakened by her children. She reports resulting irritability, daytime sleepiness, and difficulty concentrating. The provider asks Monica about caffeine use as part of the functional assessment. Monica reports she consumes four to six cups of coffee a day. Because she is tired from lack of sleep, she increased her caffeine intake to make it through the day and successfully complete all the tasks on her to-do list. Monica drinks coffee until 6 or 7 p.m. some days. The provider explains how the caffeine consumption so late in the day is contributing to her insomnia, causing a self-perpetuating cycle.

The provider evaluates if the client is compliant with medical appointments and if the presenting problem affects the client's ability to seek care. Clients who are prescribed opiates or any other medication with potential for abuse, like anxiolytics and sleeping medications, should be screened for medication misuse. Indications of medication misuse and noncompliance should be followed up with a more thorough evaluation.

Finally, the provider asks questions pertinent to the specific presenting problem. For example, in evaluating a diabetic client, the provider should assess how often the client checks his/her glucose levels, how well the client adheres to his/her meal plan, and how often he/she completes other necessary tasks like checking for skin sores. Each chapter that follows will provide an outline for the targeted questions included in a functional assessment for each specific presenting problem.

See Table 3.1 for an outline of areas to evaluate in a functional assessment and corresponding questions.

Diagnostic Evaluation

Clients referred for depression, anxiety, insomnia, or any other mental health condition require a diagnostic evaluation. This is similar to a traditional mental health assessment but is targeted specifically to the presenting problem, or any other warranted area. Clients presenting with a medical concern or a noncompliance issue may also have concurrent or resulting mental health symptoms. In this case, a diagnostic assessment is necessary to rule out possible mental health disorders. The provider should use criteria from the Diagnostic and Statistical Manual DSM-5 to rule out possible diagnoses. Screening instruments can help pinpoint the direction of the diagnostic evaluation and indicate if a risk assessment is necessary.

Table 3.1 Functional Assessment Key Points

Assessment Areas	Sample Assessment Questions
Purpose of the referral	Your primary care physician stated you have had some difficulty sleeping lately. Is that correct?
Duration of the problem	How long have you had this problem?
Triggering events	Did anything occur that triggered or started the problem?
Frequency	How often do you have this problem? Daily? If so, is it all day or sometimes?
Intensity	How intense is the problem?
	Can you rate the problem on a scale from 0–10 where 10 is the most intense possible?
	What is the most intense the problem has ever been? Least? (on the 0–10 scale)
	When does the intensity increase? Decrease?
What makes the problem better/worse	What makes the problem better? Worse?
	Physical
	Environmental
	Social
	Emotional
	Cognitive
	Behavioral
Vocational/educational functioning	How has your ability to work been affected by the problem?
	How has the problem affected your ability to go to school?

(continued)

Table 3.1 (*Cont.*)

Assessment Areas	Sample Assessment Questions
Social relationships	How has the problem affected your social relationships? (family, friends, romantic relationships)
Household duties	How has the problem affected your ability to keep up with household tasks?
Ability to care for self	How has the problem affected your ability to care for yourself? (i.e., hygiene, eating properly)
Ability to function as a caregiver	How has the problem affected your ability to care for household dependents? (i.e., children, ailing spouse)
Exercise	Do you exercise? Has the problem affected your ability to exercise?
Hobbies/enjoyable activities	How has the problem affected your ability to partake in hobbies and enjoyable activities?
Related problems	Has the problem caused any other issues? (e.g., disturbed sleep, fatigue, change in mood)
Medications	Do you take any prescribed medications?
	Do you take these medications as prescribed?
	Do you take any over-the-counter medications?
	Do you take any supplements or vitamins?
Alcohol, drug, caffeine, and/or tobacco use	How often do you consume alcohol/caffeine/tobacco? How much?
	Do you use any illegal substances?
Medical appointments	Do you regularly keep and attend all of your medical appointments?

Pattern Identification

Determining the client's pattern or personality style helps the provider effectively guide treatment and prevent relapse. Pattern is defined as the predicable, consistent, and self-perpetuating style and manner in which individuals think, feel, act, cope, and defend themselves (Sperry, Brill, Howard, & Grissom, 1996; Sperry, 2006). Patterns can be either maladaptive or adaptive. Maladaptive patterns are inflexible and ineffective and are characterized by reflexive responses to situations. Failing to address a client's maladaptive pattern can lead to the presenting problem returning once the client's pattern is triggered again. For example, Jake is referred to the provider to manage his weight. Part of his treatment plan includes regular exercise. Jake begins going to the gym regularly until one day he perceives that a woman at the gym seemed to laugh at him. Jake displays an avoidant pattern and withdraws from others when he does not feel safe. Because of this, Jake stops going to the gym altogether and becomes noncompliant with his treatment plan. Had the provider addressed Jake's avoidant pattern, he would have been more likely to maintain his treatment gains.

To elicit the client's pattern, the provider asks how the client would describe himself as a person and how others would describe him. Some clients may present with more than one pattern, one of which is more prominent than the other. Clients with maladaptive patterns that lead to serious impairment might meet criteria for a personality disorder diagnosis. The provider should rule out possible personality disorders during the assessment process.

Eliciting the client's pattern in a 10–20-minute session can be a challenge. The provider must pay attention to how the client describes themself, the factors that precipitated the client seeking treatment, and factors that maintain the client problem as these are related to the client's pattern. During the functional assessment, the provider elicits information about the client's daily functioning and social relationships. To evaluate client pattern while conducting the functional assessment, the provider should observe client beliefs and emotional, cognitive, and behavioral patterns. This way, the provider can more effectively identify client patterns in short-term therapy sessions.

Medical Treatment Noncompliance

For referrals concerning compliance, a more specialized kind of assessment is necessary. Compliance refers to the client's behavior in regard to adhering

80 Ultra-Brief Interventions

to a medical treatment plan and following physician advice. The provider should determine both the level of noncompliance, and the reasons behind it. Behaviors may include taking medications, making recommended lifestyle changes, or attending medical appointments. Factors to consider in an evaluation regarding compliance include the nature of the treatment plan, the person's perception of and adjustment to the illness, and the physician's accessibility to and relationship with the client.

Another important factor is the influence of a client's family dynamics on compliance. Families may be too involved or not involved enough in a person's medical treatment. Families that are not involved enough may undermine treatment by failing to provide adequate support. Overinvolved families, however, may interfere with the client's ability to take responsibility for their own treatment. Other family issues that could potentially affect treatment compliance include dysfunctional interactions or dynamics, poor communication patterns, or families unintentionally undermining client progress. In such cases, understanding compliance requires an understanding of the therapeutic triangle – that is between the client, provider, and family (Sperry, 2014). Table 3.2, below, outlines assessment areas and sample questions for treatment noncompliance.

Medication Misuse Assessment

Although opioid prescription rates have dropped significantly since 2012, opioids are still commonly prescribed, at the rate of 58.5 morphine milligram equivalents (MME) prescribed per 100 persons in 2017 (CDC, 2018). Up to 35% of primary care patients experience persistent pain (Morasco & Dobscha, 2008), and opioid medications are often the treatment of choice. Taking these medications over long periods or in high doses increases the likelihood of addiction to these medications, overdoses, and death (CDC, 2018). More than 40% of overdose deaths in 2016 involved prescription medications (Seth, Scholl, Rudd, & Bacon, 2018).

Many of these medications are prescribed in primary care settings, meaning these settings must also screen for the possibility of misuse. Matteliano and Chang (2015) found that of 120 primary care patients with chronic pain who were prescribed opioids, 54% appeared nonadherent to their prescription regimen as indicated by results of urine drug analyses. Additionally, 23% were found to be lacking the expected levels of opioids, while 12.5% tested positive for opioids other than those that were prescribed. Morasco and Dobscha (2008) found 78% of 127 chronic pain patients in primary care self-reported

Table 3.2   Noncompliance Assessment

Medication Adherence	How did your doctor instruct you to take your medications?
	How have you been taking your medications?
	What gets in the way of you taking your medications as prescribed?
Diet, Exercise, and Lifestyle Changes	What dietary/exercise changes has your doctor instructed you to make?
	To what extent have you made these changes?
	What gets in the way of you making these changes?
Compliance with Medical Appointments	Have you attended all of your medical appointments, including referrals, as your doctor instructs you?
	What gets in the way of you attending your appointments?
Attitude Towards Treatment Plan	How comfortable are you with the treatment plan the doctor has prescribed?
	Do you believe the treatment plan will work?
Relationship with Physician	Do you feel like the doctor considers your needs and opinions?
	Is your doctor available to you when you need him/her?
	Do you feel you have a good relationship with your doctor?
Adjustment to Diagnosis	How have you felt about having to deal with this diagnosis?
	To what extent do you feel you have been able to accept your diagnosis?
	What are some of your thoughts about your diagnosis?

(continued)

82 Ultra-Brief Interventions

Table 3.2 *(Cont.)*

Family Influence	How has your family reacted to your diagnosis?
	Has your family been supportive of your treatment?
	Would you like your family to be more involved in your treatment? Less involved?
	Do you find that your family members do things that get in the way of you following your treatment plan?
	Would you and your family members be willing to discuss your treatment plan together?

at least one indicator of medication misuse. Though these medications were once considered safe to prescribe for chronic pain, newer evidence points to worse outcomes long-term. Maintenance on opioid prescription medications can lead to decreased effectiveness of the medication and decreased patient pain thresholds (Morasco & Dobscha, 2008).

Although anyone can be at risk of misusing their prescription medications, factors associated with increased probability of opioid misuse include history of a substance use disorder, younger age, personal and family history of legal problems, anxiety, and beliefs about opioid medications (Morasco & Dobscha, 2008; Matteliano, Marie, Oliver, & Coggins, 2014). The provider should keep these factors in mind when screening for medication misuse. If medication misuse is suspected, the provider should screen for improper use or use of medications other than the way they were prescribed, medication-seeking behaviors, improper handling of medication, and high-risk behaviors. Improper use includes taking more medication than prescribed and using medications with alcohol and other substances. Medication-seeking behaviors include trying to obtain prescriptions from multiple doctors or asking for early refills. Improper handling of medication includes hoarding or sharing medication, and high-risk behaviors include selling or stealing medications and overdosing (Matteliano et al., 2014). The provider should screen for current or past substance abuse disorders as those with these histories are three to six times more likely to abuse their opioid prescriptions (Morasco & Dobscha, 2008). Table 3.3 outlines useful questions for medication misuse assessment and a

Table 3.3 Medication Misuse Assessment

Improper Use	Have you ever taken more medication than was prescribed?
	Have you ever run out of medication before you were supposed to?
	Do you ever use alcohol or other substances with your medication?
	Have you ever taken your medication other than the form in which it was prescribed, e.g. snorting, smoking?
Medication Seeking	Have you ever requested a refill on your medication before you were due for one?
	Have you requested an increased dose of your medication?
	Have you ever attempted to receive prescriptions for the same medication from more than one doctor?
	Have you ever lost your prescription medication, requiring another prescription?
Improper Handling	Have you ever saved unused medication for later use?
	Have you ever taken medication that was prescribed for someone else?
	Have you ever given your medication to someone for whom it was not prescribed?
High-Risk Behaviors	Have you ever bought or gotten medication from someone without a prescription?
	Have you ever sold or given another person your prescription medication?
	Have you ever stolen medication?
	Do you have a history of substance use problems?
	Have you ever overdosed on your medication?

84 Ultra-Brief Interventions

case example is provided in Chapter 7. The provider can also use the Current Opioid Misuse Measure (COMM) to assess medication misuse. This instrument also screens for impairments in functioning, and negative personal and social consequences resulting from opioid misuse. The COMM is detailed further in Chapter 7.

Risk Assessment

Clients referred for mental health symptoms like depression, posttraumatic stress, and anxiety can all be at risk of self-harm and should be assessed for suicide risk. Additionally, clients presenting with chronic pain should also be assessed for risk, as these patients are three times more likely to report suicidal thoughts than those who do not live with chronic pain (Tang & Crane, 2006). If the client indicates thoughts of suicide or self-harm, the provider must follow up with a thorough assessment of risk. Clients can have either passive or active suicidal ideation. Passive suicidal ideation is marked by thoughts that the person would not mind or would prefer if life ended but does not necessarily include a plan, while active suicidal ideation is marked by thoughts of wanting to harm oneself.

The provider should assess if the client has a self-harm plan, the means to carry out the plan, and history of previous suicide attempts. Intensity, duration, and frequency of suicidal thoughts should be determined. Finally, the provider should assess for protective factors. Some clients will report that they would not follow through on suicidal thoughts because of their religious beliefs, commitment to their loved ones, or other personal reasons (American Counseling Association, n.d.). When suicidal ideation is indicated, the provider can administer a standardized instrument like The Columbia Suicide Severity Rating Scale (C-SSRS). The C-SSRS is detailed in Chapter 5. Table 3.4 outlines assessment areas and questions for suicide risk assessment.

Cultural Assessment

Cultural differences are known to affect use of medical and mental health care services as well as clinical outcomes. Racial, ethnic, gender, and socioeconomic factors can all contribute to clients' presenting problems, the rate at which people seek out and utilize mental health care, and the individual experience of mental health care symptoms. Behavioral health providers must be aware that primary and integrated care settings may be the only way

Table 3.4   Risk Assessment

Suicidal Thoughts	Do you ever have thoughts of hurting yourself or that life is not worth living?
	Do you have thoughts like wishing you were no longer alive? (Passive)
	Do you think about wanting to take your own life? (Active)
	When was the last time you had these thoughts?
	How often do you have these thoughts?
	When you have these thoughts, how intense would you say they are on a scale from 0–10?
	How long do these thoughts last when you have them?
	Are you having these thoughts right now?
Plan and Means	Have you thought of methods for killing yourself?
	Have you decided on a method?
	Have you planned for how you would kill yourself?
	Does your plan involve harming someone else?
	Do you have the means or tools you need to carry out your plan?
	Do you have access to guns or other weapons?
Preparation	Have you decided on a date to kill yourself?
	Have you made arrangements or begun putting your affairs in order?
	Have you written a suicide note?
	Have you spoken to people about your suicidal thoughts and/or plans?

(continued)

Table 3.4 (Cont.)

History	Have you attempted suicide before? What did you do?
	What did you hope the outcome would be?
	What were the details of this event?
	Has anyone in your family attempted or completed suicide?
	Have any of your loved ones or acquaintances recently attempted or completed suicide?
Protective Factors	Do you want help for these suicidal thoughts?
	Are you open to accepting help from your doctor and myself?
	Is there a reason you would not follow through on your plans?
	Are you spiritual or religious? How do you view suicide through your spiritual or religious perspective?

some clients access mental health care and, therefore, clients must be accurately screened for mental health symptoms. Providers should also be aware of how culture influences client presentations and treatment plan compliance.

Cultural factors are related to differing rates of mental health symptoms commonly seen in integrated care and mental health care settings. Caucasian clients were found to be at higher risk for prescribed benzodiazepine misuse than Hispanic, Asian, and African-American patients (Cook et al., 2018). Non-Hispanic Caucasian and Native American and Alaskan clients are also more likely to overdose on opioid medications than African-American or Hispanic clients (CDC, 2018). Additionally, adolescent clients who are sexual minorities are more likely to report severe mental health problems, posttraumatic stress symptoms, and self-harming behaviors (Hirschtritt, Dauria, Marshall, & Tolou-Shams, 2018). African Americans are three times more likely to have diabetes than Caucasians, as well as higher rates of other disorders including heart disease and stroke (DHHS, 2001).

Cultural factors also affect whether and how people seek mental health care. Many non-white clients are hesitant to seek mental health services. For this reason, it is important to screen these clients for mental health symptoms in settings they are more likely to visit, like primary and integrated care. Still, these issues are prevalent with 17.4% of Asian-American men and 17.2% of Asian-American women reporting a lifetime prevalence of depression, anxiety, or substance abuse, though few receive any mental health services. For people of certain cultures and ethnicities, seeking help for mental health symptoms is primarily a social task, rather than an individual task (Pescosolido & Boyer, 2010). Primary care-based mental health services were shown to improve the likelihood that these patients would receive care (Nguyen & Bornheimer, 2014).

Among African-American clients, family dynamics can have a strong influence on whether clients seek out and follow through with mental health care. African Americans overwhelmingly underuse mental health services and families often decrease utilization of services by expressing negative attitudes. Family members may normalize or minimize symptoms and be opposed to the client seeking treatment (Villatoro & Aneshensel, 2014). When family members do support treatment, however, African-American clients are more likely to seek out and use mental health care services (Hines-Martin, Brown-Piper, Kim, & Malone, 2003).

Finally, culture affects how people experience, define, and express mental health symptoms. People of various ethnicities may be more prone to somatization and display mental health symptoms as physical symptoms. Somatic symptoms are more common in African-American and Asian clients. This is likely related to the stigmas around mental health conditions in these cultures (DHHS, 2001). Somatization was also found to be prominent in collectivistic cultures rather than individualistic cultures (Chang, Jetten, Cruwys, & Haslam, 2016). People of different ethnicities can also present with culture-bound syndromes. Attaques de nervios, or nerves, are common descriptions for intense emotional reactions marked by symptoms of anxiety and panic in Hispanic clients (APA, 2013). Similar symptoms experienced by African-American people, sometimes accompanied by fits of screaming, crying, or fainting, are typically referred to as "falling out" (DHHS, 2001). The provider should be aware of somatic reactions to mental health symptoms and the ways in which people of different cultures experience and describe symptoms. Table 3.5 details common somatic symptoms.

88 Ultra-Brief Interventions

Table 3.5 Common Somatic Symptoms of Mental Health Conditions

Headaches	Shortness of Breath
Muscle Pain & Tightness	Dizziness
Stomach Aches	Fainting
Chest Pain	Fatigue
Digestive Problems	Localized Pain
Numbness & Tingling	Weakness
Nausea	Paralysis

Assessment of Goals

Assessment of goals helps direct the focus of treatment planning and all subsequent sessions. Goals vary depending on the presenting problem and client resources and motivation, but share several common elements.

First, goals should be specific. Clients are more likely to attain concrete, measurable goals. For example, a vague goal would be to increase activity level as much as possible while a specific goal would be to walk for 15 minutes, five days a week. Second, goals should be both long-term, or distal, and short-term, or proximal. The client may have only one or two long-term goals, like losing 15 pounds, but multiple short-term behavioral goals. Short-term goals are practical and achievable and lead to attainment of long-term goals. A good short-term goal for weight loss would be to swap sports drinks for water.

Third, goals should be collaborative. Clients who take an active role in goal setting are more likely to attain their goals. Even attaining small goals increases client self-efficacy, leading them to work towards larger goals (Bodenheimer & Handley, 2009). The provider should prompt the client to identify things he/ she would like to achieve. The provider can make suggestions or list options, depending on the presenting problem. For example, if the presenting problem pertains to weight management, the provider can make recommendations about small behavioral changes that will accelerate a lifestyle change. The provider and client work together to narrow down long- and short-term goals that are both challenging and achievable.

Finally, clients have been found to respond better to goals that are related to their everyday lives rather than medical goals. Clients are more likely to attain goals that are tied to their social relationships, daily functioning, and emotional regulation (Lenzen et al., 2016). For example, a weight loss goal can be linked to having more energy to play with grandchildren, rather than improved cholesterol levels. Clients are also more amenable to goals that do not use medical or psychological terminology. Some clients may find this language intimidating or confusing. Goals should be specified in plain language that clients can understand. The client's level of motivation should be considered when determining goals, as clients who are not used to goal setting, or who have been unsuccessful in the past, are less likely to attain their goals. The provider's attitude towards and level of interest in the client can be a major motivating and confidence-building factor in goal setting (Lenzen et al., 2016). The provider should express genuine interest in and concern for the client during assessment of goals.

Ongoing Assessment and Progress Monitoring

Progress monitoring has become increasingly important in the counseling field as managed care companies hold counselors accountable for the success of their treatments (Meier, 2015). Additionally, it is estimated that treatment fails in up to 50% of cases (Persons & Mikami, 2002). With the added challenge of having to complete interventions in short-term therapy, behavioral health providers must be vigilant in monitoring client progress. Tracking client progress can help focus treatment and indicate when more or different interventions are necessary. Standardized instruments should be administered prior to each session to track symptoms. Client self-report measures like the Mood Scale and Subjective Unit of Distress Scale (SUDS) can be helpful, as are client logs. Activity, eating habits, frequency of relaxation exercises, and compliance with homework assignments can be monitored through client logs. Chapters 5 through 10 detail progress monitoring procedures for various client presentations. Table 3.6 outlines measures and worksheets used for progress monitoring.

Conducting the Assessment

As previously stated, assessments in integrated care and mental health care settings require the provider to obtain all necessary information and establish a therapeutic alliance in just 10–20 minutes. For this reason, they must be focused and skillfully conducted.

90 Ultra-Brief Interventions

Table 3.6 Tools for Progress Monitoring

Depression	Mood log
	Activity log
	Mood Scale
	Standardized instruments
Anxiety & PTSD	Subjective Unit of Distress Scale (SUDS)
	Controlled breathing log
	Progressive muscle relaxation log
	Standardized instruments
Chronic Pain	Subjective Unit of Distress Scale (SUDS)
	Standardized instruments
Sleep Problems	Controlled breathing log
	Progressive muscle relaxation log
	Standardized instruments
Weight Problems	Body Mass Index
	Food journal
	Activity journal
	Goal log
	Weight loss zones
	Standardized instruments
Diabetes	Goal log
	Food journal
	Activity journal
	Standardized instruments

Effective Information Gathering

New providers are taught to ask open-ended questions but, while these kinds of questions are useful and effective, behavioral health providers must learn to ask more focused closed-ended questions. Closed-ended questions are designed to gather pertinent information quickly. Additionally, the provider uses fewer reflective statements during the assessment. While the counselor can clarify vague information or confusing client statements, purely reflective statements should be limited. The provider should remember that the purpose of this interaction is to gather critical information for use in treatment planning and requires the provider to take a directive role. Assessment questions for various client presentations are provided in Chapters 5 through 10.

Provider Demeanor and Interview Qualities

Though the initial session is brief and comprised mostly of closed-ended questions and focused tasks, there are still steps the provider can take to build the necessary therapeutic alliance with the client. Clients are more likely to be willing to participate in an assessment and adhere to a treatment plan when they feel the provider takes a genuine interest in them as a person (Lenzen, 2016). Clients also feel more comfortable with providers who use collaborative language and avoid overuse of medical or psychological jargon (Lenzen, 2016). The provider should also recognize that client motivation varies and should use Motivational Interviewing techniques to broach difficult subjects and work with client resistance. Asking client permission can be extremely helpful in reducing resistance and increasing client trust. The provider can also display care and empathy in the way he/she approaches the client. A warm handshake or even a light touch on the shoulder, if appropriate, can communicate care.

Use of Screening Instruments

Screening instruments are assessment tools that are easily administered, and scored, and provide useful insight into a client's presenting problem. Some screening instruments can be helpful in arriving at a diagnosis. Most often, these instruments are completed in paper and pencil format and clients are asked to rate their recent experience with the presenting symptoms on a scale of severity or intensity. Screening instruments should be both valid and reliable, meaning they have demonstrated they measure what they intend to measure and that measurement is consistent. Instruments should be apropos to the presenting problem and be administered prior to each session for use in progress monitoring. For example, a client presenting with depression will provide valuable information on the effectiveness of his/her treatment by way of his/her weekly scores on an instrument like the Patient Health Questionnaire-9. Table 3.7 lists valid and reliable instruments useful for assessment and progress monitoring. These instruments are described in further detail in their respective chapters.

92 Ultra-Brief Interventions

Table 3.7 Recommended Screening Instruments

Presenting Problem	Screening Instrument
Depression	The Patient Health Questionnaire-9 (PHQ-9)
Anxiety	The Generalized Anxiety Disorder Questionnaire-7 (GAD-7)
Posttraumatic Stress	The PCL PTSD Checklist
Chronic Pain	The PEG Scale
Insomnia	The Insomnia Severity Index
Weight Problems	The Weight-Related Eating Questionnaire (WREQ)
Diabetes	The Diabetes Distress Scale (DSS)
Medication Misuse	Current Opioid Misuse Measure (COMM)
	The Drug Abuse Screening Test (DAST)
Suicide Risk	The Patient Health Questionnaire-9 (PHQ-9)
	Columbia Suicide Severity Rating Scale (C-SSRS)

Implications for Treatment Planning

Adequate assessment leads to effective treatment planning and measurable results in short-term therapy. Understanding the presenting problem's consequences on the client's daily functioning helps determine which ultra-brief interventions the provider will use. For example, a client with panicky symptoms will benefit from calming interventions like controlled breathing, while a client experiencing social withdrawal would benefit from increasing activity through behavioral activation.

Identifying the client's pattern helps providers select treatments, know how to approach a client, and foresee possible obstacles. For example, a client who is more paranoid or mistrustful of treatment may be more resistant to working with the behavioral health provider. This kind of client needs validation and needs to feel a sense of control in the session, which can be achieved using motivational interviewing and an empathic, patient, and collaborative provider demeanor.

Proper assessment sometimes directs further evaluation. Screening for risk or medication misuse can prompt the need for a more thorough evaluation. Assessment also informs the provider as to when culturally-sensitive treatments are indicated. A thorough assessment will ensure highly effective interventions in short-term therapy.

Relation to Case Conceptualization

Although behavioral health sessions in integrated settings differ from traditional counseling in both their goals and duration, providers will benefit from creating at least brief case conceptualizations for clients. A brief case conceptualization specifies what the presenting problem is, the presenting problem's precipitant, client pattern, predispositions, and perpetuants, or factors that maintain the problem. For example, David presents with depression (presentation) after a business failing in which he lost a substantial amount of money (precipitant). David has a pattern of perfectionism, holding himself to high standards and scolding himself for perceived shortcomings (pattern). David's mother suffered from depression (biological predisposition). He displays an obsessive-compulsive personality style and believes he can only rely on himself (psychological predisposition). David grew up as a lonely child, feeling like his peers misunderstood him (social predisposition) and currently has few friends, reinforcing his view of others and himself (perpetuants). An effective plan for David would include behavioral activation and a shift towards a less perfectionistic pattern.

Putting It All Together

Assessment is critical to providing effective treatment in short-term therapy. A useful assessment gathers information about the client's presenting problem and its effect on the client's daily functioning, while also establishing a therapeutic relationship. To achieve this in a 20–30-minute session, the provider must communicate concern and interest in the client while deciding which forms of assessment are necessary. Every client requires a functional assessment, or an assessment of the problem's impact on social, personal, academic, and vocational functioning. The functional assessment is structured and consists of closed-ended questions. When the presenting problem is a mental health symptom, a diagnostic evaluation is indicated. With other presenting problems, the provider must determine if a diagnostic evaluation is warranted as well.

Pattern identification is also important with every client. Understanding the client's pattern is crucial for treatment planning and anticipating obstacles. Additionally, accurately identifying the client's pattern helps the provider focus sessions towards pattern change. This focus increases the likelihood that

94 Ultra-Brief Interventions

clients will be compliant with medical treatment and will not relapse into the behaviors that once contributed to their presenting problem.

Clients who are prescribed a medical treatment regimen by their physicians need to be screened for noncompliance. Clients with diabetes, chronic pain, and other conditions will likely have dietary, exercise, and medication plans given to them by the primary physician. The provider should assess the client's level of compliance with these plans as well as reasons for noncompliance. Similarly, clients may be prescribed opioids or other medications that have the potential for misuse. In this case, the provider should assess for medication misuse, starting with screening for improper use and moving on to screening for medication-seeking behavior, improper handling of medication, and screening for high-risk behaviors, if indicated.

As with a diagnostic evaluation, not every client requires a risk assessment. Clients presenting with depression, posttraumatic stress, anxiety, or other mental health problems should be screened for risk. Additionally, providers should screen chronic pain clients for risk, as these clients are at higher risk of suicidal thoughts. If suicidal ideation is reported, the provider should follow up with a full risk assessment.

A cultural assessment includes observing and paying attention to cultural factors, and is important for each client, to varying degrees. The provider should keep in mind that culture affects both symptom presentation and treatment planning. Families of different cultures play important roles that can either support or hinder treatment. Clients from collectivistic cultures are more likely to display somatic symptoms in lieu of emotional displays. The provider should keep in mind that certain physical symptoms can be indicators of depression or anxiety.

Finally, all clients must be assessed for their treatment goals, both long-term and short-term. Short-term goals are particularly important as they are easier to conceptualize and achieve. The provider should tie client goals to real-life outcomes that the client finds personally valuable. Technical language should be avoided, and the client and provider collaborate on setting goals. Progress towards these goals, as well as presenting symptoms, is then tracked through a process of progress monitoring. Standardized screening instruments can be used for both assessment and progress monitoring.

Due to time constraints in short-term therapy, a lot must happen in a very short assessment session. Using effective screening instruments and questions will help guide the direction of the assessment, so it is completed in a timely fashion. Because primarily closed-ended questions, and few reflective statements, are used, the provider must communicate care throughout the interaction and both socialize the client to the process and put the client at ease by asking permission and using motivational interviewing strategies. A detailed case example of an assessment of a client presenting with chronic pain illustrates this process.

Case Example

Sandy is a 46-year-old Caucasian female patient in an integrated care clinic who was referred by her physician to the clinic's behavioral health provider for evaluation of her chronic pain. Sandy lives with her husband and is a stay-at-home mom to her two teenage children. She maintained a part-time job as a massage provider but recently took a leave of absence because of her back pain. Sandy attended her medication refill appointment for opioid pain medication and agreed to try behavioral health interventions for her pain. The prescribing physician brings the behavioral health provider into the exam room to meet Sandy and the behavioral health provider shakes her hand. The physician then explains how the provider could help her. The provider briefly explains her role in treating chronic pain and asks if the client would like to further discuss these possible interventions. Sandy agrees, expressing that the pain has hindered her life in many ways.

The behavioral health provider meets with Sandy one-on-one and has her complete the PEG scale to measure pain intensity and interference. The PEG is outlined in the chronic pain chapter. PEG is an acronym for pain intensity (P), interference with enjoyment of life (E), and interference with general activity (G). On the PEG, Sandy reports average pain of 6 in the last week, a 7 for pain's interference with her life in the past week, and a 6 for interference with general activity, on a 0–10 scale. The provider explains that this session will be brief, about 20 to 30 minutes, and is meant to help the provider better understand the client. She socializes Sandy to the assessment process and the role of directed questions. Sandy agrees to continue the assessment.

The provider asks Sandy how she would describe her pain and gives her a list of adjectives that can be used to describe pain. Sandy says she has gnawing, tugging pain in her sciatic area, usually only on the right side, with intermittent stabbing pain in her lower back. The provider asks when the pain began and how long the pain has been present. Sandy indicates her pain began at work one day when she was performing a massage and her back started hurting. By the end of the day, she could not stand up straight. Sandy later had an MRI that confirmed she has a herniated disc but she does not know what caused that condition. The pain started about eight months ago and Sandy describes it as being "unrelenting" since then. When asked what she means by unrelenting, Sandy states she has the pain every day for most of the day.

The provider asks Sandy to rate her pain on four scales from 0–10 and Sandy answers the following: over the last two weeks on average – 6; highest level of pain in the last two weeks – 7; lowest level of pain in the last two weeks – 5; current level of pain – 5. Sandy indicates that work and chores increase her level of pain and nothing but her medication seems to decrease her pain.

The provider asks how the pain has affected Sandy's mood and Sandy responds that she finds herself feeling sad often. She states she feels defeated and like the pain will never go away. The provider asks about how others have responded to Sandy's pain and Sandy states that her family has been very understanding and her husband helps her a lot. She adds that her mother comes over to her home a few times a week to help her with household chores as well. He asks Sandy to describe a typical day and how pain affects it. Sandy is asked to reflect on her work, social life, hobbies, and necessary tasks. Sandy states, "I used to be very active. I had my massage clients and took care of my kids. I made sure my husband always had dinner after work. I just love taking care of everyone. But, these days it seems like everyone is taking care of me. They have been so nice. I can't complain. But I don't do much of anything. I just try to rest. I just feel I can't do all these things with all this pain. My kids have had to make their own lunches and stuff for school. They are in high school but I feel so guilty that I'm not being the mom I should be and know I can be. I am worried they are pulling away from me but I just have so much pain and I am so tired lately." The provider empathizes with Sandy and asks if she would describe herself as someone who likes to take care of others to maintain relationships. Sandy agrees, and the provider determines she displays a dependent personality style.

The provider asks Sandy how she has tried dealing with the pain, to which Sandy responds she just lays in bed or on the sofa with a hot pack. Because Sandy is prescribed opioid medications, the provider asks questions about medication use. He asks how often Sandy takes her prescribed medication. Sandy responds that she does not take it much at all. She says, "I am home alone all day, which I don't like. I use that time to talk on the phone or through video chats. I have friends that live in different time zones I can talk to and other moms that have time during the day. I like to talk to people while I'm home and the medication just makes me sleep. So, I actually don't take it a lot. Only when the pain is so bad I can't sleep at night. Like a couple of nights a week." The provider commends Sandy for investing herself in her social relationships and points out how this distraction helps her pain. He asks if Sandy still has medication left from her previous prescription prior to today's refill appointment and Sandy states she has saved up about 30 pills. "I don't need them but if I do, I have them. I don't like to feel like I don't have them in case I need them," she states. The BHC asks if she ever gives her medication to people for whom it is not prescribed and she says, "oh, no, I keep it locked up. My kids don't even know I take it. I take it after they go to bed." The provider asks if Sandy uses alcohol or other medications or substances and Sandy says she is only a social drinker and has not been very social lately so has not been drinking much and never drinks alcohol with her medication. The provider determines medication misuse is probably not an issue at this time and does not warrant any further assessment, but makes a note for the prescribing physician that the client is not using all of her medication.

Because Sandy mentioned feeling sadness and guilt, the BHC decides to do a diagnostic evaluation for depression. She explains the rationale and asks Sandy if this is ok. Sandy agrees and the provider asks her to fill out the Patient Health Questionnaire-9 (PHQ-9). Sandy scores a 9, indicating the higher end of mild depression. He continues to discuss the results of the PHQ-9 with Sandy and asks about diagnostic criteria. Sandy states she feels sad most of the day, nearly every day; has feelings of guilt and worthlessness; feels tired most of the day, nearly every day; lacks interest and pleasure in things she once used to enjoy; and has an increased need for sleep. She has experienced these symptoms for roughly the last six weeks. Sandy denies suicidal ideation and did not indicate such on the PHQ-9. Therefore, the provider determines no further risk assessment is necessary at this time.

Next, the provider moves on to her expectations of treatment and asks Sandy what she would like to see improve. Sandy states she would like to have less pain and for her mood to improve. The BHC states those are great long-term goals and asks if Sandy has any ideas for small steps she can take to achieve those goals. Sandy states, "well, like you said when I'm distracted, I do feel less pain. I guess that's true. I can do something that distracts me. My husband and I used to go to dinner on Friday nights and I haven't done that in several months. I could probably do that if he was willing to go somewhere close to the house." The provider agrees this is a good idea and sets a short-term goal of going to dinner with her husband one time in the next week. Sandy agrees and then he informs her that next time they will review things she can do to change her experience of pain as well as boost her mood. Finally, the provider asks her if she has any questions, briefly responds, and ends the session.

Concluding Note

The goal of assessment in mental health and integrated care settings is to gather pertinent information and plan and implement treatment in brief sessions. The provider, whether mental health provider or behavioral health provider, focuses the assessment based on the client's presenting problem, chart or referral information, and responses on screening instruments and questions. While some form of functional assessment is standard, the provider's assessment focus may or may not include a thorough diagnostic or risk assessment for every client. The assessment process is facilitated by a caring and collaborative approach to the client, which builds trust and rapport in this short session, and by asking primarily closed-ended questions. Chapters 5 through 10 illustrate assessment processes for various client presentations.

References

American Counseling Association. (n.d.). Suicide Assessment. Retrieved from www.counseling.org/docs/trauma-disaster/fact-sheet-6---suicide-assessment.pdf?sfvrsn=2

American Psychiatric Association. (2013). *Diagnostic and statistical manual of mental disorders* (5th ed.). Arlington, VA: American Psychiatric Publishing.

Bodenheimer, T., & Handley, M.A. (2009). Goal-setting for behavior change in primary care: An exploration and status report. *Patient Education and Counseling*, 76, 174–180.

Centers for Disease Control and Prevention. (2018). Opioid Overdose: Prescription Opioid Data. Retrieved from www.cdc.gov/drugoverdose/data/prescribing.html

Chang, M.X., Jetten, J., Cruwys, T., & Haslam, C. (2016, October 20). Cultural identity and the expression of depression: A social identity perspective. *Journal of Community and Applied Social Psychology*, 27(1), 16–34. https://doi.org/10.1002/casp.2291

Cook, B.A., Creedon, T.A., Wang, Y.B., Lu, C.C., Carson, N.A., Jules, P.A., ... Alegria, M.B. (2018, June). Examining racial/ethnic differences in patterns of benzodiazepine prescription and misuse. *Drug and Alcohol Dependence*, 187, 29–34.

Department of Health and Human Services (DHHS). (2001). *Mental health: Culture, race, and ethnicity: A supplement to mental health, a report of the Surgeon General.* (2001) Rockville, MD: Department of Health and Human Services (DHHS). Retrieved from www.webharvest.gov/peth04/20041015192359/www.surgeongeneral.gov/library/mentalhealth/cre/sma-01-3613.pdf

Doherty, W., & Baird, M. (1983). *Family therapy and family medicine: Toward the Primary Care of Families.* New York, NY: Guilford.

Hines-Martin, V., Brown-Piper, A., Kim, S., Malone, M. (2003). Enabling factors of mental health service use among African Americans. *Archives of Psychiatric Nursing*, 17(5), 197–204.

Hirschtritt, M.E., Dauria, E.F., Marshall, B.D., & Tolou-Shams, M. (2018). Sexual minority, justice-involved youth: A hidden population in need of integrated mental health, substance use, and sexual health services. *Journal of Adolescent Health*, 63, 421–428.

Hunter, C.L., Goodie, J.L., Oordt, M.S., & Dobmeyer, A.C. (2017). *Integrated behavioral health in primary care: Step-by-step guidance for assessment and intervention* (2nd ed.). Washington, DC: American Psychological Association.

Lenzen, S.A., van Dongen, J.J., Daniels, R., van Bokhoven, M.A., van der Weijden, T., & Beurskens, A. (2016). What does it take to set goals for self-management in primary care? A qualitative study. *Family Practice*, 33(6), 698–703.

Matteliano, D., & Chang, Y. (2015, February). Describing prescription opioid adherence among individuals with chronic pain using urine drug testing. *Pain Management Nursing*, 16(1), 51–59.

Matteliano, D., St. Marie, B.J., Oliver, J., & Coggins, C. (2014, March). Adherence monitoring with chronic opioid therapy for persistent pain: A biopsychosocial-spiritual approach to mitigate risk. *Pain Management Nursing*, 15(1), 391–405.

Meier, S.T. (2015). *Incorporating progress monitoring and outcome assessment into counseling and psychotherapy: A primer.* New York, NY: Oxford University Press.

Morasco, B.J., & Dobscha, S.K. (2008). Prescription medication misuse and substance use disorder in VA primary care patients with chronic pain. *General Hospital Psychiatry*, 30, 93–99.

Nguyen, D., & Bornheimer, L.A. (2014, October). Mental health service use types among Asian Americans with a psychiatric disorder: Considerations of culture and need. *The Journal of Behavioral Health Services & Research*, 41(4), 520–528.

Persons, J.B., & Mikami, A.Y. (2002). Strategies for handling treatment failure successfully. *Psychotherapy: Theory/Research/Practice/Training*, 39, 139–151.

Pescosolido, B.A., & Boyer, C.A. (2010). Understanding the context and dynamic social processes of mental health treatment. In T.L. Scheid, & T.N. Brown (Eds), *A handbook for the study of mental health* (pp. 420–428). Cambridge: Cambridge University Press.

Seth, P., Scholl, L., Rudd, R.A., & Bacon, S. (2018, March). Overdose deaths involving opioids, cocaine, and psychostimulants – United States, 2015–2016. *Morbidity and Mortality Weekly Report*, 67(12), 349–358.

Sperry, L. (2014). *Behavioral health: Integrating individual and family interventions in the treatment of medical conditions.* New York, NY: Routledge.

Sperry, L., Brill, P., Howard, K., & Grissom, G. (1996). *Treatment outcomes in psychotherapy and psychiatric interventions.* New York, NY: Brunner/Mazel.

Tang, N.K., & Crane, C. (2006, May). Suicidality in chronic pain: A review of the prevalence, risk factors, and psychological links. *Psychological Medicine*, 36(5), 575–586.

Villatoro, A.P., & Aneshensel, C.S. (2014). Family influences on the use of mental health services among African Americans. *Journal of Health and Social Behavior*, 55(2), 161–180.

Pattern-Focused Therapy in Mental Health and Integrated Care Practice

4

This chapter describes Pattern-Focused Therapy, a brief, targeted, and effective approach that we have found to be successful in implementing the new practice model. It is consistent with the demand for short-term therapy consisting of very brief sessions that include ultra-brief interventions. We have also found it to be an excellent vehicle for delivering these interventions.

This chapter begins with an overview of Pattern-Focused Therapy including its origins, components, and its therapeutic process and strategy. Then, it illustrates the application of this approach with extended case material and a session transcription for use in either mental health or integrated care settings within a 30-minute time frame.

Overview of the Approach

Pattern-Focused Therapy is a brief therapeutic approach for easily and effectively identifying and changing an individual's maladaptive pattern of thinking, feeling, and behaving to a healthier and more adaptive pattern. It accomplishes this by replacing the non-productive thoughts or interpretations and behaviors that underlie the maladaptive pattern with more adaptive ones. Other modalities such as behavioral rehearsal, cognitive restructuring, exposure, skill training, reframing, and interpretation can be employed as adjunctive treatments.

This form of therapy and counseling emphasizes patterns. Pattern is the predicable, consistent, and self-perpetuating style and manner in which individuals think, feel, act, cope, and defend themselves (Sperry, Brill, Howard, & Grissom, 1996; Sperry, 2006). Patterns can be maladaptive or adaptive. Maladaptive patterns tend to be inflexible, ineffective, and inappropriate, and cause symptoms, impairment in personal and relational functioning, and chronic dissatisfaction (Sperry, 2010). If such a pattern is sufficiently distressing or impairing it can be diagnosed as a personality disorder. In contrast, an adaptive pattern reflects a personality style that is flexible, appropriate, and effective, and is reflective of personal and interpersonal competence (Sperry & Sperry, 2012).

The clinical value of this approach is threefold. First, it has much wider applicability than most other CBT approaches. For example, it can be used with almost all client presentations and diagnoses. The exceptions are acute psychosis and greatly impaired cognition, such as dementia (McCullough, 2000). Second, it does not require that individuals have the capacity for insight, a capacity that is assumed in CBT (and other) approaches that emphasize cognitive change strategies like cognitive restructuring or disputation. In this regard it is a "cognitive and behavioral replacement" treatment approach rather than a "restructuring" approach. This means that it is easier and quicker to substitute or replace a problematic thought or behavior with a more useful thought or behavior, than to slowly and meticulously dispute or restructure it. As the client shifts to healthier thoughts and behaviors, the underlying pattern shifts to a healthier and more adaptive one. Third, this focused treatment approach is relatively easy to learn and master, particularly with effective supervision.

Origins

Pattern-Focused Therapy was developed by Len Sperry (Sperry, 2016). It is derived from four sources: the pattern focus in Biopsychosocial Therapy, the questioning strategy of Cognitive Behavioral Analysis System of Psychotherapy (CBASP), specific questions from Motivational Interviewing (MI), and clinical outcomes measures. CBASP is designated as an empirically supported treatment by the Society of Clinical Psychology of the American Psychological Association.

Biopsychosocial Therapy

Biopsychosocial Therapy is an integrative approach developed by Len Sperry (1998) that incorporates biological, psychological, and socio-cultural factors in planning and implementing psychological treatment. This approach emphasizes a therapeutic process that is pattern focused. It involves three change strategies: pattern identification, pattern change, and pattern maintenance (Sperry, 2000, 2006).

Cognitive Behavior Analysis System of Psychotherapy

Cognitive Behavior Analysis System of Psychotherapy is a psychotherapy approach developed by James McCullough (2000). It is a third wave cognitive behavioral approach that was originally targeted to chronic depression. Today, it is considered applicable to most presentations. Also known as CBASP, it focuses on identifying and changing hurtful thoughts and behaviors with more helpful ones. From it a specific questioning sequence has been derived that consists of processing nine sets of questions (McCullough, 2000; 2014).

Motivational Interviewing

Motivational Interviewing is a therapeutic strategy developed by William Miller (Miller & Rollnick, 2002) for helping individuals in discovering and resolving their ambivalence to change. Specific techniques involve seeking permission, rolling with resistance, rating of level of importance, and rating of level of confidence (Miller & Rollnick, 2002).

Clinical Outcomes Measurement

Outcomes assessment and progress monitoring in psychotherapy and counseling is increasingly utilized in clinical practice today (Meier, 2015). Clinical outcomes measurement is an essential element of Pattern-Focused Therapy and includes assessment of the therapeutic relationship in addition to treatment outcomes (Sperry, Brill, Howard, & Grissom, 1996; Sperry 2010).

Components

Components refers to the core elements and active ingredients of a therapeutic approach that effect change. Pattern-Focused Therapy involves three such components: patterns, pattern identification, and pattern shifting.

Pattern

Pattern can be defined as the predicable, consistent, and self-perpetuating style and manner in which individuals think, feel, act, cope, and defend themselves (Sperry, Brill, Howard & Grissom, 1996; Sperry, 2006). Patterns can either be maladaptive or adaptive. Patterns that are maladaptive tend to be inflexible, ineffective, and inappropriate, and cause symptoms and impairment in personal and relational functioning, as well as chronic dissatisfaction. "If such a pattern is sufficiently distressing or impairing it can be diagnosed as a personality disorder. In contrast, an adaptive pattern reflects a personality style that is flexible, effective, and appropriate" (p. 817). This approach to pattern derives from Biopsychosocial Therapy (Sperry, 2006).

Pattern Recognition

Effective therapy requires changing maladaptive patterns and a critical part of this change is for clinicians to become adept at pattern recognition. It has been noted that clients and patients can and do recognize patterns:

> Most patients readily accept the idea that there is a 'pattern' underlying their behavior. The word is reassuring, for it suggests that there is order and meaning to behavior and experience. Educating patients about these patterns helps them to distance themselves from events and promotes self-observation. At the same time, pattern recognition promotes integration by connecting events, behaviors, and experiences that were previously assumed to be unconnected. (Livesley, 2003, p. 274)

Therapists can determine the client's pattern from the assessment interview, observation, and psychological assessment. It should not be surprising that patterns reflect an individual's core personality style. Accordingly, therapists who recognize an individual's basic personality style are likely to

104 Ultra-Brief Interventions

easily identify that individual's corresponding maladaptive patterns. A chart listing the most common maladaptive and adaptive patterns based on personality styles is available (Sperry & Binensztok, 2018).

Pattern Shifting

A second component of Pattern-Focused Therapy is pattern shifting. Shifting refers to a change from a maladaptive pattern to a more adaptive pattern. The shift occurs with repeated application of the query sequence, which is a strategy for processing therapeutic material. Shifting from a maladaptive to a more adaptive pattern indicates that second order change has occurred. While CBASP fosters consequential thinking and replacement of problematic thoughts and behaviors, it does not identify maladaptive patterns that intentionally focus on shifting to more adaptive patterns. Accordingly, the most it can achieve is symptoms resolution, or personal or relationship stabilization, which are first order change goals. In contrast, because its focus also includes pattern shifting, Pattern-Focused Therapy can also achieve second order change goals.

Basic Premises

Pattern-Focused Therapy is based on four premises. First, individuals unwittingly develop a self-perpetuating, maladaptive pattern of functioning and relating to others. Subsequently, this pattern underlies a client's presenting issues. Second, pattern change is an essential component of evidence-based practice. Third, effective treatment involves a change process in which the client and therapist collaborate to identify the maladaptive pattern and shift it to a more adaptive pattern. At least two outcomes result from this change process: increased well-being and resolution of the client's presenting issue (Sperry & Sperry, 2012). Fourth, *replacing* non-productive thinking and behaviors with more productive ones can quickly lead to effective therapeutic change. This contrasts with other therapeutic approaches that endeavor to directly restructure or challenge cognitions, as with Cognitive Therapy, or approaches that focus on directly modifying behavior, as with Behavior Therapy.

Therapeutic Process and Strategy

This form of psychotherapy and counseling emphasizes patterns. Pattern is the predicable, consistent, and self-perpetuating style and manner in which individuals think, feel, act, cope, and defend themselves (Sperry, Brill, Howard, & Grissom, 1996; Sperry, 2006). Patterns can be maladaptive or adaptive. Maladaptive patterns tend to be inflexible, ineffective, and inappropriate, and cause symptoms, impairment in personal and relational functioning, and chronic dissatisfaction (Sperry, 2010). If such a pattern is sufficiently distressing or impairing it may be diagnosed as a personality disorder. In contrast, an adaptive pattern reflects a personality style that is flexible, appropriate, and effective, and is reflective of personal and interpersonal competence (Sperry & Sperry, 2012).

Pattern-Focused Therapy begins with establishing a collaborative relationship and educating the client in the basic premises of this approach. Central to the assessment and case conceptualization process is the identification of the maladaptive pattern, and then planning treatment that focuses on pattern change. Other key factors considered in planning treatment are the level of readiness for change, severity, skill deficits, and strengths and protective factors.

A basic therapeutic strategy in the change process is to analyze problematic situations reported by clients in terms of their maladaptive pattern. Clients are first asked to describe the situation and their resulting interpretations (thoughts) and behaviors. Then, they are queried about their expected outcome in contrast to the actual one that resulted.

As the counseling process begins, clients inevitably report that they did not achieve their expected outcome. Parenthetically, a marker of subsequent therapeutic change is that clients increasingly experience, as a result of shifting to a more adaptive pattern, that they are achieving their expected outcome. They are then asked about their interpretations and if each helped or hurt them in getting what they expected. If not, they are asked what alternative interpretations would have helped them achieve. Their reported behaviors are analyzed as to whether the behavior helped or hurt in achieving their expected outcome. If not, the focus is on identifying alternative behavior which could achieve that end. Finally, the client's level of importance of changing the maladaptive pattern and level of confidence in doing so are assessed and therapeutically processed.

A hallmark of third wave approaches is sensitivity to the therapeutic relationship. Pattern-Focused Therapy places a high value on the development and maintenance of an effective and growing therapeutic relationship. Accordingly,

106 Ultra-Brief Interventions

near the end of each session the client rates the therapeutic relationship on the Session Rating Scale (SRS). The results are shared, compared to previous session ratings, and the therapist and client discuss how their working together might be improved (Sperry, 2016a, 2016c).

The treatment process, query sequence, and therapeutic strategy can be summarized as follows.

Treatment Process

- Identification of presentation, triggers, and predisposition, i.e., individual psychodynamics, family or system dynamics, values, strengths and protective factors.
- Functional assessment and pattern identification.
- Case conceptualization that incorporates pattern and protective factors and strengths.
- Implementation of strategy for pattern shifting.

Query Sequence

- Specify maladaptive pattern as context for processing a specific concern/situation.
- Elicit the situation: beginning, middle, and end.
- Elicit thoughts/interpretation of the situation.
- Elicit behaviors: words, actions, and paralanguage.
- Elicit what client desired/wanted to happen.
- Identify what actually happened.
- Ask if client got the desired outcome.
- Seek permission to review situation and how it might have turned out differently.
- Ask if client's interpretation(s) helped or hurt in getting desired outcome; if they say "hurt," ask what alternative interpretation(s) would have helped.
- Ask if client's behavior(s) helped or hurt in getting desired outcome; if they say "hurt," ask what alternative behavior(s) would have helped.
- Ask how important it is to change maladaptive pattern (1–10 scale) and process; ask how confident they are to change that pattern (1–10 scale) and process.

Therapeutic Strategy

Here is the treatment strategy for this Pattern-Focused Therapy. Each therapy session of 15–30 minutes involves five steps and proceeds in this approach. The steps are:

1. Each session, and particularly the first, requires a strong therapeutic relationship to be established and maintained utilizing various relationship engagement and enhancing strategies that include permission seeking and related MI questions.
2. Simultaneously, starting in the second session, each session begins with a brief review of progress on treatment goals since the last session with the Outcomes Rating Scale (ORS). Client's ratings are discussed in relation to the client's maladaptive pattern and the goal of shifting to a more adaptive pattern.
3. Then a query sequence (Sperry, 2016b; Sperry & Binensztok, 2018) is utilized to analyze the client's thoughts and behaviors in specific problematic situations, in terms of whether they help or hurt the client in achieving his/her desired outcome. This is related to the maladaptive-adaptive pattern.
4. Typically, ultra-brief interventions appropriate to specific situations are introduced and practiced in the session and assigned as a between-session activity (homework). Progress in implementing the intervention between sessions is discussed at the beginning of the next session.
5. Near the end of the session, mutually agreed upon between-session activities (homework) is set. Then, the MI "importance" and "confidence" questions and answers are processed. The effectiveness of the therapeutic relationship in that session is assessed with the Session Rating Scale (SRS), and processed for how the therapist could be more responsive.

Typically, one problematic situation can be therapeutically processed within 10–12 minutes, whereas two situations might be processed in 20 or so minutes. When an ultra-brief intervention is indicated, there is usually sufficient time within a 30-minute session to address all five steps in either a mental health or integrated care setting.

The following case examples illustrate how this approach is implemented. Chapters 5–10 also include case transcriptions of this approach.

108 Ultra-Brief Interventions

Pattern-Focused Therapy in Action: The Case of Gerry

This is an actual case involving a college student working with a therapist at a university counseling and psychological services center. Details are modified to protect the individual's identity. Clients are typically seen here for an average of 10–15 individual sessions. The therapist is a student in the second internship course of his graduate program. He utilizes Pattern- Focused Therapy with its distinctive blend of CBASP, Motivational Interviewing, and focus on shifting from a maladaptive to a more adaptive pattern. Therapy with Gerry was provided in a mental health setting in 30-minute sessions.

This section includes background information and a brief case conceptualization. It is followed by transcriptions from the third and fourth sessions. As noted below, only part of the session is included. Commentaries on both sessions are provided.

Background

Gerardo M., who prefers to be called Gerry, is a 19-year-old single Cuban American male college student who reports experiencing debilitating social anxiety and increasing social isolation. Lately, there have been increased demands on him to be more socially involved, such as being asked to join a student club and assigned a verbal report in one of his classes. While he can tolerate most solitary and family activities, he reports experiencing considerable anxiety in situations involving others he does not know well, particularly those in his classes and his dormitory. Being around others has been anxiety producing since childhood, but his anxiety levels have increased dramatically since he has been away from home at college. He describes his mother as more emotionally supportive and less demanding and critical than his father. His mother took him out of public school in first grade and subsequently home schooled through high school. As a result, he has had minimal contact with others until moving into the freshman dormitory. He is self-referred for counseling at the university counseling center, and this is his first experience of therapeutic counseling.

Case Conceptualization

Gerry's increased social isolation and anxiety symptoms appear to be his reaction to demands for increased social involvement. Throughout his life, Gerry has feared unreasonable demands and criticism, and isolated himself and avoided situations to be safe. When circumstances require it, he will minimally and conditionally relate to others. As a result, he lacks some basic relational skills and has a limited social network. His reaction and pattern can be understood in light of a demanding, critical, and emotionally unavailable father and the teasing and criticism of peers. His family history of anxiety and panic disorder may biologically predispose him to social anxiety and social isolation, as does the under development of relational skills. This pattern is maintained by his shyness, limited social skills, and social isolation.

He is a highly acculturated third-generation Cuban American from a moderately acculturated family of business owners. Therapy goals included reducing anxiety symptoms, increasing interpersonal and friendship skills, and establishing a supportive social network in his dormitory. Pattern-Focused Therapy addressed his maladaptive pattern while social skills training focused on increasing relational skills. Gerry meets DSM-5 criteria for Social Anxiety Disorder and Avoidant Personality Disorder. As far as his treatment goal for short-term therapy, it is to shift from his maladaptive pattern of isolating from others to feel safe to a more adaptive pattern of feeling safer around others while growing more confident in relating to them.

Transcription 1

This is the second session in a planned six session treatment with Gerry. As the first session was ending, Gerry agreed to a homework assignment that would increase his sociability by making eye contact and greeting someone he had not formally met before. This proved to be very difficult and distressing for him based on his SUDS used in this session. SUDS stands for Subjective Units of Distress Scale and is a common self-rating measure of distress on a 1 to 100 scale, with 90–100 representative of being so psychologically and physiologically overwhelmed that an individual cannot concentrate or cognitively process. In this case, SUDS is a key functional assessment and indicator of a client's progress. For Gerry, experiencing moderately stressful situations with SUDS levels of 60 would be a significant improvement over levels of 90 that he reported in the beginning of this session.

As the therapist learned of Gerry's highly distressful reaction, he considered utilizing the ultra-brief intervention of Behavioral Activation which would more gently increase Gerry's social connectedness. Near the end of the session it is introduced. Observe how the therapist begins by explaining the intervention's rationale. Next, both collaborate to a list of social activities that would stretch Gerry without high SUDS levels. Then, the activities are

110 Ultra-Brief Interventions

scheduled with backup activities identified which increase likelihood that activities will be completed. Gerry is asked to rate and log each one on a scale from 0–10 based on his level of confidence during the activities. As treatment progresses, the number and duration of activities increases. Chapter 2 provides a fuller description and illustration of the use of Behavioral Activation.

Pattern-Focused Therapy treatment focuses on therapeutically processing a challenging situation that reflects the client's maladaptive responses and pattern. The query sequence is the therapeutic strategy for processing such situations, particularly those involving a prescribed intervention, whether ultra-brief or not. In the case of Gerry, problematic interpretations or thoughts and behaviors are processed in light of Gerry's maladaptive pattern of avoidance and isolation to be safe. This processing is illustrated in this and the following transcription.

> THERAPIST In our last session we discussed your pattern of avoidance and isolation to be safe and you agreed that the price you've paid for feeling safe is too high. (Yeah). We also agreed that a reasonable goal of our work together was for you to feel safer but also allow to grow in the process (Yeah). So, can we review your assignment from your last session? (Sure). It was to make eye contact with someone and greet that person. Is that right?
>
> GERRY Yeah. I went to a convenience store down the street from the dorm on Tuesday night, and as I went through the checkout line, I said hello to the clerk and asked her how she was doing.
>
> THERAPIST Okay, so what were your interpretations or thoughts right then?
>
> GERRY My first thought was "I'm not normal because I am here alone." My SUDS was at least 90.
>
> THERAPIST Okay. So your interpretation was "I'm not normal because I am here alone." Let's also look at your behaviors. What did you do in that situation?
>
> GERRY While in the store, I kept my head down the entire time and looked at the floor, except when I looked at the clerk and made eye contact with her.
>
> THERAPIST What else did you do?
>
> GERRY I just kept my head down and didn't talk to anyone except when I said "hi" and asked her how she was doing. I probably said it very softly.
>
> THERAPIST Did the clerk respond?
>
> GERRY Yeah, she said she was doing fine. But then I couldn't think of anything else to say so I looked back down and was quiet, nervously quiet.

Pattern-Focused Therapy **111**

THERAPIST So your behaviors in this situation were to keep your head down and look at the floor and not to talk to anyone except when you greeted the clerk.

GERRY Yes.

THERAPIST So, what did you want to happen?

GERRY To get a few groceries and toothpaste without any stress.

THERAPIST And what happened?

GERRY I got my stuff but as I was leaving my SUDS was about 85 or 90. But, I was able to make eye contact and ask her how she was doing.

THERAPIST Did you achieve your desired outcome then?

GERRY Sort of. I was able to make eye contact with the clerk and speak to her, but I wasn't able to talk to anyone else or even look at anyone else and I still experienced a lot of stress.

THERAPIST It sounds like you may have had two desired outcomes. One was to get groceries without experiencing any stress. Another was to make eye contact and greet a person while in the store. Is that accurate?

GERRY I guess so. I was able to look at the clerk and ask her how she was doing. But I still experienced a lot of anxiety while in the store, and I couldn't think of anything else to say to the clerk.

THERAPIST Do you think that both going to the store and not experiencing any stress was a realistic desired outcome for you?

GERRY No, I can see now that it was not.

THERAPIST What might have been a more realistic desired outcome for you at that time?

GERRY Probably make eye contact, say "hi" while trying to tolerate my anxiety a little better.

THERAPIST That does sound more realistic. (Pause). So, did you get it?

GERRY I suppose so. But I couldn't think of anything else to say, and my SUDS was about 90 when I tried to talk. That bothered me a lot.

THERAPIST Okay, then, let's go back through your interpretations to see which ones were helpful and hurtful in getting the outcome of greeting the clerk, while tolerating any anxiety. Your first interpretation was, "I'm not normal because I'm here alone." Was that thought helpful or hurtful to you in this situation?

GERRY Hurtful.

THERAPIST How was it hurtful?

GERRY Because I kept my head down and didn't speak to anyone because they would look at me and think I was weird since I was alone.

THERAPIST Can you think of any thoughts, then, that you could replace the hurtful thought with that would be helpful to you in this situation?

112 Ultra-Brief Interventions

GERRY I am normal.

THERAPIST Good. How would that thought have been helpful to you?

GERRY Well, if I kept telling myself that I was normal and not weird for being there alone, and that it was okay to feel anxious, I might have kept my head up and made eye contact. And, I would have been more likely to say hello.

THERAPIST So telling yourself "I am normal, and I am not weird for being here alone or feeling anxious" would have made it easier for you to keep your head up, make eye contact with others, and to talk?

GERRY Yes.

THERAPIST It seems, though, that in this situation you were able to do that. You made eye contact with the checkout clerk and greeted her.

GERRY But I still felt a lot of anxiety, which really bothered me, and that made it harder to look up.

THERAPIST Do you think that your replacement thought would have made you feel less anxious, then, or help you accept the anxiety you felt?

GERRY Probably. It would have been a lot easier for me.

THERAPIST Then let's move to your behaviors. One of them was to keep your head down the entire time, except when you made eye contact with the clerk. Do you think this was helpful or hurtful to you in achieving your desired outcome?

GERRY Hurtful. I probably would have been more likely to make eye contact with other people and maybe even say hi if I didn't look down the entire time.

THERAPIST But you were able to make eye contact and speak to the clerk. So, how was it hurtful?

GERRY While I was looking at the ground, I just kept thinking about how I wasn't normal and that I just wanted to leave.

THERAPIST So keeping your head down actually made you think more negatively?

GERRY Yes. If I had my head up and looked at others, I might have been distracted and not thought those things repeatedly.

THERAPIST Then, what behavior would have been helpful to you in this situation?

GERRY If I kept my head up, I could have made eye contact and greeted others.

THERAPIST So thinking that "I am normal, and I am not weird for being here alone, and it's okay to feel anxiety" rather than, "I'm not normal because I am here alone, and I shouldn't feel anxiety." And had you kept your head up you would have been more likely to get your desired

Pattern-Focused Therapy **113**

outcome, which was to make eye contact and feel less anxious. Is that accurate?

GERRY Yeah, that is accurate.

THERAPIST This situation and how you responded to it nicely captures your old pattern of avoidance and isolation to be safe.

GERRY (pause) I see it.

THERAPIST I am glad to hear that. So, before we end for today let's spend a few minutes on how you can feel more confident and safer around others but also allow to grow in the process.

GERRY Okay, that sounds good. I would like to be confident about following through.

THERAPIST Good. Sometimes when a challenge seems too daunting we put it off and the more we do that the less confidence and motivation we have to follow through the next time.

GERRY Yes, that makes sense. I can see that.

THERAPIST So, the technique I would like you to try is called behavioral activation. What that means is by intentionally becoming more active or activated, you'll start to feel more motivated and confident. Becoming activated with positive behaviors activates your physiology which lets you feel better. Does that make sense?

GERRY Yeah. It does. But is it really that simple?

THERAPIST Yes, if it's done right. (Pause). I'm going to help you schedule some activities to start. At first, you don't want to take on too much. For example, it is much better to plan and walk around the block than to plan to run a mile and not do it. Even a small activity can have a big effect. Especially those that stretch you a bit in being around other people.

GERRY Yeah, I don't want to take on too much at once.

THERAPIST Right. So, I'd like to start by scheduling two activities that you can complete this week. Aim for something you can do in about 15 minutes. What are some things you know you can do and would feel good about doing?

GERRY Well, I like to take walks and lift weights. Those are things I've been totally neglecting since I started college.

THERAPIST Those sound quite reasonable. So let's first focus on taking walks. What if you decided to make it a priority to walk around the university quad this week?

GERRY Yeah, I think it would take about 15 minutes to walk around the quad three times.

THERAPIST Which day of the week will you be doing that?

GERRY Probably Wednesday.

114 Ultra-Brief Interventions

THERAPIST Okay, good. What about a backup activity if for some reason you cannot complete that activity, because of weather or something?

GERRY Oh, I guess I could walk back and forth to the convenience store about four blocks from here.

THERAPIST Great. Now what about a second activity?

GERRY Well I got up to 140 pounds bench pressing last summer at home before I started here. But, I've been reluctant to work out in the university gym with all those jocks standing around and possibly making snide comments. But, I did find out there is a small weight room in the basement of our dorm. Hardly anybody seems to use it in the mornings.

THERAPIST So, you'd feel more comfortable and motivated to bench press in your dorm's weight room. Okay, that's good. And that should take you about 15 to 20 minutes. (Yes). And what day of the week works best?

GERRY I think Tuesday morning would be good, because most classes are scheduled on Tuesday and Thursday mornings.

Therapist Okay. So, what will be your backup activity?

GERRY I think walking to the convenience store and back would stretch me in being around others and not just laying around my dorm room.

THERAPIST Good. So, you are going to walk around the quad on Tuesday mornings and do bench pressing on Thursday mornings. Those will activate you in being out in public rather than laying around your dorm. (Yeah, that's doable). I'm giving you this log, so you can track your progress. I want you to write the date and the scheduled activity. Then I want you to give each activity two ratings, on a scale from 0 to 10. The first is how much you completed the activity, whether not at all, somewhat, or completely. You can rate that from 0 to 10. Then, I would like you to rate your confidence in doing this activity out in public from 0 to 10, with 0 being none and 10 being the most confident. Do you have any questions? (No). How does that sound?

GERRY That sounds good. It seems simple enough.

THERAPIST Okay, glad to hear that. I anticipate you will find these activities a bit challenging but also doable, and that your confidence in being around others will increase. (Pause). So, on a 1–10 scale, how important is it for you to engage in these activities this week? (9). And on the same scale, how confident are you that you will accomplish both? (Between 6 and 7).

THERAPIST Wow! You are almost there the first, and over halfway there on the second. Very good. I look forward to our next meeting.

GERRY I do too. I'd like to think I can do it.

Commentary

In this session, the therapist used the query sequence to process the previously assigned task of making eye contact and greeting another person. Gerry's thoughts and behaviors demonstrated in this segment clearly reflected his maladaptive pattern of avoidance and isolation to be safe.

Because the assigned task was too anxiety provoking for Gerry, the therapist introduced Behavior Activation near the end of this session. Because it was perceived by Gerry as less anxiety producing, it is not surprising that his answers to the MI questions on importance and confidence were quite high. Such scores suggest that it is quite likely he will be successful with these activities.

Transcription 2

This transcription is from Session 3. It continues the process of pattern shifting and processing problematic situations that occurred during the week following Session 2. Recall that Gerry's maladaptive pattern is to avoid and isolate himself from others and that the goal of this short-term therapy is a pattern shift so that Gerry can feel safer around others while growing more confident in relating to them. Near the beginning of this session, after briefly checking in with Gerry, the therapist begins focusing on the maladaptive pattern utilizing the query sequence. This session focuses on these activities, and as it emerges that Gerry is considering making a casual date with a classmate, the therapist introduces the ultra-brief intervention of behavioral rehearsal, which is also known as role-playing. Chapter 2 provides a full explanation and illustration of how to utilize this ultra-brief intervention.

> THERAPIST So, let's continue discussing your old pattern of avoidance and isolation to be safe and work on the more adaptive pattern of connecting with others in a way in which you feel safer. So, how has it been since we met last?
>
> GERRY Well, it's been okay, I guess. I went to the convenience store again yesterday.
>
> THERAPIST Good. And how did that go?
>
> GERRY Well, I still felt anxious for being there alone, and I pretty much grabbed all of the stuff I needed and then headed straight for the checkout line.
>
> THERAPIST Did you make eye contact or talk to anyone while you were there?

116 Ultra-Brief Interventions

GERRY Yeah, when I was picking out a few apples there was a clerk restocking the fruit section and she smiled at me.

THERAPIST And what did you do?

GERRY I gave her a quick smile and then I looked down.

THERAPIST And what was your interpretation of that situation?

GERRY That it was crazy that she was smiling at me, I mean, for a minute I couldn't figure out if she was smiling at me or at someone behind me.

THERAPIST What does that mean to you?

GERRY That she was just smiling because that was part of her job or maybe she thought I looked like a loser at the grocery store all by myself.

THERAPIST And so these thoughts that were racing through your head at this time sound like they were really stressful to you. What was your SUDS level like right then?

GERRY I would say probably around 75 or so. I was a little sweaty, but I couldn't believe she was really smiling at me.

THERAPIST And how was it after you smiled back and then walked away?

GERRY My SUDS went down a lot to 60 or so. I was proud of myself for smiling back at her and so I felt a little better about being there alone.

THERAPIST That's wonderful. So, by simply smiling back you eased your anxiety a little. How did it go in the checkout line?

GERRY Better this week, I guess. I looked at the checkout girl and said "hi." But this time I didn't look down right away. Instead I looked at the computer screen with my grocery total on it. She said "hi. How are you today?" and smiled at me, and then I smiled back again! Right after that I looked down.

THERAPIST And what was going through your mind at that moment?

GERRY I was like, whoa. She is looking at me right now and I have to think of something to do right away so I don't look like an idiot, fumbling around and stuttering like last time. I couldn't think of anything to say so I just smiled.

THERAPIST And how was your SUDS level?

GERRY I would probably say around an 80 but when I walked out to the parking lot I was happy that I smiled and said "hi." I felt better about having gone there, like maybe I had done a little better this week. My SUDS was down to 65 then.

THERAPIST Awesome! So, you still experienced stress, but much less than in the same situation before. You achieved the desired outcome we agreed on in our last session: that you would be able to greet and make eye contact with someone while you were there and tolerate the stress it would bring you. Is that right?

GERRY   Yeah, you're right. And then I felt better about it afterwards.

THERAPIST   That's great! It seems like you really made a lot of progress at the store. Good job! Can we go over the assignment this week?

THERAPIST   So what about the two activities you were going to do this week? (Pause). I see you have your logs.

GERRY   (smiling broadly) I'm happy how both turned out!

THERAPIST   So, on the walking assignment you scored it as 10 for completing it, and 7 for your confidence level the first time, and 8 on the second time.

GERRY   Yeah. That wasn't bad at all. At that time on Tuesday and Thursday morning there are very few students on the quad then. So, it wasn't too stressful.

THERAPIST   Very good. (Pause). Gerry, I recall that when we talked about your expectation for therapy the first time we met, you said you hoped to be able to do things with your fellow college students, like going on dates. Is that accurate?

GERRY   Yes the last couple of days I was thinking about the new flick that is coming to campus this weekend, and I wondered what it would be like to go with somebody.

THERAPIST   You were thinking about it. (Pause). Any specific plans?

GERRY   Well, I wanted to ask this girl I sit next to in my biology class if she wanted to go and see this indie film I had heard was playing on campus on Thursday. We were getting ready to leave at the end of the lecture and I grabbed my stuff and tried to talk to her, but it didn't work out very well.

THERAPIST   Okay, well, what were your interpretations or thoughts in that situation?

GERRY   That she would think I was trying to stalk her or that I was some kind of freak. I was terrified that I would say the wrong thing or not say anything at all and then class would be over. Mostly I thought that I was not normal because I couldn't find the words to ask her.

THERAPIST   So your interpretation was that you were not normal because you couldn't think of anything to say. That seems like a good interpretation for us to look at. What was your SUDS level for this thought?

GERRY   Almost a 90… I was petrified.

THERAPIST   Okay, well, what about your behaviors?

GERRY   Well, like I said, I grabbed all my stuff trying to find the words and I tried to look at her, which didn't last very long, and then all I could say was "um, hey, do you like indies?" And she must not have heard me or something or I didn't say it very loud because she gave me a funny look

118 Ultra-Brief Interventions

and goes, "huh?" and then I looked down and said "nothing." I grabbed my bag and took off down the lecture hall to the doors.

THERAPIST So your behaviors in this situation were to speak softly, look down, grab your bags and leave.

GERRY Yeah. Pretty much how I thought it would go.

THERAPIST Well, we can review this in a minute. What was your desired outcome?

GERRY To ask her if she wanted to see the independent film they were playing on campus.

THERAPIST And what actually happened?

GERRY I didn't even ask her and I ran off. And my SUDS was at a 90 for about 15 minutes until I got back to my dorm room and could shut the door and calm down.

THERAPIST So, did you achieve your desired outcome then?

GERRY No, of course not. I was so sweaty I had to take a shower and I stayed in my room all night on the computer.

THERAPIST Okay, well, then, let's go on to the next phase so we can see what might have made things different in the end. First, let's look at your interpretations and see which ones were helpful or hurtful to you in getting your desired outcome of asking someone to go see a movie. Your first interpretation was that "you were not normal because you couldn't think of anything to say in that moment." Do you think that this interpretation was helpful or hurtful in this situation?

GERRY Hurtful.

THERAPIST How was it hurtful?

GERRY Because it made me feel even more anxious and like I was going to fail again and then she would think I was weird and it would always be uncomfortable having to sit there in class with her after that.

THERAPIST Can you think of any thoughts that might have been more helpful instead?

GERRY Um, well, that I am normal. Or at least I am not a freak.

THERAPIST Good, good. Now how would that have helped you?

GERRY Well, I wouldn't have freaked out so much right before and maybe I would have been able to actually think of something to say since I wasn't so scared. I guess I would have been more likely to find something good to say and say it louder.

THERAPIST So telling yourself "I am normal and I am not weird for asking her if she likes indie films or for being anxious about it" would have made it easier for you to ask her.

GERRY Yeah, I think so.

Pattern-Focused Therapy   **119**

THERAPIST Well, you did ask her, even though she didn't hear you right away. Perhaps it was your anxiety that really bothered you and got you upset in this situation?

GERRY Yeah, definitely.

THERAPIST Well, do you think your replacement thought would have made you less upset or stressed, or maybe help you accept those feelings?

GERRY Probably.

THERAPIST So your first interpretation that you were not normal because you couldn't think of anything to say was hurtful because it actually made you anxious, which makes thinking of words difficult for anyone. If you replaced that thought with the one that says, "I am normal, and it is okay to be anxious when asking someone to see a movie" you would have been more likely to be at a SUDS level that would allow you to think more clearly and find something to say, and then ask her. Is this right?

GERRY Yeah.

THERAPIST Okay, well, let's move on to your behaviors. The first one was to grab your stuff right away. Was this helpful or hurtful in terms of getting your desired outcome?

GERRY Hurtful... Probably because it looks like I just want to rush off.

THERAPIST So what might have been a better behavior?

GERRY To take my time, and slowly gather up my books while I was thinking of how to ask her.

THERAPIST That's good, that would have given you a little more time to not be anxious and think of the words. What about speaking softly, did this help you or hurt you in terms of getting your desired outcome?

GERRY Hurt, because she didn't hear me and then she gave me a funny look and I freaked out.

THERAPIST What might have been a better behavior?

GERRY To speak louder and look at her so she could understand what I was saying.

THERAPIST Great, you are really good at this part. Then perhaps she might have said "yes, I like those movies" and you could then have asked her to go with you to see it. This would have prevented her from asking "huh?" which made you even more anxious and led you to say "nothing" and leave.

GERRY Yeah, I see.

THERAPIST So, in this situation, if you would have thought to yourself "I am normal and it is okay to be anxious when you ask someone to see a movie" instead of "I am not normal because I can't think of anything

120 Ultra-Brief Interventions

to say" and if you would have spoken louder and not grabbed up all your stuff and rushed off you would have been more likely to get your desired outcome of asking someone to see a movie with you. Is that accurate?

GERRY Sure. Definitely.

THERAPIST Would you like to practice what this situation might look like if it happens again, this time with the new interpretations and behaviors? (Yes). We'll role-play it. I could be the girl in your class and you could practice asking me.

GERRY I'll try.

THERAPIST Good, I think you can do it. Let's pretend we are sitting in class and it is almost time to leave. Everyone starts to pack up their belongings and you start to slowly put your books away. What are you thinking to yourself?

GERRY That I am normal, and it is okay to be anxious about asking someone to see a movie.

THERAPIST Good, and what are you doing?

GERRY I am slowly putting away my books and then I look up and say, "hey, do you like indie films?"

THERAPIST "Yeah, they're cool. Why?"

GERRY "Well, because they're showing one in the old theater tonight about that news reporter in Iraq. Do you want to go see it with me?"

THERAPIST "Sure, what time is it?"

GERRY "7:30. I could meet you out front if you like."

THERAPIST "That would be cool. Thanks."

GERRY Okay. I see what you mean. I could carry on a whole conversation then. What if she says no?

THERAPIST Well, your desired outcome is to just get up the courage to ask someone to see a movie. There is a chance that that person might say no, but your desired outcome is to ask. I think the more practice you get at asking people, the more chances there are for them to say yes, don't you agree?

GERRY Yeah, I mean, if she said yes then what would I say to her at the movie?

THERAPIST Well, this is something we can always work on in the future. I think you did some important work today. We've already discussed your two activity tasks. Do you also want to ask someone to see that movie, guy or girl?

GERRY Asking one of the guys in my dorm would be less stressful than setting a date with a girl. (Pause). Yeah, I do want to try. I'll let you know the result next session.

THERAPIST Looking forward to our next session. Have a nice week!

Commentary

This transcribed segment begins by focusing on Gerry's second effort to make eye contact and talk briefly with someone he did not know. The situation and his maladaptive pattern was addressed utilizing the query sequence to analyze Gerry's problematic situation. Next, the log for Behavioral Activation tasks was reviewed. Although the weight lifting task was more challenging for Gerry than the walking task, the therapist decided not to formally process it because of the press of time. Instead, he encouraged Gerry to set a stretch goal for both activities and made a mental note to process them next session. Recalling that in their first session, Gerry said he wanted therapy to help him feel more comfortable and confident in going out with a friend and finding that Gerry had failed this week at achieving this, the therapist processed this situation with the query sequence, the core therapeutic strategy of Pattern-Focused Therapy. The therapist easily incorporates role-playing, the ultra-brief intervention of Behavioral Rehearsal, to help Gerry rehearse how he might act to achieve that desired outcome.

Concluding Note

As described in this chapter, the focus of Pattern-Focused Therapy is to identify and shift maladaptive patterns to more adaptive ones. This is achieved by replacing the non-productive thoughts (interpretations) and behaviors that underlie the maladaptive pattern. Moreover, the case was made that Pattern-Focused Therapy is fully compatible with the new practice model emerging today. As illustrated in the extended case material and two transcriptions, it can be utilized effectively with complex case presentations in a relatively short time frame.

Pattern-Focused Therapy has considerable promise as a therapeutic approach that is relatively easy to learn and practice and is evidence-based. It is compatible with all brief and ultra-brief interventions and is the perfect format or vehicle for delivering those interventions. As illustrated in the case

122 Ultra-Brief Interventions

material, sessions center on processing problematic situations with the query sequence and incorporating one or more appropriate ultra-brief interventions to foster change.

References

Livesley, W.J. (2003). *Practical management of personality disorder*. New York, NY: Guilford.

McCullough, J. (2000). *Treatment for chronic depression: Cognitive behavioral analysis system of psychotherapy*. New York, NY: Guilford.

McCullough, J., Schramm, E., & Penberthy, K. (2014). *CBASP as a distinctive treatment for persistent depressive disorder: Distinctive features*. New York, NY: Routledge.

Meier, S.T. (2015). *Incorporating progress monitoring and outcome assessment into counseling and psychotherapy: A primer*. New York, NY: Oxford University Press.

Miller, W., & Rollnick, S. (2002). *Motivational interviewing: Preparing people for change* (2nd ed.). New York, NY: Guilford.

Sperry, L. (1988). Biopsychosocial therapy: An integrative approach for tailoring treatment. *Journal of Individual Psychology, 44,* 225–235.

Sperry, L. (2000). Biopsychosocial therapy: Essential strategies and tactics. In J. Carlson & L. Sperry (Eds.). *Brief therapy with individuals and couples*. Phoenix, AZ: Zeig, Tucker & Theisen.

Sperry, L. (2006). *Psychological treatment of chronic illness: The biopsychosocial therapy approach*. New York, NY: Brunner/Mazel.

Sperry, L. (2010). *Highly effective therapy: Developing essential clinical competencies in counseling and psychotherapy*. New York, NY: Routledge.

Sperry, L. (2016a). Educating the next generation of psychotherapists: Considering the future of theory and practice in Adlerian psychotherapy. *Journal of Individual Psychology,* 72(1), 4–11.

Sperry, L. (2016c). Pattern-focused psychotherapy. In L. Sperry (Ed.). *Mental health and mental disorders: An encyclopedia of conditions, treatments, and well-being*. 3 vols. (pp. 816–818). Santa Barbara, CA: Greenwood.

Sperry, L., & Binensztok, V. (2018). Adlerian pattern-focused therapy: A treatment manual. *Journal of Individual Psychology,* 74(3), 309–348.

Sperry, L., Brill, P., Howard, K., & Grissom, G. (1996). *Treatment outcomes in psychotherapy and psychiatric interventions*. New York, NY: Brunner/Mazel.

Sperry, L., & Sperry, J. (2012). *Case conceptualization: Mastering this competency with ease and confidence*. New York, NY: Routledge.

Part II

Application of Ultra-Brief Interventions

Ultra-Brief Interventions with Depression   **5**

This chapter provides an overview of depression and how it commonly presents in integrated care settings. A functional assessment of depression is reviewed and common ultra-brief interventions are identified. Finally, a case example is illustrated through four transcriptions with commentary. This chapter does not emphasize the diagnostic evaluation for depression, but rather how brief interventions can be used to address depression in these integrated settings. The role of the behavioral health provider in assessing depression in these settings is different from one completing a diagnostic evaluation. A formal diagnostic evaluation is only warranted sometimes in these cases.

Depression

Depressive symptoms can present a number of ways and may not always be severe enough to qualify for a mental health diagnosis. Some individuals experience fewer symptoms for shorter periods of time but still find that their daily functioning is affected. Those with clinically significant depression can meet criteria for the diagnosis of Major Depressive Disorder or Persistent Depressive Disorder.

Major Depressive Disorder is characterized by five of the following nine symptoms: depressed mood most days, loss of interest or pleasure, unexplained weight changes, change in sleep patterns, psychomotor agitation or retardation, fatigue, feelings of worthlessness or guilt, difficulty concentrating, and thoughts of death. These symptoms must be present for at least two weeks for the diagnosis to be met. The diagnosis includes specifiers for course and severity. Symptoms can be mild, moderate, or severe. Specifiers for anxious distress, melancholic, or atypical features are also provided in the Diagnostic and Statistical Manual – 5. The 12-month prevalence of Major Depressive Disorder in the United States is about 7% (American Psychiatric Association, 2013). Persistent Depressive Disorder is characterized by the same symptoms of major depression but is more chronic. Symptoms have to be present for at least two years, with no more than two consecutive symptom-free months.

While many physicians and providers identify depressed mood as the primary symptom of depression, many clients will primarily present with loss of interest or pleasure. Some clients will deny low mood but present with irritability and somatic symptoms, particularly depending on context, culture, and community norms. For example, increased somatization with decreased expression of emotional distress is noted in Chinese clients presenting with depression. This presentation was found to accompany collectivistic belief systems, rather than other Chinese or Asian cultural norms, therefore it is expected that clients of other collectivistic ethnicities would exhibit similar presentations (Chang, Jetten, Cruwys, & Haslam, 2016).

Assessment and Screening Instruments

Assessing depression in an integrated care setting is similar to a regular diagnostic assessment but includes more closed-ended questions and gathers information about effects on daily functioning. A risk assessment is also indicated for this diagnosis.

Diagnostic Assessment

The diagnostic evaluation of depression in these settings is like a regular diagnostic evaluation. The behavioral health provider should inquire about the symptoms of depression, including time frame. The provider can use a standardized screener like the Patient Health Questionnaire-9 (PHQ-9) to assess symptoms. The assessment should also determine if any comorbid disorders are present and evaluate the client's personality style and if any personality disorder diagnosis is indicated.

Functional Assessment

The functional assessment should include information about how depression affects the client on a daily basis and interferes with regular functioning. The provider should identify not only the symptoms of depression, but also the onset, duration, frequency, and intensity. It is important to keep in mind that there might be a medical cause for the depressive symptoms. In this case, a more thorough medical evaluation is warranted. The provider should also assess for substance use, as well as use of prescribed or over-the-counter medications.

Risk Assessment

Because thoughts of death are a common depressive symptom, it is important to assess for suicidal and homicidal ideation. If the client indicates such ideation is present, the provider must follow up with a full risk assessment that includes information about the frequency, intensity, and duration of suicidal or homicidal thoughts. The behavioral health provider should inquire if the client has a plan and a means to carry out the plan, and if attempts were carried out before. Some clients will express suicidal ideation but state that their religious beliefs, families, etc., keep them from following through on suicidal thoughts (American Counseling Association, n.d.). The suicidal ideation question on the Patient Health Questionnaire-9 is often used to assess suicide risk (Na et al., 2018) and can be a starting off point for a risk assessment conversation. This instrument can be paired with the Columbia Suicide Severity Rating Scale (C-SSRS).

Screening Instruments

The Patient Health Questionnaire-9. The Patient Health Questionnaire-9 (PHQ-9) is a 9-item questionnaire that corresponds to the nine DSM-5 criteria for Major Depressive Disorder. Each question is rated on a 4-point scale from 0 to 3 where 0 = not at all, 1 = several days, 2 = more than half the days, and 3 = nearly every day. A tenth question asks how any symptoms the client rated between 1 and 3 have interfered with the person's ability to function at work, at home, and with other people. Clients rate their experiences for the previous two weeks. The scoring for the PHQ-9 is as follows: 0–4 = minimal or none,

128 Application of Ultra-Brief Interventions

5–9 = mild, 10–14 = moderate, 15–19 = moderately severe, 20–27 = severe. The PHQ-9 is useful for screening, diagnosis, treatment planning, and progress monitoring. The first two questions of the PHQ-9 are referred to as the PHQ-2 and are used for screening since they assess for depressed mood and lack of pleasure, and at least one of those symptoms must be present for the diagnosis to be met. The full instrument is required for diagnosis and progress monitoring.

The Columbia Suicide Severity Rating Scale (C-SSRS). The Columbia Suicide Severity Rating Scale (C-SSRS) is a questionnaire used to assess suicidal ideation and risk. It consists of several forced choice (yes, no) questions and several multiple choice and free response questions. The C-SSRS assesses whether clients are having thoughts of suicide, the intensity of those thoughts, whether clients have taken any steps to create a suicide plan and prepare for suicide, and whether the client has attempted suicide previously.

Mood Scale. The mood scale requires the client to rate his/her daily or weekly mood on a scale from 0–10, where 0 is the worst mood possible and 10 is the best possible. The mood scale is useful for progress monitoring. Table 5.1, below, outlines an assessment of depression, including sample questions.

Ultra-Brief Interventions

Behavioral Activation

Behavioral Activation is a behavioral intervention used to help depressed clients improve their mood and increase their interest by breaking cycles of inactivity. Individuals experiencing depression often isolate themselves, neglect life's demands, and reduce engagement in pleasurable activities. This behavior provides no opportunity for positive reinforcement, leading to worsened depression and further disengagement from activities. Behavioral activation requires the client to schedule both pleasant and necessary activities on a weekly basis. Activities are then ranked on a 0–10 scale for level of completion and enjoyment. Alternate, or backup, activities should also be scheduled to increase the likelihood that the client will succeed in completing activities each week. Even if individuals experience low motivation and little to no pleasure during the first few activities, activities should continue to be scheduled and completed. As the client begins completing small, easy-to-achieve tasks, his/her motivation, self-efficacy, and level of interest is expected to increase.

Table 5.1 Functional Assessment of Depression

Presenting Problem	Your primary care physician stated you have been experiencing low mood/loss of interest recently. Is that correct?
Mood	How would you describe your mood?
Interest and Pleasure	Do you find you have less interest in activities you once used to enjoy? Do you find you gain less pleasure from activities you used to enjoy?
Worthlessness and Guilt	Do you have feelings of guilt or worthlessness?
Energy	Do you have less energy or find yourself feeling tired more often? Are you still tired even after getting a full night's sleep?
Sleep	Are you sleeping more or less than usual? Do you have difficulty falling asleep or are you waking up before your alarm?
Concentration	Do you have difficulty concentrating?
Appetite and Weight	Have you recently gained or lost any weight without trying? Has your appetite increased or decreased?
Psychomotor Symptoms	Do you feel restless or slowed down?
Suicidal/Homicidal Ideation	Have you had any thoughts about hurting yourself? Have you had any thoughts about hurting someone else? Frequency of thoughts Intensity of thoughts Duration of thoughts Plan Means to complete plan Beliefs or reasons not to follow through

(continued)

130 Application of Ultra-Brief Interventions

Table 5.1 (*Cont.*)

Duration	How long have you been feeling this way?
Frequency	How many times a day or week do you feel this way?
Intensity	On a scale from 0 to 10, where 0 is not at all and 10 is the most, what is the most depressed you have ever felt? What is the most depressed you have felt in the last two weeks? The least?
Triggers	Did something happen that triggered your depression?
Factors That Make the Problem Better or Worse	Physical, emotional, behavioral, cognitive, social, environmental
Functional Impairment	How has your depression affected your work, social relationships, family relationships, social/recreational activities, exercise?
Alcohol and Drug Use	Do you drink alcohol? What kind and how much? Do you use any illegal drugs or prescription drugs for reasons other than their intended use? What kind and how much?
Medications	Do you take any prescription or over-the-counter medications or any supplements?
Open-Ended Questions	Is there anything I have not asked you about that you would like me to know?

Depression Psychoeducation

Clients should be taught about the self-perpetuating cycle of depression, and how limiting their activities affects their mood. The provider should discuss how self-defeating thoughts contribute to depression, how they lead to decreased activity and how decreased activity leads to more negative thoughts. This can be likened to a downward spiral, in which thoughts and behaviors fuel one another. The provider should explain how this cycle can be broken by increasing activity, changing negative thoughts, and possibly including medication in their treatment. Clients can be taught to differentiate and identify their thoughts, emotions, behaviors, and physical symptoms. Monitoring these symptoms, as well as daily moods, in a weekly chart can help illustrate how the specific client's cognitive and behavioral patterns influence his/her mood.

Referral for Medication Evaluation

Depending on the severity of the client's depression, a referral for a medication evaluation may be necessary. Some clients will present with depression severe enough to hinder their engagement in ultra-brief interventions. In this case, a medication evaluation should be coordinated with the medical doctor, the client, and the behavioral health provider. The behavioral health provider then monitors the client's use of the medication and adherence to the medication plan.

Pattern-Focused Therapy

Pattern-Focused Therapy is used to address personality dynamics and patterns that contribute to and maintain client presenting problems. If the client's pattern is not effectively addressed during treatment, symptoms can reoccur when the pattern is triggered in the future. Thus, using Pattern-Focused Therapy helps not only alleviate factors contributing to the problem but also helps stave off relapse. For example, in the Case of Maria (outlined below), Maria's avoidant personality style and pattern of avoiding specific situations increases her social isolation and symptoms of depression. It is also a barrier to treatment as it decreases the likelihood that she will engage in therapeutic activities. Using Pattern-Focused Therapy, Maria is able to shift to a more adaptive pattern of feeling safe in social situations, allowing her to more effectively engage with others and in her scheduled activities.

Progress Monitoring and Record Keeping

Progress Monitoring

Progress monitoring is particularly important when treating depression in integrated care settings, as the length and number of sessions is often limited. In the treatment of depression, progress monitoring includes periodic reassessment

132 Application of Ultra-Brief Interventions

of symptoms, monitoring completion of homework assignments, and adherence to medication plans when needed. Standardized instruments like the Patient Health Questionnaire-9 (PHQ-9) should be administered prior to each session and responses discussed with the client. Symptoms can also be monitored using daily mood charts, in which the client rates his/her mood at intervals throughout the day. When doing homework assignments, clients should log their progress and completion of assignments in a journal or log. When using behavioral activation for major depression, the client should keep a log of scheduled activities with a rating from zero to ten for how much each activity was accomplished and enjoyed. A rating of zero means the goal was not accomplished or enjoyed and a rating of ten equals maximum accomplishment and pleasure. The client should also rate his/her overall daily mood using the mood scale, including days when no activities are scheduled.

Record Keeping

Effective record keeping helps client care run smoothly in integrated care settings. Time constraints in these settings make it necessary for notes and records to be clear, concise, and structured. Commonly used in health care settings, the SOAP note method is the most organized and concise method of record keeping. In this acronym, SOAP represents the headings Subjective, Objective, Assessment, and Plan. The Subjective heading includes the client's subjective experience. Presenting symptoms, subjective ratings of intensity, and associated complaints are recorded under the Subjective heading. The Objective heading includes any objective ratings, like those obtained from standardized instruments or medical exams. In the case of depression, results from the Patient Health Questionnaire-9 are reported under this heading. The Assessment heading includes whether the client meets criteria for a DSM-5 diagnosis as well as the client's personality style. Items in this category should be listed in order of importance. Finally, the Plan heading includes the next steps to be completed in the treatment plan, objectives for the next session, and any necessary referrals.

Case of Maria Transcriptions

Case of Maria: Session 1

Background. Maria is a 38-year-old Hispanic female referred to counseling by her primary care physician, Dr. Shapiro, for depressive symptoms. Maria was administered the Patient Health Questionnaire (PHQ-9) on which she scored 15, indicating the lower end of moderately severe depression. This session will include a functional assessment, psychoeducation, and behavioral activation.

PROVIDER: Hi Maria, how are you doing today?

MARIA: Ok, thank you.

PROVIDER: Alright. I understand you were referred by Dr. Shapiro. I would like to ask you some questions to get an idea of how you are doing. Is that ok?

MARIA: Yes, that's fine.

PROVIDER: Great, let's get started. Can you tell me how your mood has been?

MARIA: It's been low. Things feel really dark. I told that to Dr. Shapiro and that's why she suggested I come see you.

PROVIDER: Well, I'm glad you came in. When you say your mood has been low, can you tell me a little more about that?

MARIA: Sure. I just feel tired and sad a lot. I'm fed up. I've had some problems at work because of it.

PROVIDER: Like what?

MARIA: I've missed some days because I'm too tired or sad to get up in the morning. I wake up late and then I think I might as well stay in bed because I messed up the day already.

PROVIDER: I see. That sounds very challenging. How long would you say you have been feeling low?

MARIA: I don't know exactly. It's been a few months. Probably six months. But I feel sad pretty much all day, every day.

PROVIDER: What about some of the things you like to do?

MARIA: Well, I used to like to go on bike rides and go to the gym but I can't remember the last time I did that. I don't feel like doing anything anymore. My mom took me out for dinner the other week. That's something I used to really like but this time it was different.

PROVIDER: Can you describe how you felt going out to dinner this time?

MARIA: Just really empty. No joy.

PROVIDER: And how have you been feeling about yourself recently?

MARIA: I feel like a total failure. I'm worried I might get fired and the worst part is I probably deserve it.

PROVIDER: I am sorry to hear you feel this way. It must be very difficult for you. How have you been sleeping during this difficult time?

MARIA: A lot of times I can't fall asleep but then I'm exhausted and want to sleep all day. Then it seems no matter how much I sleep, I'm still tired. I've gained weight too. I'm such a mess.

134 Application of Ultra-Brief Interventions

PROVIDER: How much weight have you gained?

MARIA: About 10 pounds.

PROVIDER: Ok, going back to the sleep, have there been times when you feel you need less sleep than usual? Where you have a lot of energy?

MARIA: No, I wish!

PROVIDER: Ok, Maria. Would you say you're a nervous person?

MARIA: Not really. I'm worried about losing my job but that's about it.

PROVIDER: So, you're saying you don't really find yourself worrying much?

MARIA: That's correct.

PROVIDER: Do you have any rituals or things you feel must be done?

MARIA: No, nothing like that.

PROVIDER: Have you had any difficult experiences lately? Like a move or loss of relationship?

MARIA: Nothing drastic. I was moved into a cubicle space from an office at work a few months ago. We all were. Now we're all in one big room.

PROVIDER: I see. And you find that challenging?

MARIA: Yes. I don't like it.

PROVIDER: Have you had any unusual experiences lately?

MARIA: Not that I can think of.

PROVIDER: Or ever feel like your mind is playing tricks on you?

MARIA: No. My mind is too tired to do anything.

PROVIDER: Ok. Do you use any drugs or alcohol?

MARIA: I have a drink once in a while but that's it. No drugs. Coffee but no drugs.

PROVIDER: When you say once in a while, what do you mean?

MARIA: Maybe one or two drinks a week. I haven't even been doing that recently because it makes me feel worse the next day.

PROVIDER: Yes, it can do that. What about prescription or over-the-counter drugs?

MARIA: Just ibuprofen. I get headaches.

PROVIDER: You mentioned you had gained some weight recently. How would you describe your eating habits?

MARIA: Nothing crazy. I haven't been cooking though. I've just been eating takeout.

PROVIDER: Do you ever eat a lot in one sitting?

MARIA: No, I just kind of graze all day. Just eating leftovers or ice cream or whatever.

PROVIDER: And how has your memory been recently?

MARIA: No complaints. It's hard to concentrate but no memory problems.

PROVIDER: Have you had any thoughts that life isn't worth living?

Ultra-Brief Interventions with Depression **135**

MARIA: Sometimes I feel so sad I kind of hope I don't wake up in the morning. But I haven't thought about hurting myself. I wouldn't do that.

PROVIDER: What about thoughts of hurting someone else?

MARIA: Oh no I wouldn't do that.

PROVIDER: Ok, and how would you describe your relationships with people?

MARIA: I'm not really social. I see my family, my mom and stuff. But that's really about it.

PROVIDER: Can you tell me more about that?

MARIA: Sure. People can be so judgmental and I'm so awkward. I never know what to say.

PROVIDER: Can you give me an example?

MARIA: There are a hundred examples. People seem to know how to act. Or they like each other but laugh at me. Everything that comes out of my mouth is so stupid it's no wonder they laugh.

PROVIDER: People have openly laughed at you?

MARIA: I know they are. I guess I do have one friend, Jen. We have been friends since high school when we both got teased a lot. She is cool and doesn't judge. That's when I started pulling away from people more. It's just easier.

PROVIDER: Would you say you have a pattern of avoiding others so you don't feel judged?

MARIA: Yes, I would definitely agree with that. It is just easier not to deal with those things, you know?

Commentary. Maria's answers indicate an avoidant personality style. She has a pattern of avoiding interactions so she can feel safe and not feel judged.

PROVIDER: I see. Does that have anything to do with your dislike of the new cubicles at work?

MARIA: Yeah! It's like everyone is watching you. I can't even concentrate because I'm so out in the open. I hate it.

PROVIDER: I understand why that must be so difficult for you.

MARIA: Uh huh.

PROVIDER: Have you ever sought therapy or treatment in the past?

MARIA: No, this hasn't happened before.

PROVIDER: Can you tell me how your current symptoms of sadness and loss of interest have been affecting your daily life?

MARIA: Well, I don't do as many things anymore. I have been missing work and I worry about the consequences at my job.

136 Application of Ultra-Brief Interventions

Commentary. Maria's diagnostic interview responses are consistent with a PHQ score of 15. She meets DSM-5 diagnostic criteria for Major Depressive Disorder, Single Episode, Moderate 296.22, and it is long-standing. She also appears to have an avoidant personality style. Acculturation does not appear to be an issue. Because her presentation is more anhedonic, the provider will use behavioral activation. Medication does not appear to be warranted at this time.

PROVIDER: Well, I am glad you came here and hopefully this is the first step for you to get to feel the way you would like to. What do you hope to get out of counseling?

MARIA: I just don't want to be so sad and tired anymore. I don't even know if that's possible. I'm a lost cause.

PROVIDER: I understand sometimes it feels like an uphill battle.

MARIA: Yes, exactly.

PROVIDER: There are things that have proven to be very helpful to many people who feel depressed. One of those is actually making ourselves do some things that we once enjoyed.

MARIA: But I don't enjoy anything anymore.

PROVIDER: I understand. It can be difficult to get going. Yet many clients find that if they start by doing small things, even if they don't enjoy them at first, they slowly begin to feel better and better. Depression tends to follow a self-perpetuating cycle. When we are depressed, we no longer feel like doing things we once loved, yet it is that inactivity that makes depression worse, which leads to doing even less, and so on.

MARIA: Yes, I can see that. I can see how that's happened to me in a way. At first, I just didn't want to ride my bike anymore and now I don't even want to shower some days.

Commentary. The provider provides Maria with psychoeducation about depression and the self-perpetuating cycle of inactivity. She is able to understand how her behaviors have contributed to her low moods and agrees to behavioral activation.

PROVIDER: So, does that sound like something you might like to try?

MARIA: Yes, I might as well.

PROVIDER: Ok, that's a great start. Let's begin by making a list of some things you would like to do. Now, we don't have to jump into an hour-long bike ride. It is actually better to start small. I think you will find completing a five-minute walk is more rewarding than scheduling but not completing an hour at the gym.

MARIA: Haha. Yes, I guess that's true.

PROVIDER: How have you been affected by not biking or doing the things you used to enjoy?

MARIA: I guess it actually makes things worse. I don't get out much. When I biked I got fresh air and sun. Now I feel cooped up a lot. I think it does make me more tired and sad.

PROVIDER: Yes, I would agree. How is the lighting in your house?

MARIA: It's actually pretty dark. Sometimes I don't turn the lights on and it's just the light from the TV. Now that you mention it, it's really depressing.

PROVIDER: So, let's brainstorm some things you used to like to do but have been avoiding recently.

MARIA: Ok, biking, painting, I don't know what else.

PROVIDER: I have a list of activities that people find pleasurable. It may give you some inspiration. Would you like to look at it?

MARIA: Sure. Ok, well going out for coffee, and maybe taking some walks through nature.

PROVIDER: Ok, that sounds wonderful. Which of those would you like to start with?

MARIA: I think getting a coffee and taking nature walks.

PROVIDER: Ok, I agree those both sound like they will help you start feeling better. You may not feel better the first, or even the second time. But it is the continuity of the activities that is key. Let's see how we can break down the coffee runs and nature walks into smaller activities. Let's aim to start with just one or two things a week.

MARIA: Ok, well I actually wanted to try this new coffee drink I saw advertised.

PROVIDER: That sounds good. And what are some places you might like to walk?

MARIA: There's actually a nice park about a mile from my house.

PROVIDER: Wonderful. Let us schedule your activities. I would also like you to keep a log of your activities, with the date you scheduled them for, and rate them on a scale. So, you can look at your scheduled activities and rate whether you accomplished and enjoyed them. For example, a rating of 0 means the goal was not accomplished or enjoyed and a rating of 10 means the activity was accomplished and pleasurable. I will give you this activity log and you can list your activities and ratings where 0 equals no accomplishment or pleasure and 10 equals

138 Application of Ultra-Brief Interventions

maximum accomplishment and pleasure. I would like you to also note your overall mood for each day on the 0–10 scale, even on those days when you do not have activities scheduled.

Commentary. The provider gives Maria an activity monitoring form. Maria will list the dates of the week across the top and fill in the planned activities. As Maria either completes or does not complete these activities, she will rate them on a scale of 0 to 10 where 0 equals no accomplishment or pleasure and 10 equals maximum accomplishment and pleasure. Maria will also indicate her overall mood for each day.

MARIA: Ok, I can go get a coffee to go one day. And maybe take some walks.

PROVIDER: That is great. You can start the walks but just walking to the park and back, or even just walking around the block once. It is better to give yourself goals you can achieve more easily at first.

MARIA: Ok so I will get coffee this Friday. Then next week walk for 15 minutes on Saturday.

PROVIDER: You have done a great job. I believe you will do really well with this exercise and I am looking forward to hearing about your progress. Remember to spend some time reflecting on how you accomplish each small goal. It is important to allow yourself to enjoy the rewards of what you are doing.

MARIA: Yes, I can see how that might help. To be honest, I'm not as optimistic as you are but I am willing to try because sitting home all the time isn't helping.

Commentary. In this brief 20–30-minute session, the provider was able to do a diagnostic and functional assessment of Maria's depressive symptoms as well as introduce the behavioral activation intervention. It is expected that the behavioral activation will improve her mood, allowing us to work on her negative thinking in the upcoming sessions. Maria was cooperative in scheduling her upcoming activities and her motivation appeared to increase across the session.

PROVIDER: I'm glad to hear that. So, before we end for the day, let us recap. You are going to get a coffee to go this week and take a walk to your neighborhood park next week. You estimated each activity will take about 15 minutes, and you are going to monitor those activities and rate them on the 0–10 scale. Then you can bring the activity log with you next week and we will review it together. How does that sound?

MARIA: Yes, I got it. That sounds good. I hope I can do it.

Ultra-Brief Interventions with Depression   **139**

PROVIDER: Good, now on a scale of 0 to 10, with 0 being not at all, how important is it to you that you complete the activity scheduling and monitoring?

MARIA: I would say about an 8. I'm not sure it will work, and I feel so tired all the time, but I want to feel better.

PROVIDER: Good. Now on that same 0 to 10 scale, how confident are you that you can complete these activities?

MARIA: Oh, maybe just a 4.

PROVIDER: Ok, that's good. What do you think it would take to bump that up to a 5 or 6?

MARIA: I think if I can do the first activity, I will be a lot more confident.

PROVIDER: Ok, good. I'm looking forward to our next meeting and hearing how it went.

Commentary. S – Maria presents with depressive symptoms that cause her to feel sadness, fatigue, and loss of pleasure. Her symptoms have caused her to be absent from work and she worries about the consequences at her job.

O – She appears to be somewhat depressed and scored 15 on the Patient Health Questionnaire (PHQ-9), indicating the lower end of moderately severe depression.

A – Scores on the PHQ and results of the functional assessment reveal that she meets DSM-5 diagnostic criteria for Major Depressive Disorder, Single Episode, Moderate 296.22, and it is long-standing. She also demonstrated an avoidant personality style, with a pattern of avoiding others so as not to feel judged, which may be contributing to her depressive symptoms.

P – Treatment will focus on pleasant activity scheduling, progress monitoring, and pattern-focused therapy to address the role her pattern plays in maintaining her depression. The PHQ-9 will be administered prior to each session.

Case of Maria: Session 2

Background. The PHQ was administered again, and Maria scored 9, indicating an improvement from her initial session. In this session, I will review Maria's progress as well as plan further behavioral activation activities.

PROVIDER: Maria, how are you doing today?

MARIA: I am ok, thank you.

140 Application of Ultra-Brief Interventions

PROVIDER: I am glad to see you back and am looking forward to reviewing your activities and monitoring today.

MARIA: Yes, me too.

PROVIDER: Let's have a look at your activity log. Is that ok?

MARIA: Yes, well I had scheduled going to get coffee and walking to the park. It went ok, I guess.

PROVIDER: Alright. I see you rated getting coffee as a 6. Can you tell me a little more about how that went?

MARIA: Ok, I really wanted to try this new flavored coffee drink I saw on TV and I actually did make it there on the day I said I would.

PROVIDER: That's great. What was good about this activity?

MARIA: Well, I got the drink I wanted and that was good. I enjoyed it. I kind of wanted to sit in the café for a while but I didn't but it was nice in there.

PROVIDER: Was there anything else?

MARIA: I guess it was nice to get myself something I wanted.

PROVIDER: I agree. So, can you tell me what was not so good about this activity?

MARIA: Well, it seemed nice in there. I sat down for a couple of minutes but it didn't really make me feel good. I thought I would enjoy sitting there but I didn't.

PROVIDER: Mhmm. So, you would have liked to spend some time in the coffee shop but that wasn't very pleasurable for you?

MARIA: No, it was too crowded.

PROVIDER: I see. So, was there anything else?

MARIA: No, not really.

Commentary. Maria successfully completed her first activity and would have achieved more pleasure from it if her avoidant pattern was not triggered. The provider should work with Maria to change her maladaptive pattern, using Pattern-Focused Therapy, in future sessions.

PROVIDER: That is ok. I think it's very admirable that you were able to accomplish your goal. This was your first activity and you knew exactly what you wanted and made that happen.

MARIA: Thank you. Too bad I don't have the same to say about my other goal.

PROVIDER: Ok, let's review the other goal. You were going to walk to the neighborhood park, and I see you rated that activity a 4. Can you tell me what went well?

MARIA: Well, I did try. I got dressed and went outside and started walking towards the park. It was nice to get some fresh air. And I suppose it was nice to put my sneakers on and go out as though I was going to exercise.

PROVIDER: That sounds nice. What else was positive?

MARIA: Nothing else, really. It was just nice to get outside.

PROVIDER: Great. Now what wasn't so good about the activity?

MARIA: I didn't make it very far. I started walking towards the park but it was cold out and I was tired. I didn't feel happy, I just felt miserable. I figured what's the point anyway so I turned around after about a block and went home.

PROVIDER: Go on.

MARIA: My muscles felt really stiff. I felt sad about how out of shape I've become. That's about it.

PROVIDER: I understand. I commend you for trying and getting as far as you did. I think it shows great progress that on only your second activity, you were able to get outside and start walking even though you didn't get as far as you would have liked.

MARIA: Thanks.

PROVIDER: So, how would you describe your mood this week as compared to before you came in?

MARIA: It's a little better but I still feel pretty bad.

PROVIDER: I am glad to hear you feel better. What else can you tell me about how you have been feeling?

MARIA: I haven't been feeling as low every day. There have been some fluctuations in my moods.

PROVIDER: I see that on your activity log, your mood seemed to be lower on the days when you had no activities scheduled. For example, on this day, you rated your mood a 3 but on the day when you took the walk, your overall mood was a 5, despite the fact that you did not complete that activity.

Commentary. Using her mood rating log, the provider helps Maria see that on days when she engaged in activities, her mood was improved, even if she did not complete those activities to her satisfaction. Rather, it is the increase in activity that positively affects her mood.

MARIA: Yeah, I guess that's true.

PROVIDER: Can you see a similar pattern in your log?

142 Application of Ultra-Brief Interventions

MARIA: Yeah, I didn't realize it at the time but now that you point it out, it's obvious I rated my mood lower on the days when I didn't do anything. It's funny I didn't notice that before.

PROVIDER: Can you tell me more about what you think of that pattern?

MARIA: Yes, it is making me think that getting off the couch and actually doing something makes me feel better.

PROVIDER: Yes, I agree.

MARIA: I think it's interesting that I actually had a better mood even though I didn't finish the activity. I thought I would have to go through with it completely for it to do me any good.

PROVIDER: Interesting that just part of an activity would have that much of a positive effect for you.

MARIA: I agree. I guess that it's important to at least do something.

PROVIDER: What did you do on those days you had no activities scheduled?

MARIA: Nothing besides go to work.

PROVIDER: So, no fresh air or tasty coffee?

MARIA: Haha. No. You are right. On those days I didn't have activities, I didn't really do much to help myself feel better. When I got the coffee and took a walk, I did feel a little more connected – to myself and the outside world. It's sort of like an awakening.

PROVIDER: An awakening. I think that's an interesting way to describe it. Can you elaborate?

MARIA: Yes, like waking up your senses and feeling a little pleasure again. When I got the coffee, I actually thought about doing it again.

PROVIDER: That is a very powerful statement. It sounds like you are discovering that even some small changes and simple pleasures have a big effect.

MARIA: That's right. I definitely see that connection.

PROVIDER: I think it is also important to keep in mind that doing some activities motivates you to do more, as you mentioned with getting coffee.

MARIA: Yes, I think that is true. I didn't realize it at the time but now that I am discussing it with you, it makes more sense. It makes sense that these activities have somewhat of a cumulative effect. Every little bit counts.

PROVIDER: I agree with you and I am very impressed that you were able to not only complete or attempt the activities you scheduled, but that you were able to make these connections between your activities and your mood.

MARIA: Thank you.

Ultra-Brief Interventions with Depression 143

Commentary. Maria has been cooperative with behavioral activation and increased her motivation when she made the connection between how limiting vs increasing activities affects her mood. At this point the provider moves into scheduling next week's activities with Maria. The provider will ask her to continue to keep a log on the activity monitoring sheet given to her. The log will include the dates during the week, the scheduled activities and Maria's rating of them, and her rating of her daily overall mood.

PROVIDER: Now again on a scale of 0 to 10, with 0 being not at all, how motivated are you to complete the activity scheduling and monitoring this week?

MARIA: I would say about a 9. I would like to see how it goes.

PROVIDER: Good. Now on that same 0 to 10 scale, how confident are you that you can complete these activities?

MARIA: 5.

PROVIDER: Ok, that's an increase from last week, which is great. What do you think would help bump that to a 6 or even a 7?

MARIA: Maybe if I can actually finish my activities this week.

PROVIDER: Ok, that sounds good. I am looking forward to hearing about it.

Commentary. S – Maria reports that she completed some of her scheduled activities for the week and was able to derive some pleasure from them.

O – She scored 9 on the Patient Health Questionnaire (PHQ-9), indicating an improvement from the initial session.

A – Scores on the PHQ and results of the functional assessment reveal that she meets DSM-5 diagnostic criteria for Major Depressive Disorder, Single Episode, Moderate 296.22, and it is long-standing. She also demonstrated an avoidant personality style, with a pattern of avoiding others so as not to feel judged, which may be contributing to her depressive symptoms.

P – The following session will focus on progress monitoring and a medication evaluation. The PHQ-9 will be administered prior to each session.

Case of Maria: Session 3

Background. The PHQ-9 was administered and Maria scored 17, an increase from the first session. In this session, I will review her activities from last week

144 Application of Ultra-Brief Interventions

and the severity of her current symptoms to determine the need for a medication evaluation.

PROVIDER: Hi Maria, I'm glad to see you. How are you doing?

MARIA: I'm ok, not great though.

PROVIDER: Not great? Can you tell me a little more?

MARIA: I could barely do the activities I planned. I'm such a failure. I should have known I couldn't do it.

PROVIDER: I am very sorry to hear that you feel this way. But I must disagree with you being a failure. People often experience many ups and downs and winding roads on their journeys towards feeling better.

MARIA: I guess so.

PROVIDER: Why don't we look over your activity monitoring log from last week?

MARIA: Ok.

PROVIDER: I see that your first activity was to cook and your rating was a 3. Can you tell me what was good about that activity?

MARIA: Sure. I did manage to make the pasta that I planned to make. I was glad I could do it.

PROVIDER: Great. What else went well?

MARIA: Honestly, I can't even think of what else went well.

PROVIDER: Ok, I see something must not have gone so well, considering your rating. Can you tell me what wasn't so good about this activity?

MARIA: Well, for starters, what I cooked wasn't very good. I didn't really like it and it was hard to do. Then my mom called me and I told her what I did and she said what I made wasn't really healthy.

PROVIDER: Oh, can you elaborate on that?

MARIA: Yeah, she told me I should make something like a kale salad or brown rice. She's all into health food these days. She told me all these recipes to make and I actually went to the grocery store to get some stuff and I didn't know where to find stuff. There were so many people there and the people who worked there kept asking if they could help me find stuff. I just felt so stupid and overwhelmed that I left.

PROVIDER: I see. That sounds like an overwhelming experience. Perhaps that was not the best time for your mother's advice though it sounds well-intended.

MARIA: Yeah, she meant well and she's probably right. I don't know how she does it. I feel like such a failure.

PROVIDER: I see. I am sorry this didn't turn out as you had hoped. It sounds as though you felt defeated by your mother's advice.

Ultra-Brief Interventions with Depression 145

MARIA: Yes, it was like a criticism. I thought it was pretty good that I made anything at all and then I felt bad about what I made.

PROVIDER: Do you still believe completing the activity itself was beneficial?

MARIA: I think so, yes. Maybe I would have felt differently if I had just left it at that.

PROVIDER: I do agree that completing the cooking was a great step that was rewarding in and of itself. I see a rating of 0 for your second activity – the biking. Can you tell me more about that?

MARIA: Yeah, I felt so bad after what happened, I just stayed home all weekend and watched TV. I felt like such a failure and I was too tired and too sad to bother doing anything else. I also called in sick to work on Friday and my boss didn't sound too happy on the phone. I don't know. What's the point anyway?

PROVIDER: I am sorry to hear you are struggling. I am hopeful that you will do better considering how well you did the first week and that you did actually accomplish one of your goals this week although you did not seem very pleased with it.

MARIA: I hope you are right but I don't know.

PROVIDER: Your activity monitoring log shows you had the lowest mood – 3 – on the day you called in sick from work.

MARIA: I guess that makes sense since I didn't do anything that day. I just sat around feeling depressed.

PROVIDER: I hear you saying that you see a connection between inactivity and feeling more depressed. Is that correct?

MARIA: Yes, that's correct. Because I actually didn't feel as bad on the day I cooked even though my mom gave me that advice that upset me. I guess maybe because I actually did something, I felt better.

PROVIDER: I see you rated that day a 4 in terms of your overall mood so I would tend to agree with you. I also wonder if getting out and going to the grocery store was beneficial, despite the fact that it did not turn out as you wished.

MARIA: I think so but I think in general, I am feeling worse this week. My overall mood this week was worse than last week.

PROVIDER: Yes, I see that reflected in your activity monitoring log and in your PHQ score today. I am sorry to hear that you are experiencing this downturn in your mood.

Commentary. At this point in the session, after assessing Maria's activities and her symptoms, I decide to refer Maria back to her primary care physician, Dr. Shapiro, for a medication evaluation. I will help her get an appointment the same day and attend the appointment with her.

146 Application of Ultra-Brief Interventions

PROVIDER: As I said, ups and downs are not uncommon in this process and sometimes people need some extra help achieving these goals.

MARIA: I could use some extra help. What kind of stuff are you talking about?

PROVIDER: I think it would be wise to refer you back to Dr. Shapiro for an evaluation for medication. How does that sound?

MARIA: Yeah, maybe that would help. I would at least like to know what the doctor thinks.

PROVIDER: Ok, I am glad to hear that. I can help you see Dr. Shapiro today and attend that meeting with you. Is that ok?

MARIA: Yeah that's good.

Commentary. S – Maria reports increased sadness and a sense of defeat. She reports that she struggled to complete her scheduled pleasant activities and her symptoms prompted her to miss work again. A meeting was coordinated for her medication evaluation.

O – She scored 17 on the Patient Health Questionnaire (PHQ-9), indicating an increase from the last two sessions.

A – Scores on the PHQ and results of the functional assessment reveal that she meets DSM-5 diagnostic criteria for Major Depressive Disorder, Single Episode, Moderate 296.22. The worsening of her symptoms indicated possible need for medication.

P – She was prescribed anti-depressant medication. Treatment will continue to focus on pleasant activity scheduling and pattern-focused therapy to address the role her pattern plays in maintaining her depression. The PHQ-9 will be administered prior to each session.

Case of Maria: Session 4

Background. The PHQ was administered, in which Maria scored 7, indicating an improvement in her symptoms. For this session, I will focus on helping Maria analyze a specific situation using Pattern-Focused Therapy in order to address the role her avoidant pattern plays in her depression.

PROVIDER: Hi Maria. I am glad to hear you are feeling better. I was thinking today we could continue talking about some of your experiences with that pattern we discussed, where you avoid people and situations in order to not be judged. How does that sound?

Ultra-Brief Interventions with Depression 147

MARIA: That's fine.

PROVIDER: Ok, so we can discuss a particular situation where you saw this pattern emerge. Was there anything that happened in the past week that didn't turn out how you hoped or where you noticed this pattern?

MARIA: Yes, I wanted to do some exercise since that has been helping me feel better. I was going to take a walk around my neighborhood.

PROVIDER: Ok, can you tell me what happened from beginning to end?

MARIA: Yes, it was Saturday and I had plenty of time and the weather was actually nice. The sun was out and I thought, maybe I should take a walk. So, I went to put on my workout clothes. I haven't worn them in a long time but I thought I would make this a real workout. But then the pants were so tight and the shirt I wanted to wear had a tear in it. I don't know how that happened. I tried to find the other shirt I liked wearing to work out but I couldn't find it. I felt so frustrated and thought what's the point. I could imagine people would be looking at me like I was crazy. So, I ended up not going anywhere and watching hours' worth of TV and eating junk food instead.

PROVIDER: Ok, so you wanted to go for a walk and make it more like a work out but then when your clothes didn't fit and didn't seem to work out, you abandoned the idea and watched TV and ate snacks instead. Is that right?

MARIA: Yes, that's right.

PROVIDER: You mentioned you worried people would look at you and think ill of you because of your clothes?

MARIA: Yes. That's what I thought.

PROVIDER: Do you see this as possibly that avoidant pattern we talked about manifesting itself again?

MARIA: Yes, that's true. That pattern of not doing things because I think I'll be judged.

PROVIDER: Yes, that seems to fit. What were some of the thoughts you were having at the time?

MARIA: I thought people are going to think I look crazy.

PROVIDER: Ok, what else?

MARIA: I thought it's all or nothing. Either I'm going to go all the way and work out or I'm not doing anything at all.

PROVIDER: Ok, so you thought you were a loser and you took an all-or-nothing approach to the walk. Was there anything else?

MARIA: Yes, I thought I failed at this, I'm going to fail at everything.

PROVIDER: Yes, I can see how that can be disheartening. What were some of your behaviors? What did you do during the situation?

148 Application of Ultra-Brief Interventions

MARIA: Well, first I sort of scrutinized myself in the mirror. The pants made me look really fat so I stood in front of the mirror squeezing my thighs and thinking about how fat I looked. I used to be so in shape.

PROVIDER: Ok, you analyzed your looks in front of the mirror. What else did you do?

MARIA: I stayed home. I didn't go on the walk.

PROVIDER: You stayed home. Was there anything else?

MARIA: Yeah, like I said, I watched TV for the rest of the day and ate junk food.

PROVIDER: Ok, so you scrutinized your body, abandoned the walk, and ate some junk food in front of the TV.

MARIA: That's right.

PROVIDER: Now what did you hope to get out of this situation?

MARIA: I wanted my clothes to fit and to get a workout.

PROVIDER: Well, we can't always get our clothes to fit, unfortunately.

MARIA: Haha. Yes, that's true.

PROVIDER: So, what is an outcome that is in your control?

MARIA: I guess just getting some exercise.

PROVIDER: Ok, so your desired outcome was to get some exercise. And what actually happened?

MARIA: The complete opposite of that. I don't think eating cookies in front of the TV is a very good workout.

PROVIDER: Ok, so you wouldn't say you got what you wanted.

MARIA: No, I didn't.

PROVIDER: Ok, then would you like to go over this situation again and see how it might have turned out differently for you?

MARIA: Ok.

PROVIDER: So, your first thought was, "people are going to think I'm crazy." Did that thought help you or hurt you in getting your desired outcome of getting some exercise that day?

MARIA: It hurt. That's not a very good start. And that's the pattern like we said.

PROVIDER: What is an alternative thought you could have had?

MARIA: Reminding myself people don't care. They're doing their own thing.

PROVIDER: Ok, so people aren't necessarily paying any attention to what you're wearing?

MARIA: Yes.

PROVIDER: And how would that be helpful?

MARIA: I think it would make me less worried. Less self-conscious.

Ultra-Brief Interventions with Depression **149**

PROVIDER: I think so too. Your second thought was it's all or nothing. Did that help you or hurt you in getting some exercise that day?

MARIA: I think that's what really ended it, so it was hurtful. I obviously couldn't go all the way so I basically guaranteed I wouldn't do anything.

PROVIDER: Right, and what would have been a more helpful thought?

MARIA: Thinking if I could just do a little, it's better than nothing. That would help me do at least some walking.

PROVIDER: Ok, so something is better than nothing. And your third thought was that you are going to fail at everything. Was that thought helpful or hurtful in getting some exercise?

MARIA: It was hurtful. It made me depressed. That's when I threw in the towel.

PROVIDER: What would have been a more helpful thought?

MARIA: I think similar to the first one. I've done all these activities. There's no reason I should be a failure.

PROVIDER: Ok, good. Now, looking at some of your behaviors. You said your first behavior was to scrutinize yourself in the mirror. Was that helpful or hurtful in getting your desired outcome of getting some exercise?

MARIA: It was hurtful. It made me feel terrible!

PROVIDER: I can imagine. What would have been an alternative behavior?

MARIA: Not analyzing myself. Just taking off the pants and putting on something comfortable.

PROVIDER: Your second behavior was to stay home and not go for a walk.

MARIA: Yes, obviously that didn't help me get any exercise.

PROVIDER: Right. Then what would be an alternative behavior that would help you get what you wanted?

MARIA: Just going outside anyway. Even if I just walked a little bit.

PROVIDER: So, taking even a short walk would have helped you get more exercise than not going at all?

MARIA: Yes.

PROVIDER: And your third behavior was to watch TV all day and eat junk food. Did that help you or hurt you in getting what you wanted – some exercise?

MARIA: Of course, that hurt. I felt much worse. And the next day I didn't get any exercise because I felt so sluggish from the food I ate

PROVIDER: Ok, so what would have been a more helpful behavior?

MARIA: I think taking a short walk and limiting my TV time.

PROVIDER: Ok, so nothing too extreme but some small changes to help keep you on track.

150 Application of Ultra-Brief Interventions

MARIA: Yes, I think that would have helped.

PROVIDER: You have come up with some great alternatives. Is this something you can see yourself doing outside of the therapy sessions?

MARIA: Yes, now that I understand it, I definitely think I could.

PROVIDER: That's really good. So, on a scale from 0 to 10 where 0 is not at all and 10 is the maximum, how important is it to you to change your avoidant pattern?

MARIA: It's a 10. I really did feel better on those days when I actually got out and did things.

PROVIDER: I agree. And on the same scale, how confident are you that you can change that pattern?

MARIA: 6. It seems clear here but I worry I won't be able to do it.

PROVIDER: Ok, well you are more than halfway there. What would have to happen for that to move to a 7 or an 8?

MARIA: I think if I'm successful with one of the next activities I have scheduled.

Commentary. Maria has been compliant with her prescribed medication and arrived at the session with an improved mood. The provider determined Maria was ready to engage in Pattern-Focused Therapy to improve her maladaptive pattern. Because Maria's pattern is primarily to avoid social situations so she can feel safe, the query process was focused on a situation of this nature. Maria was compliant with the query process and was able to explore how her avoidant pattern affects her mood and behavior, as well as generate useful alternative thoughts and behaviors.

S – Maria reports a decrease in depressive symptoms and has been compliant with her medication.

O – She scored 7 on the Patient Health Questionnaire (PHQ-9), indicating an improvement since the last session.

A – She demonstrates an avoidant personality style, which contributes to her symptoms by increasing social isolation and decreasing her sense of self-worth. She was able to generate alternative thoughts and behaviors to address this pattern through pattern-focused therapy.

P – Treatment will continue to focus on pleasant activity scheduling, progress monitoring, and pattern-focused therapy to address the role her pattern plays in maintaining her depression. The PHQ-9 will be administered prior to each session.

Concluding Note

This chapter reviews depression and how it commonly presents in integrated care settings. The format for a diagnostic evaluation and functional assessment is reviewed and a case example illustrates how ultra-brief interventions are utilized to address these client concerns. Depression is a common presentation in integrated care settings and even presentations that are subclinical can cause significant distress, disruption in daily functioning, and worsening of medical conditions. A clinical evaluation and risk assessment as well as functional assessment are indicated and primary interventions include behavioral activation, psychoeducation, pattern-focused therapy, and medication treatment. Ongoing symptom monitoring using standardized instruments and the mood scale. A case example is included in this chapter to illustrate an intervention completed in four ultra-brief sessions.

References

American Counseling Association. (n.d.). Suicide Assessment. Retrieved from www.counseling.org/docs/trauma-disaster/fact-sheet-6---suicide-assessment.pdf?sfvrsn=2

American Psychiatric Association. (2013). *Diagnostic and statistical manual of mental disorders* (5th ed.).

Chang, M.X., Jetten, J., Cruwys, T., & Haslam, C. (2016, October 20). Cultural identity and the expression of depression: A social identity perspective. *Journal of Community and Applied Social Psychology*, 27(1), 16–34. https://doi.org/10.1002/casp.2291

Lew, V., & Ghassemzadeh, S. (2018). SOAP Notes. Retrieved from www.ncbi.nlm.nih.gov/books/NBK482263/

Na, P.J., Yaramala, S.R., Kim, J.A., Kim, H., Goes, F., Zandi, P.P., ... Bobo, W.V. (2018, May). The PHQ-9 Item 9 based screening for suicide risk: A validation study of the Patient Health Questionnaire (PHQ-9) Item 9 with the Columbia Suicide Severity Rating Scale (C-SSRS). *Journal of Affective Disorders*, 232, 34–40.

Spitzer, R.L., Kroenke, K., & Williams, J.B., (1999). Validation and utility of a self-report version of PRIME-MD: The PHQ primary care study. Primary care Evaluation of Mental Disorders. Patient Health Questionnaire. *JAMA: Journal of the American Medical Association*, 282(18), 1737.

Ultra-Brief Interventions with Anxiety and Trauma **6**

This chapter provides an overview of anxiety, acute emotional distress, and trauma and how these conditions commonly present in integrated mental health care settings. Included is an overview of the functional assessment and common interventions for these presentations. Finally, a case example is illustrated through four transcriptions with commentary. This chapter does not emphasize the diagnostic evaluation, but rather how brief interventions can be used to address anxiety issues in both of these settings. The behavioral health provider's role in assessment is different from one completing a diagnostic evaluation. Typically, the behavioral health provider will only occasionally be expected to perform a formal diagnostic evaluation. The rest of the time, the provider will be engaged in consultation to other staff members and provide direct services to patients.

Anxiety Disorders

Anxiety disorders commonly present in primary care settings and may account for up to 20 percent of client complaints (Hunter, Goodie, Oordt, & Dobmeyer, 2017, p. 61). While anxiety disorders are common, these symptoms occur on a spectrum and while some clients might not meet the criteria necessary for a diagnosis, anxiety symptoms may still be present. Anxiety disorders have been identified as contributory factors in a number of medical problems as well. Thus, they can be treated on their own in clinical settings or addressed as part of the treatment for other medical disorders.

Two anxiety disorders that commonly present in both integrated mental health and primary care settings are Generalized Anxiety Disorder and Panic Disorder. These disorders are characterized by fear or anxiety, or both, and associated behavioral symptoms. While fear is a key component, anxiety involves feelings of foreboding and the expectation that something bad will happen in the future. Symptoms may include worry, avoidance of situations, and physical symptoms. The DSM-5 distinguishes between anxiety and fear. Fear is defined as the emotional response to an imminent threat, which triggers an individual's fight or flight response. Anxiety is defined as a feeling of apprehension and anticipation of future events. Anxiety can produce worry, distress, or somatic symptoms.

Generalized Anxiety Disorder (GAD)

The DSM-5 defines GAD as a disorder characterized by excessive anxiety and worry that is difficult to control. This is accompanied by at least three of the following symptoms: restlessness, fatigue, difficulty concentrating, irritability, tense muscles, and poor sleep. These symptoms must be present for the majority of days for at least six months, and in relation to a variety of events and situations. Symptoms must cause significant distress and decreased functioning. The duration and intensity of the client's worry is disproportionate to the situation and represents an irrational fear. Worries often center around everyday events, including work, family and social issues, finances, personal health and that of loved ones, etc. These worries are more intense, excessive, and pervasive than those not associated with GAD. Non-pathological worrying is also less likely to include the physical symptoms associated with GAD. Physical symptoms can include shakiness, muscle aches, sweating, nausea, headaches, and stomach aches. The 12-month prevalence for GAD in adults in the United States is 2.9% (DSM).

Panic Disorder

The DSM defines Panic Disorder as characterized by recurrent panic attacks. Individuals experiencing panic attacks have a sudden, intense onset of fear and physical sensations that peak rather quickly. Often, these attacks are unexpected, seemingly have no trigger, and do not necessarily occur when the individual is already experiencing anxiety. Symptoms can include increased heart rate, sweating, shaking, shortness of breath, choking feeling, chest pains,

154 Application of Ultra-Brief Interventions

nausea, upset stomach, dizziness or faintness, chills, numbness and tingling, fear of losing control or losing one's mind, fear of dying, derealization, and depersonalization. Four or more of these symptoms are present during a panic attack. For Panic Disorder criteria to be met, at least one of the attacks must be followed by a month of constant worry about future panic attacks, and/or behavioral changes intended to avoid more panic attacks. Frequency of attacks varies as they may occur once a week for several months, daily bouts separated by months without attacks, or occasional attacks over the course of several years. Some individuals experience attacks with fewer than four symptoms, but at least one full attack (four or more symptoms) is necessary for the diagnosis to be made. The 12-month prevalence for Panic Disorder in adults in the United States is 2–3% (DSM).

Acute Emotional Distress and Posttraumatic Stress Disorder

Acute emotional distress and Posttraumatic Stress Disorder also commonly present in integrated settings. While acute emotional distress is short-lived, effective assessment and care in these settings can facilitate recovery. Posttraumatic Stress Disorder (PTSD) typically requires more intense, lengthier, and/or manualized interventions, which are unlikely to be provided in integrated care settings. Here, the behavioral health provider's role is to assess for PTSD, provide interventions for related acute anxiety and depression, and referrals for further treatment and/or a medication evaluation. The assessment for acute emotional distress and PTSD is similar to that for anxiety and includes both a diagnostic and functional assessment using closed-ended questions like those in Table 6.1.

Acute Emotional Distress

Acute emotional distress refers to subclinical levels of stress that do not meet criteria for a DSM-5 diagnosis but still cause the individual significant distress. Symptoms of acute emotional distress may be similar to those of Generalized Anxiety Disorder, Adjustment Disorder, and Acute Stress Disorder but milder in intensity and shorter in duration. Acute emotional distress is highly amenable to treatment with ultra-brief interventions, which can prevent development of a full disorder.

Posttraumatic Stress Disorder (PTSD)

The DSM defines Posttraumatic Stress Disorder (PTSD) as a disorder arising after an individual is exposed to a traumatic event like the threat of death, a natural disaster, or an assault. Common symptoms of posttraumatic stress include intrusive symptoms, in which the individual re-experiences the event either through recurrent memories, dreams, and/or dissociative reactions like flashbacks. The individual attempts to avoid stimuli associated with the distressing event and may suffer from distorted memories of the event, negative emotions, negative beliefs about the self or others, and decreased interest and engagement. The individual also experiences altered arousal and reactivity, which can include irritability, reckless behavior, hypervigilance, and an exaggerated startle response. Dissociative symptoms such as depersonalization and derealization can also be present.

Assessment and Screening Instruments

Similar to depression, assessment of anxiety in integrated settings requires both a diagnostic and functional assessment. Interview questions should be primarily closed-ended in order to gather all necessary information in a short amount of time. A risk assessment is also indicated for this diagnosis.

Diagnostic Assessment

The assessment for anxiety is similar to a regular diagnostic assessment. The provider can begin by asking if the client worries and finds it difficult to control the worry. For Generalized Anxiety Disorder (GAD), the GAD-7 screener is a useful tool to assess symptoms. The behavioral health provider should also determine if any comorbid disorders are present and evaluate the client's personality style or possible personality disorder.

Functional Assessment

The functional assessment should include information about how anxiety affects the client on a daily basis and interferes with regular functioning. Areas of interest include sleep, tension, aches and pains, difficulty concentrating,

156 Application of Ultra-Brief Interventions

etc. Triggers for symptoms should also be explored as well as factors that make the symptoms better or worse. The GAD-7 can also be used to screen for panic symptoms. The functional assessment for Panic Disorder should also address the client's related behavioral changes, worrying about future attacks, and attempts to avoid more attacks. Finally, the provider should determine if the client uses any substances that may be contributing to symptoms, such as caffeine. If the client is currently taking any prescribed or over-the-counter medication for anxiety, the provider should determine if using these medications is recommended. Table 6.1 outlines questions commonly asked in a functional assessment of anxiety.

Table 6.1   Functional Assessment of Anxiety

Presenting Problem	Your primary care physician stated you have been experiencing some anxiety recently. Is that correct?
Duration	How long have you been feeling this way?
Frequency	How many times a day or week do you feel this way?
Intensity	On a scale from 0 to 10, where 0 is not at all and 10 is the most, what is the most anxious you have ever felt?
Subjective Unit of Distress Scale (SUDS)	On a scale from 0 to 100, where 0 is not at all and 100 is the most, what is your average level of anxiety in the past week?
Triggers	Did something happen that triggered your anxiety?
Factors That Make the Problem Better or Worse	Physical, emotional, behavioral, cognitive, social, environmental
Functional Impairment	How has your anxiety affected your work, social relationships, family relationships, social/recreational activities, exercise?

Interventions with Anxiety and Trauma **157**

Table 6.1 (*Cont.*)

Changes in Sleep, Energy, Concentration, Eating Habits	How has your sleep changed since you began feeling anxious? Have you been sleeping more or less? Have you noticed any changes in your ability to concentrate? How has your appetite been?
Caffeine Use	Do you drink caffeinated drinks like coffee, tea, energy drinks, or soda? How much and how often?
Alcohol Use	Do you drink alcohol? What kind and how much?
Medications	Do you take any prescription or over-the-counter medications or any supplements?
Suicidal/Homicidal Ideation	Have you had any thoughts about hurting yourself? Have you had any thoughts about hurting someone else? Frequency of thoughts Intensity of thoughts Duration of thoughts Plan Means to complete plan Beliefs or reasons not to follow through
Open-Ended Questions	Is there anything I have not asked you about that you would like me to know?

Subjective Units of Distress (SUDS). The Subjective Units of Distress Scale is a useful, informal tool to rate a client's level of anxiety or panic. Ratings on the scale can be from 0–10 or from 0–100. This scale is useful for both clients and providers to assess the intensity of symptoms and the distress and disturbance they cause for clients. It is also a useful measure to monitor progress through therapy and after interventions.

Risk Assessment

While risk of suicide or self-harm is usually associated with depression, clients experiencing anxiety can also be at risk, especially considering the overlap of anxiety and depression symptoms and the high rate of comorbidity between these two diagnoses. Posttraumatic Stress Disorder is associated with higher rates of suicidal ideation and high suicide risk (American Psychiatric Association, 2013) so it is important to screen for risk during the assessment. When the client does present with suicidal ideation, the provider must complete a full risk assessment that includes information about the frequency, intensity, and duration of suicidal thoughts, plan and a means to carry out the plan, and if attempts were carried out before (American Counseling Association, n.d.).

Screening Instruments

The Generalized Anxiety Disorder-7. The Generalized Anxiety Disorder-7 (GAD-7) is a 7-item questionnaire that corresponds to the DSM-5 criteria for Generalized Anxiety Disorder. Each question is rated on a 4-point scale from 0–3 where 0 = not at all, 1 = several days, 2 = more than half the days, and 3 = nearly every day. Clients rate their experiences for the previous two weeks. The scoring for the GAD-7 is as follows: 0–4 = minimal or none, 5–9 = mild, 10–14 = moderate, 15–21 = severe. The first two questions of the GAD-7 are referred to as the GAD-2 and can be used to screen for anxiety but the full instrument is required for diagnosis and progress monitoring. The GAD-7 has also been shown to be useful in screening for Panic Disorder and Social Anxiety (Bardoshi et al., 2016).

PCL: PTSD Checklist. The PCL PTSD Checklist is a 17-item questionnaire widely used as a PTSD screening instrument. Respondents are asked about the severity with which a particular symptom has affected them within the last month. Each question is rated on a 5-point scale where 1 = not at all, 2 = a little bit, 3 = moderately, 4 = quite a bit, and 5 = extremely. The PCL includes subscales for Reexperiencing, Avoidance, and Hyperarousal, and is available for civilians (PCL-C) and members of the armed forces (PCL-M) The most updated version, is the PCL-5, based on DSM 5 criteria. Both instruments are available to the public and used by the Department of Veterans Affairs (Bardhoshi et al., 2016).

Interventions

Distress Tolerance Training

Distress Tolerance Training is a cognitive behavioral technique that teaches individuals to tolerate distressing emotional states. The client is taught skills needed to accept painful emotions and crises without trying to stop or change them. The client learns to observe thoughts and emotions, and self-soothe during distressing periods, reducing the likelihood that the individual will engage in self-destructive behavior. Self-soothing skills can include controlled breathing and other relaxation techniques. The client also learns to distract himself/herself from unpleasant emotions by substituting an activity, using thought stopping, or inducing other physical sensations (e.g., holding ice cubes).

Controlled Breathing

Controlled breathing is a behavioral intervention that teaches individuals to slow their breathing and restore regulated breathing rhythms to reduce stress-related symptoms. The shallow and rapid breathing patterns associated with anxiety, stress, and panic increase these unpleasant symptoms. Controlled breathing teaches individuals regulated, deep breathing patterns that calm the parasympathetic nervous system and control unpleasant symptoms. This is primarily done through diaphragmatic breathing, which has individuals take slow, deep inhales into the abdominal area and exhale slowly through the mouth. The client learns to breath out slowly, through pursed lips, and count to pace inhales and exhales.

Thought Stopping

Thought stopping is a behavioral technique used to interrupt and remove distressing thoughts. This technique decreases the frequency of distressing thoughts and the anxiety that accompanies them. The client generates a list of distressing thoughts and the provider teaches the client to issue a stop command when thoughts arise. The inhibitory behavior can be saying or thinking the word, "Stop," picturing a stop sign, or snapping a rubber band on the wrist. The client can also generate a list of pleasant images or memories with which to replace the distressing thoughts.

160 Application of Ultra-Brief Interventions

Anxiety Psychoeducation

The primary purpose of psychoeducation in this setting is to teach the client the difference between fear and anxiety and how to differentiate between a panic attack and being panicky. Using the Subjective Unit of Distress Scale (SUDS), the provider should explain that on a scale from 0–100, any score less than 20 applies to someone feeling safe; 30–40 indicates feeling apprehensive. 50+ indicates feeling increasingly apprehensive, and 90+ indicates a panic attack. Scores between 50 and 89 indicate the client is feeling panicky but not experiencing a full-blown panic attack.

For anxiety, individuals should be taught about the positives and negatives of worry, anxiety and panic warning signs, and common myths associated with anxiety and its treatment. Psychoeducation for panic includes giving the client an understanding of physical sensations commonly associated with panic, and thoughts and behaviors that trigger or increase panic.

Pattern-Focused Therapy

Pattern-Focused Therapy is useful to address client personality dynamics and patterns that underlie the presenting symptoms. The client's pattern serves to maintain the presenting problem, which can reoccur when the pattern is triggered, even after successful treatment. Addressing the client pattern using Pattern-Focused Therapy not only treats factors that may be contributing to the problem, but also helps prevent the problem from returning. For example, in the Case of Jeffrey (outlined below), Jeffrey's pattern of interacting with others contributes to and maintains his anxiety. His worries are mostly centered around others and are triggered when he is unable to take care of his loved ones or control their actions. Using Pattern-Focused Therapy, Jeffrey learns he can only control his own actions, increases his use of assertive communication, and moves to a more adaptive pattern of caring for others without sacrificing his own well-being.

Combined Medication Treatment

For some clients, psychotropic medication may be an essential part of treatment. Medication may be needed when an individual's symptoms are so intense, he/she has difficulty engaging in cognitive and behavioral interventions. In this case, a medication evaluation should be coordinated with the medical doctor, the client, and the behavioral health provider. The behavioral health provider then monitors the client's use of the medication and adherence to the medication plan.

Progress Monitoring and Record Keeping

Progress Monitoring

Because of the limited number of sessions and short duration of sessions, progress monitoring is especially important in integrated and mental health care settings. In the treatment of anxiety, panic, and stress-related disorders, progress monitoring includes reassessment of symptoms, monitoring completion of homework assignments, and adherence to medication plans when indicated. Standardized instruments like the GAD-7 should be administered prior to each session and responses discussed with the client. When doing homework assignments, clients should document their progress and completion of assignments in a journal or log.

Record Keeping

Commonly used in health care settings, the SOAP note method is the most organized and concise method of record keeping. In this acronym, SOAP stands for Subjective, Objective, Assessment, and Plan. The Subjective heading describes the client's subjective experience. Presenting symptoms, subjective ratings of intensity, and associated complaints are recorded under the Subjective heading as well. The Objective heading describes any objective ratings, like those obtained from standardized instruments or medical exams. In the case of anxiety, results from the GAD-7 are reported under this heading. The Assessment heading includes a DSM-5 diagnosis, if indicated, as well as the client's personality style. Items in this category should be listed in order of importance. Finally, the Plan heading includes the next steps to be completed in the treatment plan, objectives for the next session, and any necessary referrals.

162 Application of Ultra-Brief Interventions

Case of Jeffrey Transcriptions

Case of Jeffrey: Session 1

Background. Jeffrey is a 30-year-old Caucasian male referred to counseling by his primary care physician, Dr. Morris, for symptoms of anxiety with intermittent panic. Jeffrey was administered Generalized Anxiety Disorder 7-item (GAD-7) scale, on which he scored 12, indicating moderate anxiety. Jeffrey also reports intermittent panic symptoms and the highest score on the GAD-7 was for the item indicating feelings of foreboding. Judging by the severity of his panic symptoms, I will initially focus treatment on that area.

PROVIDER: Hi Jeffrey. I really enjoy working with Dr. Morris's patients and trust our time together will be very useful to you.

JEFFREY: I do too. I really like Dr. Morris and trust his judgment. But I do admit I'm a bit nervous about counseling.

PROVIDER: I would like to ask you some questions to get a better idea of how you are doing. Is that ok?

JEFFREY: Yes, that's fine.

PROVIDER: Great, let's get started. Can you tell me how your mood has been?

JEFFREY: It has been ok. I'm mostly nervous when I feel bad. Not sad or anything.

PROVIDER: What about your energy level?

JEFFREY: I don't really have problems with that.

PROVIDER: That's good. Was there ever a time when you felt you had a lot of energy and maybe even needed less sleep than usual?

JEFFREY: There are times I can't sleep but it's usually because I'm thinking about stuff. I don't remember ever having a lot of energy like that.

PROVIDER: Ok. You mentioned thinking about stuff getting in the way of your sleep. Can you tell me a little more about that?

JEFFREY: It's usually that I'm worried. I worry a lot about different things.

PROVIDER: Can you tell me more about some of the things you worry about?

JEFFREY: Yeah mostly I worry about other people. Like my mother. She has been alone since my dad died. She does a lot of stuff on her own but I still worry about her all the time. And I worry about my brother. He has a drinking problem. Or at least I think so.

PROVIDER: It sounds like you are a caring person but that maybe that is having some unintended consequences for you.

Interventions with Anxiety and Trauma   **163**

JEFFREY: Yes, that's a good way to say it.

PROVIDER: When you have these worries, do you ever do any little rituals to try to ease those anxious feelings?

JEFFREY: What, like turning the lights on and off? Haha. No, I don't do anything like that.

PROVIDER: Alright. How would you say you cope with some of these worries?

JEFFREY: I don't really cope. I do have anxiety attacks sometimes.

PROVIDER: I'm sorry to hear that. Can you explain to me how you experience those anxiety attacks?

JEFFREY: Yeah, for example last week, it just came out of the blue, as it often does. I was in my kitchen and then all of a sudden, I started to feel short of breath. That freaked me out and I quickly started feeling worse and worse. It felt like the walls were closing in and I was shivering and sweating at the same time. I thought I would actually stop breathing.

PROVIDER: I'm sorry to hear. That sounds very frightening.

JEFFREY: It was! It was awful.

PROVIDER: How often would you say you have these attacks?

JEFFREY: Maybe every few weeks. I feel restless and jittery a few times a week but the full-blown attacks are not as often.

PROVIDER: And how long has this been going on?

JEFFREY: Maybe almost a year.

PROVIDER: How would you say this impacts your daily life?

JEFFREY: It definitely makes it hard to concentrate at work. And sometimes I'm so distracted I can't do basic things like laundry, errands, and cooking.

PROVIDER: It sounds like it's really getting in the way of things you would like to or have to do.

JEFFREY: Yes, it is.

PROVIDER: Now if you had to rate that on a scale from 0 to 10 where 0 is the worst it could be and 10 is the best, how would you rate your ability to function with your anxiety?

Commentary. As the provider completes the functional assessment, the scaling question provides useful information about how Jeffrey is able to function daily with his anxiety. This gives insight into the severity of his symptoms and the effect on his daily life.

JEFFREY: I would say just about a 5. I'm not totally incapacitated, but it makes things pretty difficult.

164 Application of Ultra-Brief Interventions

PROVIDER: Ok, what about any one thing you particularly find frightening? Anything like that?

JEFFREY: Like bugs and spiders? No.

PROVIDER: Have you had any big changes in your life recently?

JEFFREY: No. My dad died but that was four years ago.

PROVIDER: Ok, what about any particularly frightening experiences?

JEFFREY: No, I wouldn't say so. The anxiety attacks are scary but nothing traumatic happened.

PROVIDER: Do you ever feel that your mind is playing tricks on you?

JEFFREY: I feel like I'm going crazy sometimes during the attacks but that's the only time. When that happens, sometimes I feel like I might actually go crazy.

PROVIDER: That sounds very difficult. How have you been managing thus far?

JEFFREY: I don't know. I just deal with it and then it passes but I worry because I know it will happen again.

PROVIDER: Mhmm. What about do you ever feel your mind is playing tricks on you?

JEFFREY: No, nothing of the kind.

PROVIDER: Ok. Do you use any drugs or alcohol?

JEFFREY: I have a drink once in a while.

PROVIDER: When you say once in a while, what do you mean?

JEFFREY: Just when I go out with friends. Maybe once or twice a month. I don't go out much.

PROVIDER: What about prescription or over-the-counter drugs?

JEFFREY: Not really.

PROVIDER: And what about coffee, tea, soda, or anything that has caffeine in it?

JEFFREY: I don't have much. I actually cut down my caffeine intake because I felt it was making me more anxious.

PROVIDER: Yes, that's exactly why I asked. I am glad to hear you noticed that and cut down. And generally, how would you describe your eating habits?

JEFFREY: I think my eating is usually pretty normal. I try to eat healthy but sometimes I don't eat because I lose my appetite when I'm nervous.

PROVIDER: And how has your memory been recently?

JEFFREY: No problems with that.

PROVIDER: Have you had any thoughts that life isn't worth living?

JEFFREY: No, I really don't have thoughts like that.

PROVIDER: What about thoughts of hurting someone else?

Interventions with Anxiety and Trauma **165**

JEFFREY: Oh, no I wouldn't do that. Not at all.

PROVIDER: Ok, and how would you describe your relationships with people?

JEFFREY: I am usually the person that others turn to. Maybe that sounds weird because I'm struggling to keep my own self together lately but I usually take care of everyone else.

PROVIDER: Can you tell me more about that?

JEFFREY: Yeah, everyone relies on me. My mom is alone a lot, like I said. So, I try to go to her place a few times a week and clean up her house. I call her a lot to make sure she is ok.

PROVIDER: Do you ever find yourself doing things for people that you find somewhat unpleasant?

JEFFREY: Yeah, I don't want to clean my mom's house. And my brother needs a lot of help. I try to call him to make sure he isn't drinking and driving. I even offer to pick him up and we get into arguments when he won't let me.

PROVIDER: So, when do you find time to take care of yourself while you're taking care of everyone else?

JEFFREY: Haha. I don't. I guess that's why I'm here.

PROVIDER: Would you say you have a pattern of taking care of others while somewhat neglecting yourself?

JEFFREY: Yes, I would say so.

Commentary. Jeffrey's answers indicate a dependent personality style. Most of his worries center around others and his pattern of caring for others while neglecting himself contributes to his anxiety.

PROVIDER: Yes, and I'm glad you are here. Have you ever sought therapy or treatment in the past?

JEFFREY: No, I haven't.

Commentary. Jeffrey's diagnostic interview responses are consistent with a GAD-7 score of 12. He presents with subclinical symptoms of generalized anxiety and panic. He also appears to have a dependent personality style. Acculturation does not appear to be an issue. For Jeffrey's treatment, the provider will use breathing retraining for panic symptoms and thought stopping for distressing thoughts.

PROVIDER: I'm glad you took the step to come here. What do you hope to get out of counseling?

166 Application of Ultra-Brief Interventions

JEFFREY: I don't want to worry so much and I definitely don't want to have the anxiety attacks anymore.

PROVIDER: So, you would like to reduce both your worries and those panic sensations you experience once in a while?

JEFFREY: Yes, I would. I don't know that anything will make me feel better but I'm willing to try and see.

PROVIDER: Ok, well there are a number of techniques and exercises that are particularly helpful for concerns such as yours. We can start with some of the panic symptoms and then deal with the worrisome thoughts you have been having. How does that sound?

JEFFREY: That sounds good. I could use some tools to help me deal with this.

PROVIDER: Ok, let us start by looking at the panic symptoms you have had. Can you describe them for me further?

JEFFREY: Yes, I have heavy breathing, sweating, feeling like the room is closing in on me.

PROVIDER: I am sorry to hear you are experiencing some of these difficult symptoms. Many people who experience panic start to breathe more heavily and rapidly. But that rapid breathing actually makes people feel more panicked.

JEFFREY: I can see that connection. I start to breathe really fast and it feels out of control but like I am still not getting enough air.

PROVIDER: Yes, and what we have found is that if people can learn a technique to control their breathing, they can use that when they start to feel panicked, to actually calm themselves and get some of those symptoms under control. This is something you can practice on your own in a comfortable setting.

JEFFREY: Ok.

PROVIDER: Does that sound like something you would like to try?

JEFFREY: Sure.

PROVIDER: Ok, I want you to breathe normally to start.

JEFFREY: Ok.

Commentary. First, the provider provides psychoeducation about panic symptoms and illustrates how Jeffrey's response to his symptoms only serves to exacerbate them. The provider observes Jeffrey's normal breathing in session and points out the difference between shallow and diaphragmatic breathing. The provider demonstrates this technique to Jeffrey before having him try it.

Interventions with Anxiety and Trauma **167**

PROVIDER: Watching you breathe, I see that you tend to take more shallow, shorter breaths. That can increase panic feelings. Slower, longer breaths that come from deeper in your abdominal region can actually calm you down. Have you heard of diaphragmatic breathing?

JEFFREY: I have heard of that but I don't know what it is exactly.

PROVIDER: Ok, it is breathing from your diaphragm. I can demonstrate it for you. See how the belly rises and falls with this type of breathing? Why don't you put your hand on your stomach and take a couple of normal breaths and then a couple of deep breaths. Can you feel a difference?

JEFFREY: Yes, I can feel my stomach distend with the deeper breaths.

PROVIDER: Good. That's a good way to monitor your breaths as you practice. Another thing that helps slow down the breathing is to purse your lips – pretend you are blowing bubbles. Why don't you give that a try?

JEFFREY: Ok.

PROVIDER: Good. Now let's practice the breathing just as you are doing it. You are doing very well. Try to maintain the same pace and aim for six to eight breaths per minute.

JEFFREY: Ok, I am getting the hang of it.

PROVIDER: Ok, Jeffrey, you have done very well today. I'm going to give you this form you can use to monitor your breathing exercises as you practice them. You can write in the date and how long you practiced each time.

JEFFREY: Ok, I'll do my best.

Commentary. In this 20–30-minute session, the provider was able to complete an assessment and introduce an ultra-brief intervention. Jeffrey responded well to the intervention and was able to learn and practice the controlled breathing exercise. Introducing this intervention at this point will help Jeffrey manage his most pressing and distressing symptoms, give him a sense of control over his anxiety, and instill confidence in the therapeutic process.

PROVIDER: Good, now on a scale of 0 to 10, with 0 being not at all, how important is it to you that you complete the breathing exercises?

JEFFREY: Probably a 9. I would really like for something to help with my anxiety.

PROVIDER: Great. Now on that same 0 to 10 scale, how confident are you that you can complete these exercises?

JEFFREY: I would say 6. I think I can complete them but I worry they won't work and that I'll be too stressed to even do it.

168 Application of Ultra-Brief Interventions

> PROVIDER: Ok, I understand your concern. What do you think needs to happen to bump that number to about a 7 or 8?
>
> JEFFREY: I think if I can do the breathing at least once a day this week, I'll feel more confident.
>
> PROVIDER: Ok, good. I think you will do well. I look forward to our next meeting so we can look at your progress.

Commentary. S – Jeffrey presents to therapy with constant, uncontrollable worry and intermittent panic attacks.

O – He scored 12 on the Generalized Anxiety Disorder 7-item (GAD-7) scale, indicating moderate anxiety.

A – His functional interview indicates subclinical symptoms of anxiety and panic, consistent with his score on the GAD-7 scale. His symptoms interfere with his quality of life and his ability to concentrate at work. Additionally, he displayed a dependent personality style with a pattern of taking care of others while neglecting himself.

P – Treatment will include breathing retraining and thought stopping, as well as Pattern-Focused Therapy to address his pattern's role in maintaining his anxiety and panic symptoms. Future sessions will include progress monitoring and the Generalized Anxiety Disorder 7-item (GAD-7) scale will be administered prior to each session.

Case of Jeffrey: Session 2

Background. Jeffrey was administered the Generalized Anxiety Disorder 7-item (GAD-7) scale again, on which he scored 10, indicating a decrease in symptoms since the last session. During this session, I will address Jeffrey's disturbing thoughts using a thought stopping intervention after reviewing his progress with breathing retraining.

> PROVIDER: Hi Jeffrey, welcome back.
>
> JEFFREY: Thank you.
>
> PROVIDER: How have your anxiety symptoms been this past week?
>
> JEFFREY: I would say a little better but not that much.
>
> PROVIDER: Can you describe that for me?
>
> JEFFREY: I'm still getting nervous and anxious a lot.
>
> PROVIDER: Last time you mentioned that was getting in the way of some of your daily tasks. How has that been?

Interventions with Anxiety and Trauma **169**

JEFFREY: Yes, it makes it difficult to concentrate when I work and I feel too distracted to do my chores and cook. That has been slightly better.

PROVIDER: Ok, can you rate that on a scale from 0 to 10?

JEFFREY: Yes, I'd say about a 6.

PROVIDER: I'm glad to hear it is somewhat better. Last week your rating was a 5. Can you tell me how the breathing practice went? Let's review your log.

JEFFREY: Ok, I did the breathing on four days. But it was only about five minutes a day. I guess that's not very good.

PROVIDER: I actually think that is a good start. It's impressive that you were able to do it most of the days of the week.

JEFFREY: Oh, ok, that's good.

PROVIDER: It is good. Today, I was thinking we could address some of those unwanted thoughts you were having, as we discussed the last time we met. My aim is that dealing with those thoughts, in addition to the deep breathing, will bring you more relief from your anxiety and panic.

JEFFREY: Yes, I remember discussing that. Those are very bothersome so I would definitely like to address that.

PROVIDER: Why don't we recap what some of those thoughts are?

JEFFREY: Sure. Well, primarily I worry about other people. A lot of stuff runs through my head.

PROVIDER: Can you give me some examples?

JEFFREY: I worry that my mom is alone since my dad died. What if something happens to her? Like what if she falls or chokes on her food while she is home alone and no one is there to help her? Or sometimes a thought will pop in my head at night, like what if someone breaks into her house?

PROVIDER: I can see you are a caring son. What do you do when you have those thoughts?

JEFFREY: Well, sometimes I will call her. But a lot of times she doesn't answer. Sometimes it's because she is busy and sometimes because it's late and she's already asleep. I know she can take care of herself and she isn't that old but I can't stop worrying about it.

PROVIDER: What are some other things you worry about?

JEFFREY: My brother. He is an alcoholic. I mean, he has a job and he generally takes care of himself but I personally believe he drinks too much. He would never say he's an alcoholic but there have been many times I've seen him have too much to drink.

PROVIDER: And what are some of the thoughts you have about him?

170 Application of Ultra-Brief Interventions

JEFFREY: I guess it's similar to ones I have about my mom. I worry he will drink and drive. One time I saw a television show where someone got really drunk and took a shower and they slipped in the shower and hit their head and died. Sometimes I can totally picture that happening. It seems so vivid. I imagine he's going to fall and bust his head open and of course there will be no one there to find him and take him to the hospital.

PROVIDER: I can understand why these thoughts are so distressing, particularly when they are so vivid.

JEFFREY: Yes, and then of course I have other general worries like what if something happens to me and I can't be there for my family. That would kill my mother.

PROVIDER: I can clearly see how difficult this is for you and I commend you for dealing with these thoughts thus far.

JEFFREY: Yeah, I guess I do deal with them but I wouldn't say I'm doing that well. I usually just feel really bad until something else distracts me. Sometimes it can last for hours.

PROVIDER: Hopefully some of the tools we use here can help you better deal with these thoughts and decrease the anxiety you feel associated with them.

JEFFREY: Yes, that would be great.

PROVIDER: Good. Now that we have listed your thoughts, I'm going to show you how to do an exercise we refer to as thought stopping. The idea is that by stopping the thoughts in their tracks, you don't allow them to get out of hand and lead to the hours of anxiety that you described experiencing. When you're doing this exercise, you will learn to command the thoughts to stop and eventually find that you are more in control of your thoughts as opposed to them being in control of you.

JEFFREY: Ok, I hope this works but I have to be honest, I'm pretty skeptical.

PROVIDER: It's normal to be skeptical, especially since you have been dealing with this for quite some time. We will explore it together and see how it works for you.

JEFFREY: Ok, we'll see.

PROVIDER: Now, you said one distressing thought is of someone breaking into your mother's house and hurting her.

JEFFREY: Yes, that's probably the worst one.

PROVIDER: Ok, now I want you to focus on that thought and I will start by issuing the stop command. What I want you to do is really focus on

Interventions with Anxiety and Trauma   **171**

that thought of someone breaking into your mother's house and when you have it fully in focus, I want you to hold up one finger. Ok?

JEFFREY: Yes, that makes sense.

Commentary. When Jeffrey concentrates on his thought and raises his finger, the provider will loudly say, "Stop!" This will startle Jeffrey and distract him from his distressing thought. They will repeat this exercise about 20 times in a row. Then the provider will instruct Jeffrey on how to practice thought stopping on his own.

PROVIDER: Stop!

JEFFREY: Oh my god! Ok. That was a surprise! I knew you were going to say something but I didn't expect it to be that loud.

PROVIDER: Ok, how did you find that?

JEFFREY: It did get me off the scary thought. It sort of brought me back to reality.

PROVIDER: And now where is the thought?

JEFFREY: Oh, it's gone. That's pretty neat.

PROVIDER: Ok, so we are going to do this again, about 20 times in total over the next ten minutes so you can really start getting used to it and be prepared to do it on your own when you need it.

JEFFREY: Alright.

PROVIDER: So, I want you to concentrate on the thought again. Let it be the same thought of someone breaking into your mother's house and when you are really concentrating on it, raise one finger.

Commentary. After completing this exercise 20 times, the provider instructs Jeffrey to do it on his own when disturbing thoughts arise.

PROVIDER: Ok, Jeffrey, you have done so well today. I know it isn't easy but you hung in there and I am proud of the progress you have made.

JEFFREY: Thank you. I am actually pretty proud of myself too.

PROVIDER: Now, is this something you can see yourself doing when you have some of those unpleasant thoughts?

JEFFREY: Yeah, I can remind myself to do that.

PROVIDER: The way you can do it on your own is to yell, "Stop!" to yourself in your head. You don't actually have to say it out loud for it to work. I would suggest, though, that you start by practicing in a private place where you actually can say it out loud. So, concentrating on

172 Application of Ultra-Brief Interventions

those thoughts and saying the "Stop!" command. You can even picture a stop sign when you do it.

JEFFREY: Ok, I can practice some. I'll try picturing the stop sign too.

PROVIDER: Good, then you can begin using the "Stop!" command in your head whenever a distressing thought comes up. Another thing that can help is replacing the upsetting thought with a pleasant one after the "Stop!" command.

JEFFREY: Oh, ok. That would be nice.

PROVIDER: Can you think of some pleasant images that would be helpful?

JEFFREY: I can think of petting my cat. Or someplace pleasant that I really like.

PROVIDER: Can you give me some examples?

JEFFREY: I like the beach. And one time my friends and I took this trip to the south of France. I remember we sat at this beautiful outdoor café. I like thinking of that.

PROVIDER: That sounds lovely. Now there is one additional component to this exercise.

JEFFREY: What is that?

PROVIDER: It is unreasonable to say you will not worry at all, but we don't want you to have to worry all day. So, what we are going to do is set up a time for you to worry, about 20 minutes every morning and 20 minutes every night. It is helpful to set a timer so that you can stop when the 20 minutes are up.

JEFFREY: Ok so you want me to actually worry?

PROVIDER: I want you to schedule your time to worry. What is a good time in the morning that works for you? You want to pick a time that you can do every day.

JEFFREY: I think 7:30. I usually can't sleep past 7 and that's before I have to be at work.

PROVIDER: Ok, so you can set a reminder and worry from 7:30 to 7:50. What about in the evening?

JEFFREY: Probably 9 p.m. I'm usually home by then.

PROVIDER: Ok, so 7:30 a.m. to 7:50 a.m. and then 9 p.m. to 9:20 p.m. I will give you a form so you can monitor your worry time each day.

JEFFREY: Ok. I think this is a little strange but I'll try it. I should do that in addition to the breathing exercises and stopping my thoughts when they come up?

PROVIDER: Yes.

JEFFREY: Ok, I'll try.

Interventions with Anxiety and Trauma   173

Commentary. After addressing Jeffrey's panic symptoms in the previous session, the provider introduced two ultra-brief interventions to help Jeffrey deal with his anxious thoughts in this session. Jeffrey was responsive to thought stopping and, though he was somewhat skeptical, agreed to try the worry time.

PROVIDER: Good, now on a scale of 0 to 10, with 0 being not at all, how important is it to you to complete the worry activity and the thought stopping?

JEFFREY: I think 8.

PROVIDER: Good. Now on that same 0 to 10 scale, how confident are you that you can complete these exercises?

JEFFREY: Maybe 5. I don't know that I can keep the worry to those specific times. I can definitely worry but I don't know that I can do it for only 20 minutes at a time.

PROVIDER: That is understandable. What would it take to move that number from a 5 to perhaps a 6 or even a 7?

JEFFREY: I think if I can see myself actually stop the thoughts and worry just for that short amount of time I'll feel much more confident.

PROVIDER: It seems you have taken to this really well and have done a great job today. I expect practicing these exercises will bring you a lot of relief.

JEFFREY: Yes, I feel somewhat hopeful about it.

PROVIDER: Good. I look forward to hearing about your progress the next time we meet.

Commentary. S – Jeffrey reports decreased anxiety symptoms. He was able to practice breathing retraining and learn the thought stopping technique.

O – He scored 10 on the Generalized Anxiety Disorder 7-item (GAD-7) scale, indicating a decrease since the last session.

A – His GAD-7 score and progress review indicates his anxiety and panic symptoms have decreased. His functional interview indicated subclinical symptoms of anxiety and panic, consistent with his score on the GAD-7 scale. Additionally, he displayed a dependent personality style.

P – Treatment will continue to focus on breathing retraining and thought stopping. Pattern-Focused Therapy will be used to address his pattern's role in maintaining his anxiety and panic symptoms. Future sessions will include progress monitoring and the Generalized Anxiety Disorder 7-item (GAD-7) scale will be administered prior to each session.

174 Application of Ultra-Brief Interventions

Case of Jeffrey: Session 3

Background. Jeffrey was administered the Generalized Anxiety Disorder 7-item (GAD-7) scale, on which he scored 15. This score indicates a 5-point increase from the previous session and a 3-point increase from the initial session. Because of this increase in severity, the provider will assess Jeffrey's progress and refer him back to his primary care physician for a medication evaluation.

PROVIDER: Hi Jeffrey, it is nice to see you again.

JEFFREY: Hi, nice to see you too.

PROVIDER: Well, first I would like to review your progress. How would you rate your daily functioning this past week on the scale from 0 to 10?

JEFFREY: I don't know. It wasn't so great. I would say 4 or 5.

PROVIDER: So that's a decrease from last week?

JEFFREY: Yeah, this week wasn't so good.

PROVIDER: I'm sorry to hear that. Can you tell me more about that?

JEFFREY: Yes, I found it very hard to concentrate. I got almost no work done and now I'm very behind on my deadlines. That, of course, makes me more anxious.

PROVIDER: That sounds very frustrating. Can you tell me how the worry time went? I'd like to review your log.

JEFFREY: Sure. I did it for a day but that's it. So, for the rest of the days I worried all the time, or most of the day. It didn't really work out.

PROVIDER: Ok, and how about the thought stopping? How did that work out for you?

JEFFREY: Well, actually that did work out ok. I was able to do it some of the time, which is a plus. Most of the time, though, I didn't try or it just didn't seem to work. I would keep saying, "stop," but I didn't feel any better and the thoughts didn't stop.

PROVIDER: I am sorry to hear you had such a difficult time. How was it with the controlled breathing exercises?

JEFFREY: To be honest, I didn't even do them this week. I tried one day, and it went ok. I wrote that in my log. But once I felt I couldn't do the worry times and that stopping the thoughts wasn't working, I thought what's the point. So, I just kind of gave up on everything. I can't say it would not have worked, but I thought it just wasn't worth trying since everything else was going so poorly.

Interventions with Anxiety and Trauma **175**

PROVIDER: Right. I think it is still good that you made some attempt. I agree it can be difficult to continue when you feel you are getting minimal relief.

JEFFREY: Yes, that's a good way to put it.

PROVIDER: I really am sorry to hear that things have gotten a little worse for you and I commend you for coming back here and continuing to try. Sometimes people find they need an extra leg up to deal with their anxiety while they are practicing these exercises. I think it would be helpful if I referred you back to Dr. Morris for a medication evaluation.

JEFFREY: Maybe that would be helpful.

PROVIDER: It may help calm some of those symptoms so you can really put these exercises into practice. I can arrange for you to see Dr. Morris today and I can accompany you.

JEFFREY: Ok, yes. You can help me explain how I've been doing.

Commentary. Considering his symptoms have worsened, Jeffrey may need the assistance of medication so he can be more responsive to the ultra-brief interventions. At this point I will escort Jeffrey to see the primary care physician and we will meet together to discuss his need for medication.

S – Jeffrey reports increased anxiety and panic symptoms. He reports he was able to complete the thought stopping exercise but experienced minimal relief.

O – He scored 15 on the Generalized Anxiety Disorder 7-item (GAD-7) scale, indicating an increase in symptoms from the last two sessions.

A – His anxiety and panic symptoms appear to have increased and interfere with his daily functioning and his ability to concentrate at work.

P – He will be referred for a medication evaluation. Treatment will continue to include breathing retraining and thought stopping with allotted worry times. Pattern-Focused Therapy will be used to address his pattern's role in maintaining his anxiety and panic symptoms. Future sessions will include progress monitoring and the Generalized Anxiety Disorder 7-item (GAD-7) scale will be administered prior to each session.

Case of Jeffrey: Session 4

Background. Jeffrey was administered the Generalized Anxiety Disorder 7-item (GAD-7) scale, on which he scored an 8. He has been stable on his medications and his GAD-7 score indicates a decrease in symptom severity.

176 Application of Ultra-Brief Interventions

In this session, the provider will help address his dependent pattern using Pattern-Focused Therapy and help him practice using behavioral rehearsal.

> PROVIDER: Hi Jeffrey, glad to see you. I see your score on the questionnaire indicates you have been feeling better.
>
> JEFFREY: Yes, I would say I'm feeling better, especially since the last time I saw you.
>
> PROVIDER: That's great news. On a scale from 0 to 10, how has your daily functioning been?
>
> JEFFREY: I would say 6 most days and some days a 7.

Commentary. Now that Jeffrey's symptoms have improved and he is managing his medication well, the provider can use Pattern-Focused Therapy to address Jeffrey's maladaptive caretaking pattern. Because Jeffrey's anxiety is largely related to interactions with his family, in which he is overly concerned with others while ignoring his own needs, the query process will be tailored to a situation of this kind.

> PROVIDER: Ok, so that's definitely an improvement. I'm glad to hear this. Do you remember we discussed your pattern of taking care of everyone else and ignoring your own needs?
>
> JEFFREY: Yes, I do.
>
> PROVIDER: I was thinking we could discuss that for our session today. How does that sound?
>
> JEFFREY: That sounds good.
>
> PROVIDER: Ok, can you think of a recent situation in which that pattern might have been at play?
>
> JEFFREY: Um, yes. There was an incident at my mother's house.
>
> PROVIDER: Ok, can you tell me more about that – what happened from beginning to end?
>
> JEFFREY: Sure. I was at my mom's house and I guess she needed something from the kitchen cabinet. She didn't ask me to get it, which I gladly would have. Instead, I walk into the kitchen, and there she is standing on a chair, reaching into the cabinet! I freaked out and felt my heart jump.
>
> PROVIDER: Ok, then what happened?
>
> JEFFREY: Well, I yelled at her, "Mom, you're crazy! What are you doing?" She acted like it was no big deal. She sort of laughed it off like I was being silly. We ended up getting into an argument when she realized

Interventions with Anxiety and Trauma **177**

I was serious. She told me I was acting like a baby and I needed to grow up. I was so upset!

PROVIDER: Is that all of what happened?

JEFFREY: Yes.

PROVIDER: Ok, so let me see if I heard you. You went over to your mother's house and when you walked into the kitchen, you saw her standing on a chair, trying to reach something in the cabinet overhead. This frightened you and you told your mother not to do that but she laughed off your concerns. Then you ended up getting into an argument. Is that right?

JEFFREY: Yes, that's it.

PROVIDER: Ok, can you tell me some of the thoughts that were going through your head at the time?

JEFFREY: Yes, I thought she's going to fall and kill herself!

PROVIDER: Ok, she's going to fall. What else?

JEFFREY: I thought who knows what other dangerous things she does when I'm not there! Now I have more to worry about.

PROVIDER: Ok, so you thought she might be doing other potentially dangerous things that you haven't witnessed.

JEFFREY: Right.

PROVIDER: Anything else?

JEFFREY: Honestly, I thought she doesn't care if she gives me a heart attack with this sort of behavior.

PROVIDER: Ok. And what were some of the things you did?

JEFFREY: I yelled at her, "Mom, what are you crazy?!"

PROVIDER: You yelled, ok. What else?

JEFFREY: I called her a crazy old lady. I hate to say it but I did.

PROVIDER: Alright. Was there anything else?

JEFFREY: Yeah, when she got down off the chair, I slammed it back at the table.

PROVIDER: Ok. Sounds like a pretty frustrating situation. What were you hoping to get out of this situation?

JEFFREY: I want her to stop doing crazy stuff like standing on chairs.

PROVIDER: Do you think that is really in your control?

JEFFREY: I guess not. I can't control everything she does.

PROVIDER: That's true. What do you think is an outcome that could have been in your control?

JEFFREY: I would have liked it if she at least listened to my concerns.

178 Application of Ultra-Brief Interventions

PROVIDER: Ok, so a good outcome would have been effectively expressing your concerns to your mother?

JEFFREY: Yes.

PROVIDER: And what actually happened?

JEFFREY: Just what I said, we ended up in an argument that led nowhere.

PROVIDER: So, would you say you got what you wanted?

JEFFREY: No, not at all.

PROVIDER: Ok, so would you like to go back and reexamine this situation and perhaps come up with some ways it could have turned out differently?

JEFFREY: Sure. I'd like some other solutions.

PROVIDER: Great. So, your first thought was, "she's going to fall and kill herself." Do you think that thought helped you or hurt you in getting what you wanted – expressing your concerns effectively?

JEFFREY: It didn't help because that's when my anxiety started to increase. Then I can't think straight.

PROVIDER: Ok, so it hurt because it triggered your anxiety. What is an alternative thought that would not trigger your anxiety?

JEFFREY: Um, I suppose she looked pretty stable on the chair. She probably wasn't going to fall.

PROVIDER: Ok, so thinking, "she isn't going to fall." And how would that thought be helpful to you?

JEFFREY: I wouldn't get so worried.

PROVIDER: Ok, now what about your second thought, "who knows what other dangerous things she does when I'm not there." Did that thought help you or hurt you in getting what you wanted?

JEFFREY: It hurt because then I wasn't just worried but I was also angry at her.

PROVIDER: Ok, so that made you upset. What is an alternative thought?

JEFFREY: If I just didn't think about it. Or thought she can take care of herself.

PROVIDER: So, she can take care of herself. How would that thought be helpful to you?

JEFFREY: Well, she's a grown woman. That way I wouldn't have to worry and be angry.

PROVIDER: Ok, good. And your third thought was that she's going to give you a heart attack. Did that thought help you or hurt you in communicating effectively?

Interventions with Anxiety and Trauma **179**

JEFFREY: It hurt. Now that you say it out loud it sounds kind of silly.

PROVIDER: So, what would be an alternative thought?

JEFFREY: It's not really about me. What she's doing has nothing to do with me and she's not trying to hurt me.

PROVIDER: Ok, so it's not about you and she isn't trying to hurt you. How is that thought helpful?

JEFFREY: I wouldn't have gotten so worked up.

PROVIDER: Yes, I agree. You are doing very well. Now let's look at your behaviors. Your first behavior was yelling at your mother like, "are you crazy?" Do you think that helped you or hurt you in communicating your concerns effectively?

JEFFREY: It hurt. That was really the beginning of the argument. She hates when I yell.

PROVIDER: Ok, then what would be an alternative behavior?

JEFFREY: Maybe if I don't want her on the chair, I could just offer to get what she needed.

PROVIDER: Ok, so offering to help her?

JEFFREY: Yeah, that would be more helpful than yelling.

PROVIDER: Ok, good. Your second behavior was calling her a crazy old lady. Do you think that help or hurt you in getting your desired outcome of communicating your concerns?

JEFFREY: Well, when you put it that way, it hurt. It's not really communicating if I'm just calling her names.

PROVIDER: Then what would have been an alternative behavior?

JEFFREY: Not call her names. Just maintain my cool.

PROVIDER: Ok, and your final behavior was slamming the chair back under the table. Was that helpful or hurtful in achieving your desired outcome?

JEFFREY: That was definitely hurtful. That increased the tension and that's when my mom lost her cool.

PROVIDER: Ok, so pretty challenging to communicate your concerns effectively when you have both lost your cool?

JEFFREY: Yes, definitely.

PROVIDER: So, what is an alternative behavior that would have helped you get what you wanted?

JEFFREY: I could have stayed calm and expressed myself. I could have said, "Mom, you're worrying me. Can we talk about this?"

180 Application of Ultra-Brief Interventions

PROVIDER: Ok, so that way you are setting the stage for expressing your concerns?

JEFFREY: Yes.

PROVIDER: I think you have definitely come up with some great alternative thoughts and behaviors. Is this something you can see yourself applying in certain situations?

JEFFREY: Yes, I think it would help me get what I actually want.

PROVIDER: Good. So, on a scale from 0 to 10, where 0 is not at all and 10 is all the way, how important is it for you to change that pattern of taking care of others while neglecting yourself?

JEFFREY: I would say 10. It is really important. I would love to be able to deal with some of these situations before they make me upset and anxious.

PROVIDER: Excellent, so it is very important. Now on the same 0–10 scale, how confident are you that you can change that pattern?

JEFFREY: Oh, I think only 5.

PROVIDER: Ok, so halfway there. What needs to happen to make that a 6 or 7?

JEFFREY: Well I am worried I won't be able to change my behaviors when my mom is actually getting on my nerves or worrying me.

PROVIDER: I understand your concern. It can be challenging to monitor and change our behaviors in the moment. Many people find it helpful to rehearse and practice how they would like to behave in certain situations. Does that sound like something you would like to try?

Commentary. Engaging in behavioral rehearsal will not only give Jeffrey a chance to practice his new skills and alternative behaviors, but also help increase his confidence in his ability to change his pattern to a more adaptive one. The behavioral rehearsal focuses on Jeffrey's primary area of concern – his caretaking behavior and associated worries.

JEFFREY: Sure, that sounds good. I can use the practice.

PROVIDER: Ok, are there any upcoming events where you may have the opportunity to use these new skills?

JEFFREY: Um, yes, actually. I am supposed to go to dinner with my mother and brother. I'm looking forward to it but at the same time it can be very stressful.

Interventions with Anxiety and Trauma **181**

PROVIDER: Can you tell me more about that?

JEFFREY: Yes, I worry about my brother's drinking. Usually I say something and then we argue. I also hate that my mom insists on driving herself. We always argue and I just end up getting myself worked up and worried.

PROVIDER: Ok, you said you guys end up in an argument. Can you describe what usually happens?

JEFFREY: Well, for example I would offer to pick my mom up and she would say no and I would tell her she's too old to be driving at night and that offends her. Then I would yell and go on about how stubborn she is.

PROVIDER: Ok, so think about applying the alternatives we thought of in this session. Let's do a little role-play. Let's pretend I am your mother and you can practice how you would like to respond.

JEFFREY: Ok, so Mom can I pick you up for dinner?

PROVIDER: No thank you. I will drive myself.

JEFFREY: Um, are you sure I can't give you a ride? It would be easier for you.

PROVIDER: No, I like driving myself.

JEFFREY: Ok. I just want you to know that I worry about you and I want to make sure you are ok.

PROVIDER: I really appreciate that. It is nice to know you care about me but you need to give me a little more credit. I can take care of myself.

JEFFREY: Ok, I understand. Please feel free to ask me if you ever do need some assistance.

PROVIDER: Ok, thank you. So, how did that feel, Jeffrey? You were able to come up with some good responses, similar to those we discussed about the previous situation.

JEFFREY: Yes, I felt good about it.

PROVIDER: How do you feel about applying this when you actually speak to your mother?

JEFFREY: I think it will go well. I just need to slow down and remember that my mother really can take care of herself. I just want her to know I am there for her.

PROVIDER: I agree. I look forward to hearing how it goes.

Commentary. S – Jeffrey reports decreased anxiety and panic symptoms. He has been stable on his medication.

- O – He scored 8 on the Generalized Anxiety Disorder 7-item (GAD-7) scale, indicating decreased anxiety since the last session.
- A – His daily functioning appears to be improving. His functional interview indicated subclinical symptoms of anxiety and panic, consistent with his score on the GAD-7 scale. Additionally, he displayed a dependent personality style, with a pattern of taking care of others while neglecting his own needs. Jeffrey was able to use Pattern-Focused Therapy to generate some alternative thoughts and behaviors that will help him change his dependent pattern.
- P – Treatment will continue to include medication, breathing retraining, thought stopping, and Pattern-Focused Therapy. Future sessions will include progress monitoring and the Generalized Anxiety Disorder 7-item (GAD-7) scale will be administered prior to each session.

Concluding Note

This chapter reviews symptoms and disorders that commonly present in integrated care settings, including anxiety, panic, posttraumatic stress, and acute stress. Anxiety disorders and posttraumatic stress disorder require both a diagnostic evaluation and a functional assessment. Clients with these presentations should be screened for risk of self-harm. Primary interventions include controlled breathing, thought stopping, and pattern-focused therapy. Clients' progress should be monitored using standardized screening instruments and a medication evaluation completed if indicated. A case example illustrates the assessment, interventions, and progress monitoring in four ultra-brief sessions.

References

American Counseling Association. (n.d.). Suicide Assessment. Retrieved from www.counseling.org/docs/trauma-disaster/fact-sheet-6---suicide-assessment.pdf?sfvrsn=2

American Psychiatric Association. (2013). *Diagnostic and statistical manual of mental disorders* (5th ed.).

Bardhoshi, G., Erford, B.T., Duncan, K., Dummett, B., Falco, M., Deferio, K., & Kraft, J. (2016). Choosing assessment instruments for posttraumatic stress disorder screening and outcome research. *Journal of Counseling and Development*, 94(2), 184–194.

Hunter, C.L., Goodie, J.L., Oordt, M.S., & Dobmeyer, A.C. (2017). *Integrated behavioral health in primary care: Step-by-step guidance for assessment and intervention* (2nd ed.). Washington, DC: American Psychological Association.

Lew, V., & Ghassemzadeh, S. (2018). SOAP Notes. Retrieved from www.ncbi.nlm.nih.gov/books/NBK482263/

Plummer, F., Manea, L., Trepel, D., McMillan, D., & Simpson, A. (2016). Screening for anxiety disorders with the GAD-7 and GAD-2: A systematic review and diagnostic metaanalysis. *General Hospital Psychiatry, 39,* 24–31.

Ultra-Brief Interventions with Chronic Pain and Medication Misuse **7**

This chapter provides an overview of chronic pain and how it commonly presents in integrated settings. An overview of the functional assessment and common interventions for chronic pain is included. The issue of medication misuse is explored, including assessment of medication misuse and creation of a medication contract. Finally, a case example is illustrated through four transcriptions with commentary. In working with chronic pain in these settings, the behavioral health provider's role is to complete a functional assessment and provide psychoeducation and brief interventions that help clients understand and manage pain more effectively. A formal diagnostic evaluation is typically not performed in this setting, unless warranted by client presenting problems.

Chronic Pain

Chronic pain is defined as pain that is persistent and lasts longer than six months, whereas acute pain results from an injury and generally resolves, and recurrent pain refers to repeated pain episodes. Chronic pain was long thought of as an entirely physical condition with a biological cause but it is now widely understood that psychological factors play a major role in how individuals experience pain. With the introduction of the gate control theory of pain (Melzack & Wall, 1965), practitioners came to understand how emotions, attitudes, beliefs about pain, stress, and environmental factors influence pain perception. The gate control theory shows how pain signals themselves are

Chronic Pain and Medication Misuse **185**

not always intense enough to "open" the neurological gate leading to the transmission and interpretation of these signals by the brain. Combined with psychological and environmental factors, sensory information can become intense enough to cross this neurological threshold and open the gate, leading to the perception of pain (Moayedi & Davis, 2013). Therefore, an injury itself is not always sufficient for the perception of pain. Some individuals experience an injury with no pain, while others experience pain with no physical cause. Examples include an individual cutting his hand but not feeling the pain until he brought attention to the injury, or a person experiencing intensified pain upon receiving an injection because of fear, stress, and the expectation of pain.

Addressing chronic pain is crucial in primary care settings as this is where pain issues most commonly present. Chronic pain is highly prevalent and patients experiencing pain extensively use health care services, yet guidelines for effectively assisting these patients are not always utilized (Dobkin & Boothroyd, 2008). Chronic pain has been linked to reduced employment and quality of life (Oakman, Kinsman, & Briggs, 2017), as well as poor sleep quality, which can in turn lead to increased pain (Sezgin et al., 2015).

Despite its frequent appearance in primary care settings, protocols for assisting individuals with chronic pain have not been widely adopted. The US Department of Defense created a course of action, based on empirical findings, for addressing chronic pain patients in primary care settings. Individuals diagnosed with chronic pain, those with new prescriptions for narcotics, those who have been prescribed narcotics for the previous four months, or those who are changing their medications or medication schedules are referred to a behavioral health provider. The behavioral health provider completes a functional assessment and implements ultra-brief cognitive and behavioral interventions in approximately four sessions. The patient is then scheduled for continuing follow-up visits as needed (Hunter, Goodie, Oordt, & Dobmeyer, 2017).

Medication Misuse

Misuse of prescription medication refers to use that is different from that indicated by the prescriber. Patients might use more medication than intended, hoard medication, use the medication more often than prescribed, or for symptoms other than those for which the medication was intended. Commonly prescribed for chronic pain, opioids are the most frequently misused prescription medications. Opioids include drugs like oxycodone (OxyContin) and hydrocodone, and work by binding to opiate receptors in the brain to reduce pain sensations (National Institute on Drug Abuse [NIDA], 2014). Prescription of opioids can lead to misuse, addiction and dependence, and death. Individuals most at risk are those with a history of substance abuse, those with concurrent prescriptions for nervous system depressants such as benzodiazepines, or those with existing respiratory problems as opioids slow the respiratory system (Volkow & McLellan, 2016).

Assessment and Screening Instruments

The assessment for chronic pain focuses on the nature and intensity of the pain, and the impact the pain has had on the client's daily functioning. Chronic pain clients should also be screened for suicide risk. Clients prescribed opiate pain medications may be assessed for medication misuse, when indicated.

Functional Assessment

The functional assessment of chronic pain should consist of specific, closed-ended questions. Information to be gathered includes the nature of the pain, pain frequency, duration, and intensity, as well as factors that make the pain better or worse. The impact the pain has had on the patient's daily functioning should be determined as well as any resulting behavioral or psychosocial changes. The provider can also use a screener like the PEG Pain Scale, a 3-item instrument used to assess pain intensity and interference.

Medication Misuse Assessment

In the case that a patient is, or is at risk of, misusing a prescribed medication, an assessment of medication use should be completed. In this case, it is important to determine how the patient is using the medication and if he/she is prescribed any other medications that may increase risk for use or overdose. Use of alcohol and illicit drugs should be assessed and risk of potential self-harm through overdose should be determined for individuals with a history of depression or suicidal ideation.

Risk Assessment

Individuals who live with chronic pain are up to three times as likely to report suicidal thoughts. The highest risk individuals are those whose pain is more intense and has a higher frequency and longer duration. Feelings of helplessness and hopelessness, and catastrophic beliefs about pain were found to correlate with higher suicide risk (Tang & Crane, 2006). For this reason, it is important to complete a risk assessment for clients who present with chronic pain. If the client indicates suicidal ideation, the provider will follow up with a full risk assessment that includes information about the frequency, intensity, and duration of suicidal thoughts (American Counseling Association, n.d.).

See Table 7.1 for an outline of the functional and risk assessment for chronic pain and medication misuse.

Table 7.1 Functional Assessment of Chronic Pain and Medication Misuse

Nature of the pain	How would you describe your pain? (Shooting, stabbing, dull, throbbing, etc.)
Location of the pain	Where in your body do you feel the pain?
Onset	When did the pain begin?
Duration	How long have you had the pain?
Frequency	How often do you have the pain? How many days per week? How often during a day?
Subjective rating of pain intensity	On a scale from 0–10, where 10 is the most excruciating pain and 0 is no pain, how much pain have you experienced: • Over the last two weeks on average • Highest level of pain in the last two weeks • Lowest level of pain in the last two weeks • Current level of pain
Factors that increase pain	What increases your level of pain?

(continued)

Table 7.1 (*Cont.*)

Factors that decrease pain	What decreases your level of pain?
Medical conditions relating to pain	Do you know what caused this pain?
	What has your primary care doctor informed you about the origin of the pain?
Psychosocial changes	How has the pain affected your mood/emotions?
	How have others responded to your pain?
	How would you like loved ones to respond to your pain?
Daily functioning across various domains	Describe your usual day and how the pain affects it.
	How has the pain affected your work? Family life? Social life? Hobbies?
Coping strategies	How have you tried dealing with the pain? (medical treatments, alternative medicine, exercise, substance use, etc.)
Medication frequency	How often do you take the medication your primary care physician prescribed?
	Is this more frequently than the physician prescribed?
Medication dosage	How much of your medication do you typically take?
	Is this more than the physician prescribed?
Medication hoarding	Do you ever save up your medication in case you need it in the future?
Alcohol/drug use	Do you drink alcohol? What kind and how much?
	Do you use any illegal drugs or prescription drugs for reasons other than their intended use? What kind and how much?

Chronic Pain and Medication Misuse **189**

Table 7.1 *(Cont.)*

Use of other medications or supplements	Do you take any prescription or over-the-counter medications or any supplements?
Suicidal ideation	Have you ever had thoughts about hurting yourself or that life is not worth living? Frequency of thoughts Intensity of thoughts Duration of thoughts Plan Means to complete plan
Open-ended questions	Is there anything I have not asked you about that you would like me to know?

Screening Instruments

The PEG Pain Scale. The PEG Pain Scale is a 3-item instrument used to assess pain intensity and interference. Each question is rated on an 11-point scale from 0–10 where 0 = no pain, and 10 = pain as bad as you can imagine. Clients are asked to rate their average level of pain in the past week, the extent to which the pain has interfered with enjoyment of life in the past week, and the extent to which the pain has interfered with general activity in the past week.

Current Opioid Misuse Measure (COMM). The Current Opioid Misuse Measure (COMM) is a 17-item instrument used to assess a patient's misuse of medication by determining its effect on social, emotional, and general functioning. Each question is rated on a 5-point scale from 0–4, where 0 = never, 1 = seldom, 2 = sometimes, 3 = often, 4 = very often. This patient self-report instrument also measures contextual factors, like emotional volatility and recent history of arguments. These questions are meant to measure the effect of medication misuse on the client's functioning, but may not necessarily point to medication abuse. This screening tool is best paired with an interview about how the client is using medications.

Ultra-Brief Interventions

Psychoeducation about pain is a primary behavioral health intervention for chronic pain in integrated and primary care settings. Pattern-focused therapy is useful for ameliorating maladaptive patterns that might trigger, exacerbate, and maintain chronic pain or increase the risk of medication misuse. For those patients who are misusing their medication, a contract for proper use can be drafted and agreed upon by the patient, the doctor, and the behavioral health provider.

Chronic Pain Psychoeducation

Many patients have misconceptions about chronic pain and about factors that make pain better or worse. These misconceptions often lead to behaviors that worsen clients' experience with pain. For this reason, psychoeducation about pain must be the first intervention after the functional assessment. The behavioral health provider should explain the difference between pain and suffering. The experience of pain itself does not guarantee that an individual will suffer related mental, emotional, social, and vocational detriments. Clients should be educated about the gate control theory of pain and about changes they can make to control pain. Individuals who are informed about pain and factors that affect how it is perceived are better equipped to manage pain and reduce its interference in their functioning.

Gate Control Theory of Pain. The behavioral health provider should inform clients that the way people typically think about pain is erroneous. Individuals often believe pain is entirely a result of physical injury and that, short of resolving the injury or using painkillers, nothing can be done to decrease or control pain. The Gate Control Theory teaches clients that physical pain signals are only one factor that contribute to the perception of pain. The theory states that a neurological gate opens, letting pain signals pass through, leading to the perception of pain sensations. Factors other than neurological signals can open or close the gate. Pain sensations can be modulated by an individual's thoughts, expectations, attitudes, attention, and mood (Melzack & Wall, 1965). Clients can be given examples of how these factors influence pain perception. For example, when an individual is distracted from his/her pain, he/she often ceases perceiving it. Negative thoughts, fearful expectations, social withdrawal, anxiety, depression, and anger are all factors that help open the "gate" and allow pain signals to pass through, while positive emotions and thoughts, relaxation exercises, distractions, pleasurable activities, and a belief that the individual is in control of the pain can all close the "gate." When the gate is closed, pain signals are not perceived (Hunter et al., 2017).

Understanding Pain. Individuals often have misconceptions about pain perception and how to control and cope with pain. Clients commonly believe that only rest is good for pain, and that pain is going to interfere with their enjoyment of life. These thoughts and behaviors, however, only serve to make pain worse. Clients should be taught which behaviors can help them control their pain. Clients can be given examples of common beliefs about pain as a way to explore and restructure their pain beliefs.

Pattern-Focused Therapy

Pattern-Focused Therapy addresses client personality dynamics and patterns that serve to increase and maintain chronic pain. For example, a client with a pattern of avoiding others because of fears of being criticized may avoid social activities and group exercise activities that can help decrease his/her chronic pain. Even after successful treatment, if left unchanged, a client's pattern can be triggered leading to relapse of symptoms. Addressing the client pattern using Pattern-Focused Therapy helps treat factors contributing to the current problem and prevent the problem from reoccurring. For example, in the Case of Linda (outlined below), Linda's pattern of being perfectionistic contributes to her pain. Linda engages in self-criticism and does not engage in physical activities unless she can do them to her unreasonable standards. Her thoughts and behaviors help open the neurological gate and increase her experience of pain. As Linda's pattern becomes more adaptive, she improves her self-talk and outlook about her pain and engages in physical activities that decrease her level of pain.

Medication Contract

For clients who are misusing, or are at risk of misusing, their pain medications, a medication contract can be drawn up and agreed upon by the client, the prescribing physician, and the behavioral health provider. The contract should outline the client's rights and responsibilities and allow the client to agree to refrain from taking medication should he/she have a history of addiction, and if the physician decides to limit or cease prescription of a medication.

192 Application of Ultra-Brief Interventions

Reasons to cease or modify a prescription can include the client's behaviors, the client's use of other substances, if the client obtains pain medications from another physician, development of tolerance, or if the client fails to keep medical appointments. The contract should outline safety risks and side effects of medication and provide information about physical and psychological dependence, tolerance, and withdrawal. The contract should specify how much medication will be prescribed and the exact manner in which the patient is expected to use the medication. The client is encouraged to keep a log of when he/she takes medication, along with specific doses taken.

Progress Monitoring and Record Keeping

Progress Monitoring

Progress monitoring in chronic pain treatment includes tracking severity of symptoms, level of functional impairment, and adherence to medication plans when needed. Standardized measures like the PEG Pain Scale are used to monitor progress and should be administered prior to each session. Additionally, tools like client journals or logs can be used to monitor activities, moods, and pain beliefs.

Record Keeping

The behavioral health provider should keep concise yet detailed notes to communicate information about clients to other staff. Commonly used in health care settings, the SOAP note method is a structured way of record keeping. In this acronym, SOAP represents the headings Subjective, Objective, Assessment, and Plan. The Subjective heading includes the client's subjective experience. Presenting symptoms, subjective ratings of intensity, and associated complaints are recorded under the Subjective heading. The Objective heading includes any objective ratings, like those obtained from standardized instruments or medical exams. The Assessment heading includes whether the client meets criteria for a DSM-5 diagnosis as well as the client's personality style. Items in this category should be listed in order of importance. Finally, the Plan heading includes the next steps to be completed in the treatment plan, objectives for the next session, and any necessary referrals.

Case of Linda Transcriptions

Case of Linda: Session 1

Background. Linda is a 52-year-old Caucasian female referred by her primary care physician, Dr. John, for lower back pain. Linda was administered the PEG: a 3-item scale for assessing pain intensity and interference. On a scale from 0–10, Linda rated her average pain intensity as 7 for last week. She marked 8 for her pain's interference with enjoying life and 7 for interference with general activity. During this session, the provider will conduct a functional assessment and provide Linda with psychoeducation on chronic pain.

> PROVIDER: Hi Linda, I always enjoy working with Dr. John's patients so I am glad to meet with you today. I'm going to start out by asking you some questions so I can get a better idea of how you've been feeling. Is that ok?
>
> LINDA: Yes, hi. Sure, I'll be glad to answer the questions.
>
> PROVIDER: Ok, thank you. Let's start with your mood. How would you describe your mood recently?
>
> LINDA: Oh, it's a little low. I don't get out much anymore, so you know. Not much to look forward to.
>
> PROVIDER: How often would you say you feel that way?
>
> LINDA: Pretty much just on the weekends. That's when my husband and I would go out and have fun. I haven't been able to do that stuff since I hurt my back.
>
> PROVIDER: What kinds of things did you used to enjoy doing?
>
> LINDA: We used to take walks on the beach or we would take drives up the coast. I can't sit in a car for that long now.
>
> PROVIDER: Ok, and what about during the week?
>
> LINDA: Well, I work during the week. I work in the front office of a school and I'm pretty good at my job. I also get to see my friends there. Better than staying home all day.
>
> PROVIDER: Ok, so work has been more rewarding for you?
>
> LINDA: Yes. It is still hard to sit for that long but they let me bring in my special pillow for my chair.
>
> PROVIDER: Oh well that's nice.
>
> LINDA: Yeah.
>
> PROVIDER: Have you had any times where your mood was really high or you had a lot of energy?

194 Application of Ultra-Brief Interventions

LINDA: No, I haven't.

PROVIDER: Would you say you are a nervous person?

LINDA: No, I wouldn't say I'm nervous. I like for things to be done right but I'm not nervous about it.

PROVIDER: Ok, and when you say you like for things to be done right, what do you mean by that?

LINDA: Well, like I said, I'm good at my job. That's because I'm organized. All the paperwork goes through me and everyone who works with me knows they should double-check their work because I always find mistakes.

PROVIDER: Ok. Just a few more questions. Do you use any substances?

LINDA: No, I don't do anything like that. I hardly ever even take the pain medication. I rarely drink.

PROVIDER: Good. Now have you felt recently that life wasn't worth living?

LINDA: Oh no. I don't think like that.

PROVIDER: Ok, good. And how would you describe your relationships with other people?

LINDA: They're fine. I'm the mom of the family, you know. Some of my kids still come home from college for me to do their laundry. They know no one does it the way I do.

PROVIDER: So, you take pride in your work?

LINDA: Yes! Of course. You have to pay attention to the details. That's what most people don't do. My girlfriends at work tease me sometimes. They say, "Linda you're such a perfectionist."

PROVIDER: How do you feel that description fits you?

LINDA: Yeah, I guess I would say I'm a perfectionist, sort of. But I know when to put things down and live my life too. I might be working on something but if my husband says all of a sudden he wants to go out, I can do that too.

PROVIDER: Would you say you have a pattern of wanting things to be done a certain way?

LINDA: Yes, absolutely.

Commentary. Linda's description reveals an obsessive-compulsive personality style, with a pattern of wanting things to be done a certain way.

PROVIDER: Ok, now I see you were referred by Dr. John for lower back pain and it seems from the PEG form you filled out that your pain has been interfering with things you have to do and things you enjoy. Can you tell me more about that?

Chronic Pain and Medication Misuse **195**

LINDA: Yes, like I said, it's hard to get out and go for drives and walks like I used to. It's harder to clean the house. I can't even pick up my dog!

PROVIDER: How else does your pain affect your daily life?

LINDA: It makes it harder to clean the house and do other things I need to do. Also, it holds me back from doing things I like, like walking the dog or going out on the weekend with my husband. It's also just really annoying and makes me upset to think about sometimes.

PROVIDER: That sounds very challenging. If you had to put your level of pain on a scale from 0 to 10, what would you rate it on average?

LINDA: I would rate it a 7.

PROVIDER: How would you rate your pain right now?

LINDA: Probably a 6.

PROVIDER: Ok. Is your pain constant or does it fluctuate?

LINDA: It fluctuates.

PROVIDER: What makes it better?

LINDA: Lying down in the right position.

PROVIDER: And what makes it worse?

LINDA: Bending over a lot. Trying to do things in spite of the pain. That irritates it. Sitting in the car for a long time.

PROVIDER: And how do you usually cope with it?

LINDA: Well, I try to distract myself. Because like I said, it can really get me down not to do anything over the weekend. That's why I offer to do my kids' laundry, so they come down and we can at least be together. It can be lonely. And then I think, is this it? Am I just going to be living with this now?

PROVIDER: And where is the pain usually located?

LINDA: Oh, it's my lower back down here. And it goes down my leg sometimes.

PROVIDER: How would you describe the pain?

LINDA: It's throbbing, deep. Sometimes shooting down my leg on the left side. Or it feels like my back is weak, like it's going to give out.

PROVIDER: I am sorry to hear you are dealing with this. How often do you have this pain?

LINDA: Most days of the week. It started about a year and a half ago.

PROVIDER: Do you know what is causing this pain?

LINDA: Yeah, I have a herniated disc. I had an MRI scan.

PROVIDER: What would be different if you didn't have this pain?

LINDA: I could do a lot more. I never used to think about doing the chores around the house. I would just do them. I mean now if I have to pick something up, I can't just do it. I have to think about it. How am I going

196 Application of Ultra-Brief Interventions

to reach for it? And I would be able to have fun again, going out with my husband and my kids.

PROVIDER: How has your husband responded to your pain?

LINDA: He's very supportive. He does stuff for me if I need it. But it's taken a toll on him. He says it's ok, but I can see. He misses being able to go out too. He goes golfing with the neighbors but not much else.

PROVIDER: How would you like other people to respond to you and to the pain?

LINDA: Um, I would like people to be more understanding. My husband could offer to do more stuff around the house so I don't have to. I feel like I'm always doing things for other people. I would like people to do some favors for me when I am dealing with the pain.

PROVIDER: I understand. That is certainly a reasonable request. What have you done to help yourself deal with the pain?

LINDA: I got some balm for achy muscles. And some seat cushions to make it more comfortable for me. Also, when I do the stretches I learned in physical therapy, that helps.

PROVIDER: That's good that you have found some relief.

LINDA: Yeah but not enough. That's why I'm here.

PROVIDER: Yes, I'm glad you're here. Pain is a multifaceted issue. We used to see pain as really the outcome of a physical problem or injury but now we are finding the root causes are more intricate than this. Sometimes people have physical injuries with no pain or pain in spite of having no injuries. Did you ever cut yourself and not feel any pain until you looked down and saw the cut?

LINDA: Yes, that's happened to me.

PROVIDER: That's because so many factors are involved with feeling pain. Lack of attention, adrenaline, and even our mood can influence how or if we feel pain, sometimes more than the physical injury itself. Understanding and paying attention to these factors can give people more control of their own pain.

Commentary: The provider gives Linda a handout explaining the gate control model of pain and reviews it with her.

PROVIDER: Scientists and doctors now understand that there is something that acts like a gate between the physical injury and the brain, as you can see in this handout. The gate controls how and when pain signals travel up and down your spinal cord. If the gate is open, the signals can travel freely and the person will perceive more pain, but if the gate is closed, pain signals do not get through. Even if the gate is somewhat closed,

Chronic Pain and Medication Misuse **197**

only some pain signals get through. Different factors affect whether the gate is open or closed. Emotions, thoughts, and expectations are all things that can affect if the gate is open or closed.

LINDA: Yes, I can say that's true. I do feel worse when I'm angry or upset.

PROVIDER: Right, and pain can intensify those feelings which, in turn, intensify the pain. Negative thinking can also open the gate. People feel more pain when they pay more attention to it and have negative thoughts about it. Have you ever had a headache and then listened to music or talked on the phone and then realize the headache is gone?

LINDA: Yeah, that's happened to me. Talking on the phone. I hang up and realize, oh, my headache is gone.

PROVIDER: Right. And behavioral and physical factors can also open and close the gate. For example, a person might stop exercising because of pain but then muscles get weaker and stiffer, which can contribute to more pain. Also, not doing things that you enjoy and bring you pleasure can stir negative emotions like boredom and depression. That opens the door for you to focus on your pain. The neurological signals from your herniated disc are still there, but we can help reduce the toll the pain takes on your emotions and your life. Many clients report a better quality of life from this treatment. Does that sound like something you would be interested in?

LINDA: Yes, I would love that. I like the way you said it, me being in control of my life, not the pain being in control.

PROVIDER: I'm going to give you this handout. We can look over it together. It is about understanding chronic pain and what you can do to manage it.

LINDA: Ok.

PROVIDER: As you can see, some of the factors we talked about are on this handout. Things you can do to manage pain and that can actually make pain worse when you neglect them. Which of these stands out to you?

LINDA: Yes, I don't use any relaxation techniques. Maybe that's something that would help. Also like we talked about, I don't get out and do those things I used to like anymore. I'm probably more out of shape too. And it says avoid cycles of overactivity and underactivity. I do that. I usually wear myself out and then can't move for a few weeks.

PROVIDER: Ok. I'm glad you were able to identify some things on this list that might be helpful to you. Do those sound like things you would like to work on?

LINDA: Yes, anything that helps.

198 Application of Ultra-Brief Interventions

PROVIDER: Good. How is this handout helping you see how these factors fit together?

LINDA: Well it's that connection between body and mind. I can see how a lot of this emotional stuff affects the physical stuff.

PROVIDER: That's exactly right. So, it seems we have identified some goals you would like to work on to help manage your pain.

LINDA: Yes.

PROVIDER: Typically, we meet once every two weeks or so, depending on what you need, and I may give you some homework assignments and ask you to keep track of your pain and your activities. How does that sound?

LINDA: That sounds fine.

PROVIDER: Ok, Linda, then I'll see you next time and we will start working on the areas we identified.

Commentary. S – Linda presents to counseling with chronic lower back pain. She describes her pain as throbbing and deep, sometimes shooting down her left leg.

O – On the PEG scale from 0–10, she rated her average pain intensity as 7 for last week. She marked 8 for her pain's interference with enjoying life and 7 for interference with general activity.

A –The functional assessment revealed chronic pain has caused her sadness, a decreased ability to partake in leisure activities, and difficulty completing daily tasks. Additionally, she displayed an obsessive-compulsive personality style, with a pattern of wanting things to be done a certain way.

P – Treatment will focus on pain management techniques. Pattern-Focused Therapy will be used to address her pattern's role in managing her chronic pain. The PEG will be administered at each session.

Case of Linda: Session 2

Background. Linda was administered the PEG: a 3-item scale for assessing pain intensity and interference. On a scale from 0–10, Linda rated her average pain intensity as 6 for last week. She marked 7 for her pain's interference with enjoying life and 5 for interference with general activity. This session will focus on psychoeducation and helping Linda analyze her pain-associated self-talk.

Chronic Pain and Medication Misuse 199

PROVIDER: Hi Linda, I'm glad to see you again. I thought we could start today's session by reviewing the handout on pain beliefs.

LINDA: Alright.

PROVIDER: Which of these beliefs stood out to you?

LINDA: Well, first of all that pain is ruining my life and will ruin my future. My husband and I were planning to take a road trip and buy a boat once we retire. I don't see how I'm going to be able to do that with my back. This handout says that I can control my pain and my future. I hope so but I don't know if it's true.

PROVIDER: I understand your concern. What else stood out?

LINDA: The best intervention for pain is rest and inactivity. We did discuss this last time and it says it on this handout too. That I limit myself because I'm in pain but that actually causes more pain. I always thought if it hurts, then you should stay off it and give it time to heal.

PROVIDER: Right, that's something many people think but doctors have found just the opposite to be true. It isn't good to over-exert yourself but too little activity can be just as harmful. We discussed increasing activity as one of your goals.

LINDA: Yes, that's true. I would like to work on that.

PROVIDER: Can you tell me about the last time you felt like doing something active?

LINDA: Yes, my husband wanted to take the dog for a walk on the beach last week. I used to love that. I wanted to go. It was Friday after work and a really nice day out.

PROVIDER: Did you go?

LINDA: No, I didn't. I decided to stay home while he went out.

PROVIDER: What do you think kept you from going?

LINDA: Well, it's funny my back didn't hurt that bad that day. It was actually a pretty good day, but there was some pain. But the day before was really bad. So here I was just having one ok day after a few really bad ones and I didn't want to irritate my back and make it worse.

PROVIDER: Because it was just starting to feel better.

LINDA: Yes, that's right.

PROVIDER: And how was it the next day?

LINDA: Um, it was actually worse, now that you mention it. So, yeah, I guess I didn't irritate it but it turned out bad anyway.

PROVIDER: You didn't take the walk because you worried about irritating your back but your back worsened anyway. It's interesting how we worry about something because we think it will turn out a certain way but those ideas are often inaccurate.

200 Application of Ultra-Brief Interventions

LINDA: Yes, that's true.

PROVIDER: The ways we talk to ourselves has a lot to do with how well we can manage pain. Also, the ways in which we address some of those automatic thoughts that can be distressing.

LINDA: Next time I can keep in mind that the exercise can help me in the long run, even if I'm worried I might feel worse tomorrow.

PROVIDER: That's true. That is a great alternative thought. How do you see that helping you?

LINDA: Well, maybe just not overthinking it. Just going for the walk and enjoying it.

PROVIDER: What do you usually think before having a pain episode?

LINDA: Sometimes it happens out of the blue. But sometimes I can feel some pain or I know when I reached for something, oh I'm going to have pain after this. Then I think I should have known better. I get mad at myself for doing stuff I know will end up hurting my back.

PROVIDER: That does sound frustrating. And yet, when you were playing it safe by not taking the walk, you had pain anyway.

LINDA: Yeah. Well, there are some things I know aren't good for my back. But yeah, I guess you can't always predict it. And you can't control everything. It's going to happen.

PROVIDER: And sometimes it won't.

LINDA: Yeah, sometimes I have pain and sometimes I don't. Sometimes it's hard to do everything right to avoid it.

PROVIDER: Of course, it is important to do those things that help you feel better. How do you feel when you get angry at yourself though?

LINDA: Oh, I feel bad.

PROVIDER: Do you think that correlates to your pain?

LINDA: Yeah, that's true. Anger makes pain worse.

PROVIDER: So, you mentioned worry and sometimes anger at yourself leading up to pain. What do you think during pain episodes?

LINDA: I get really upset. I usually think, this is taking over my life. It's just awful. I hate it. I can't stand it.

PROVIDER: How do those thoughts help you cope with the pain?

LINDA: They don't. Again, they probably make it worse.

PROVIDER: Are there any thoughts that do help you cope with the pain?

LINDA: Sometimes I try to think about times when it was better. Like oh, it gets worse but it gets better. But then I usually just get more upset thinking about how much worse I feel now.

Chronic Pain and Medication Misuse **201**

Commentary. The provider gives Linda a handout on managing self-talk during pain episodes and they review it together.

LINDA: I can see some of the thoughts I have are on this handout.

PROVIDER: Yes, and some alternative thoughts. You did mention a helpful thought. It can help to continue to avoid all-or-nothing thinking. You know there are times in the past when you were able to manage your pain and that means you have the ability to continue to manage pain. Can you see yourself pinpointing some of these thoughts when you have them and redirecting them to the more helpful ones?

LINDA: Yes, I can do that. I also really like the suggestion of rating the pain instead of thinking about how awful or unbearable it is.

PROVIDER: Yes. What is it about that that appeals to you?

LINDA: Well, it's like taking my mind off it. Instead of thinking about how terrible it is, I can separate myself from it a little bit.

PROVIDER: So, it's a distraction?

LINDA: In a way, yes.

PROVIDER: That's very good. Distraction can be very effective in managing negative self-talk. What are some other things that might be good distractions for you?

LINDA: I think playing with my dog, talking to my husband.

PROVIDER: Ok, so before we meet next time, I would like you to do one of those things you have been avoiding. I would like you to write down some of the self-talk associated with the activity. I will also give you this handout for monitoring pain. When you have pain, I want you to write the date and time, rate the pain on a scale from 0 to 10, write in how long the pain lasted and what led up to it, if you know. Then write down your thoughts related to the pain, as well as your emotional reactions and some of your behaviors.

LINDA: Ok, I can do that. Maybe I'll take that walk with my husband.

PROVIDER: Ok. I look forward to hearing about it.

Commentary. S – Linda reports her pain has decreased since the last session.

O – On the PEG scale from 0–10, she rated her average pain intensity as 6 for last week. She marked 7 for her pain's interference with enjoying life and 5 for interference with general activity.

A – She was able to identify ways her self-talk relates to her pain perception, as well as generate alternatives to stressful thoughts.

202 Application of Ultra-Brief Interventions

P – Treatment will continue to focus on pain management techniques and progress monitoring. Pattern-Focused Therapy will be used to address her pattern's role in managing her chronic pain. The PEG will be administered at each session.

Case of Linda: Session 3

Background. Linda was administered the PEG: a 3-item scale for assessing pain intensity and interference. On a scale from 0–10, Linda rated her average pain intensity as 6 for last week. She marked 7 for her pain's interference with enjoying life and 7 for interference with general activity. In this session, the provider will help Linda address her obsessive-compulsive pattern using Pattern-Focused Therapy.

PROVIDER: Hi Linda, I am glad to see you again. Why don't we start today's session by reviewing your pain scale from last week?

LINDA: Sure. My highest pain was on Thursday, that was 6. My best day was Tuesday at a 3.

PROVIDER: A 3. That is pretty low for you. What do you think contributed to you having less pain that day?

LINDA: Well, I just had a good day at work that day. We had a little party for one of my coworkers. She's having a baby. It was really nice and the day kind of just went by.

PROVIDER: So, being distracted helped you not notice the pain?

LINDA: Yeah, I guess so.

PROVIDER: Ok, what was some of your self-talk associated with the pain?

LINDA: I wrote down – I can't stand this. I hate it. This is never going to go away.

PROVIDER: Ok, and what were some of the emotions that you noted along with that?

LINDA: I wrote that I felt sad, angry.

PROVIDER: That is understandable.

LINDA: Yeah. I'm trying to deal with it. But it isn't easy.

PROVIDER: I agree it isn't easy, but you have been coping well given the circumstances. I would like to move on to what I was thinking we should focus our session on today.

LINDA: Ok.

Chronic Pain and Medication Misuse **203**

PROVIDER: If you remember we were talking about your pattern of wanting things to be a certain way. Did anything come up recently where you saw that pattern?

LINDA: Yes, for example, I wanted to go for a walk with my husband and the dog. The weather was just beautiful. But my back hurt too much. It was very upsetting because I had to stay inside while it was so nice out.

PROVIDER: How was that experience for you?

LINDA: It was depressing. I know we talked about me doing stuff even though I have pain and how that helps with the pain but it's hard and I start to worry about my back.

PROVIDER: I understand. It sounds like a challenging situation for you. Would you like to explore that situation further so we can help you deal with these issues better in the future?

LINDA: Sure.

PROVIDER: Ok, well why don't you tell me what happened that day in more detail so I can get a clear picture of the situation?

LINDA: Ok, like I said my husband wanted to take a walk. Actually, my husband and I were enjoying some coffee. It was Sunday morning. And like I said it was just beautiful out. Warm but not too hot, sunny. He suggested we take our dog out and get some fresh air and a walk by the beach. I struggled with it but I said, "nah, you go ahead without me." So, he did. He went for a walk and he said he missed me. I felt bad but that's just the way it is sometimes.

PROVIDER: Is that all of what happened?

LINDA: Pretty much. He said he ran into some of our friends. I would have liked to see them.

PROVIDER: Ok, so you were enjoying some time with your husband when he suggested you take a walk by the beach. You declined because of your back trouble and he went along without you where he ran into some friends, which made you regret not going. Is that correct?

LINDA: Yes, that's right.

PROVIDER: Ok. Can you tell me what were some of the thoughts you were having at the time?

LINDA: Well, I thought, oh my back hurts too much.

PROVIDER: Ok, what else were you thinking?

LINDA: I thought if I go walking it will only make my back feel worse and then I won't be able to clean the house.

PROVIDER: Alright. Was there anything else?

LINDA: Yeah, I thought this pain is ruining my life!

204 Application of Ultra-Brief Interventions

PROVIDER: Ok so some of the thoughts going through your head at the time were, "my back hurts too much. Walking will only make it worse. And this pain is ruining my life." Is that right?

LINDA: Yes.

PROVIDER: Ok, and now what were some of your behaviors? What did you do?

LINDA: Well, first off, I didn't go for the walk. I also didn't tell my husband why. I assumed he knew.

PROVIDER: Ok, anything else?

LINDA: I just lay on the couch, which actually made my back feel worse. I think I wasn't in a good position.

PROVIDER: Ok, so to recap, you didn't take the walk and you didn't tell your husband why. Then you lay on the couch which ended up hurting your back.

LINDA: That's right.

PROVIDER: Ok, so looking back, what did you want to get out of that situation?

LINDA: Well, it would have been nice to take the walk.

PROVIDER: Right. But the conditions weren't exactly as you would have liked them.

LINDA: Yeah. If I was pain-free that would be better.

PROVIDER: I agree, being pain-free would be much better. Remember we discussed your pattern of wanting things to be just right. Do you think that pattern may have played a role in this situation?

LINDA: Now that you mention it, it makes sense. If everything was just the way I wanted it, I would have gone.

PROVIDER: Right. So, what actually happened in the situation?

LINDA: I sat around, lonely and depressed and actually ended up hurting my back anyway.

PROVIDER: So, would you say you got what you wanted?

LINDA: Of course not!

PROVIDER: Ok, so would you like to go back and take another look at the situation and see how it may have turned out differently?

LINDA: Sure.

PROVIDER: Ok, well you said your first thought was that your back hurt too much to go on the walk. Would you say that thought helped you or hurt you in getting what you wanted – taking the walk?

LINDA: It hurt because it didn't even let me get started.

PROVIDER: Ok, so what would have been a different thought?

Chronic Pain and Medication Misuse 205

LINDA: If I reminded myself that my back hurts but a walk would get my mind off the pain.

PROVIDER: Ok, so remembering the role distraction plays in pain management. How would that thought have helped you?

LINDA: It would have been more encouraging.

PROVIDER: Ok, your second thought was that the walking would make your pain worse. Did that thought help you or hurt you in taking the walk?

LINDA: It hurt me because it's more of that self-defeating thinking.

PROVIDER: So, what would have been a more helpful thought?

LINDA: If I reminded myself that exercise actually helps the pain. I would have been less worried about the pain that way.

PROVIDER: That's good. Now, your final thought was this pain is ruining your life. Did that thought hurt you or help you take the walk?

LINDA: It hurt. It was very depressing to think about.

PROVIDER: What would have been an alternative thought?

LINDA: This pain is manageable and it doesn't have to take over the rest of my life.

PROVIDER: I like that statement. How do you think that would have helped?

LINDA: It's encouraging. Not so depressing.

PROVIDER: I agree. Those alternative thoughts are all very empowering. Now, let's take a look at your behaviors. You said your first behavior was to decline the walk. Did that help you or hurt you in getting what you wanted?

LINDA: Well, that's a silly question because it obviously did not help me take the walk.

PROVIDER: Right. What could you have done instead?

LINDA: Gone on the walk anyway.

PROVIDER: Ok, and then you said you did not tell your husband why you declined. Did that help you or hurt you in taking the walk?

LINDA: It hurt me. I guess if I had told him what I was worried about he could have helped me. He's very supportive and he knows what I'm dealing with.

PROVIDER: Ok, so communicating with him would have helped you get support?

LINDA: Yes.

PROVIDER: And your final behavior was to lie on the couch. Did that help you or hurt you in getting what you wanted?

LINDA: It hurt me. Literally. I did feel worse after that which is ironic.

206 Application of Ultra-Brief Interventions

PROVIDER: Ok, what could you have done instead?

LINDA: I could have gone on the walk, or at least not just lie around. I could have done something else a little more active.

PROVIDER: And how would that have been helpful?

LINDA: It's good for the back, just like it says in that handout you gave me last time. Exercise is good for the pain and rest is not necessarily good.

PROVIDER: Good, I'm glad to hear you have been able to incorporate the information from those handouts. You came up with some great alternative thoughts and behaviors.

LINDA: Thank you.

PROVIDER: Earlier, we were talking about your pattern of wanting things to be just right. On a scale from 0 to 10, where 0 is not at all important and 10 is extremely important, how important is it for you to change that pattern?

LINDA: I would say 9. Not all the way at a 10 because I think things should be done right, but I do recognize now that wanting everything to be a certain way ends up holding me back from the things I want to do.

PROVIDER: That's a good insight. Now on the same scale from 0 to 10, how confident are you that you can change this pattern?

LINDA: Oh, I think only a 5.

PROVIDER: Ok, so 5 is halfway there, which is good. What do you think it would take to make you more confident – say about a 6 or a 7?

LINDA: I think if I can actually make myself get some exercise, even just a little.

PROVIDER: Ok, as I said you came up with some great alternatives and I look forward to hearing how some of these situations turn out differently for you in the future.

Commentary. S – Linda reports her pain has decreased since the last session.

O – On the PEG scale from 0–10, she rated her average pain intensity as 6 for last week. She marked 7 for her pain's interference with enjoying life and 7 for interference with general activity.

A – She was able to identify alternative thoughts and behaviors through Pattern-Focused Therapy.

P – Treatment will continue to focus on pain management techniques and progress monitoring. Pattern-Focused Therapy will continue to be used to address her pattern's role in managing her chronic pain. The PEG will be administered at each session.

Case of Linda: Session 4

Background. Linda was administered the PEG: a 3-item scale for assessing pain intensity and interference. On a scale from 0–10, Linda rated her average pain intensity as 4 for last week. She marked 7 for her pain's interference with enjoying life and 5 for interference with general activity. In this session, Linda reveals she has been struggling to manage her prescribed medication.

PROVIDER: Hi Linda, I see you have been experiencing less pain from your PEG rating but it is still interfering with your ability to enjoy life and complete general tasks. Can you tell me more about that?

LINDA: Yes, well I found I have to take my medication a lot more. That really helps with the pain but then when I'm medicated I'm often too tired to do anything.

PROVIDER: Why don't we review your electronic health record together to see which medication you are prescribed and how you are supposed to be taking it.

LINDA: Ok.

PROVIDER: I see you are prescribed OxyContin and are to take 20mg three times a day. How often have you been taking it?

LINDA: Um, I've been taking about four pills a day, sometimes five. At first, there was a period where I didn't need it that much. They seem to prescribe more than you need. I did fill all the prescriptions though and I saved up the medication so I can have it when I need it.

PROVIDER: You saved up the medication. Can you tell me more about that?

LINDA: Yes, well I got worried that my pain would get really out of hand and then I would need the pills but maybe not have refills left and then I would have to wait while I was in all that pain so I figured better to get them while they're prescribed and save them for a rainy day, you know?

PROVIDER: I understand your concern. And now you find yourself needing them more?

LINDA: That's right. It's not so much that the pain is out of hand, it's that I'm really tired of dealing with it. I know we talked about all that stuff that pain is not necessarily forever and it doesn't have to ruin your life but sometimes you just get tired of putting up with it and waiting for it to go away.

PROVIDER: What about other substances? Do you drink alcohol?

208 Application of Ultra-Brief Interventions

LINDA: I do but not that often. Only when we are out with friends, on the weekend or something. I haven't been drinking while I take the pain meds though. So, I haven't had a drink in a couple of weeks.

PROVIDER: It's good that you are not mixing the two. In the past year, have you used any illegal drugs?

LINDA: Oh no, I don't do that.

PROVIDER: What about any prescription drugs for nonmedical reasons?

LINDA: No, like I said, I just use it for the pain.

PROVIDER: Does anyone in your family have a history of abusing substances or prescribed medications?

LINDA: Not that I know of.

PROVIDER: Ok, now you mentioned the medication makes you tired. How else has it been affecting your life?

LINDA: Well, it makes it difficult to do my chores. I can't cook or drive when I'm on it. And I'm too tired to go out. My husband also says I don't make a lot of sense when I'm on the medication so we don't talk much then.

PROVIDER: It sounds like it interferes with a lot of the things you like to do.

LINDA: Yeah, and all of the things I have to do.

PROVIDER: I understand that you are concerned about your treatment and managing your pain and I would like to help you manage as best you can. But I am concerned about the way you are using your medication and that you've been experiencing some difficulty using it as it was designed to be used. I am concerned about both the short-term and long-term consequences of medication misuse which can include addiction, liver problems, and tolerance so that the medication does not work for you any longer.

LINDA: Yeah, I know it can be a dangerous drug. I definitely don't need those problems on top of the problems I already have.

PROVIDER: Remember, as we discussed, there are many tools you can learn in these sessions that can help you manage the pain and perhaps find you no longer need any medication.

LINDA: Yes, that's true. I do remember that from our conversations and the handouts. It can be discouraging sometimes.

PROVIDER: I understand it must be very discouraging when the pain persists.

LINDA: Yes.

Chronic Pain and Medication Misuse 209

PROVIDER: I would like for us to have a medication agreement, between you, me, and Dr. John. It will outline how and when you will use the prescribed medication. How does that sound?

LINDA: Ok, I think that sounds fine.

PROVIDER: Ok, now this is something we will come up with together, that will suit your needs, while helping you protect yourself from some of those ill effects of using this medication incorrectly.

LINDA: Ok. I'm willing to do that.

Commentary. S – Linda reports her pain has decreased since the last session but she is increasingly dependent on her prescribed opiate medication.

O – On the PEG scale from 0–10, she rated her average pain intensity as 4 for last week. She marked 7 for her pain's interference with enjoying life and 5 for interference with general activity. She is prescribed OxyContin 20mg three times per day.

A – She has been misusing her medication but has no personal or family history of substance abuse. She demonstrates an obsessive-compulsive personality style.

P – I am already working with her on medication management but a medication agreement is needed to specify the amount of medication she is to take, as well as when she will take it. The primary care physician will create a flow chart to monitor medication refills. Treatment will continue to focus on pain management techniques and progress monitoring. Pattern-Focused Therapy will continue to be used to address her pattern's role in managing her chronic pain. The PEG will be administered at each session. Medication compliance will be monitored.

Concluding Note

Chronic pain is a complex problem and frequently presents in integrated care and mental health settings. Clients presenting with chronic pain often benefit immensely from behavioral interventions and psychoeducation. Clients are taught about the various factors that affect how the brain perceives pain signals and how to change their thoughts and behaviors to control how they experience pain. Pattern-Focused Therapy is used to ameliorate client patterns and personality factors that may inhibit successful treatment. When medication misuse is suspected, the provider evaluates how the client has been using his/

210 Application of Ultra-Brief Interventions

her medication and creates a medication contract to outline how medication will be prescribed and used.

References

American Counseling Association. (n.d.). Suicide Assessment. Retrieved from www.counseling.org/docs/trauma-disaster/fact-sheet-6---suicide-assessment.pdf?sfvrsn=2

Dobkin, P.L., & Boothroyd, L.J. (2008). Organizing health services for patients with chronic pain: When there is a will there is a way. *Pain Medicine*, 9(7), 881–889.

Hunter, C.L., Goodie, J.L., Oordt, M.S., & Dobmeyer, A.C. (2017). *Integrated behavioral health in primary care: Step-by-step guidance for assessment and intervention* (2nd ed.). Washington, DC: American Psychological Association.

Krebs, E.E., Lorenz, K.A., Bair, M.J., Damush, T.M., Wu, J., Sutherland, J.M., ... Kroenke, K. (2009). Development and initial validation of the PEG, a three-item scale assessing pain intensity and interference. *Journal of General Internal Medicine*, 24(6), 733–738.

Lew, V., & Ghassemzadeh, S. (2018). SOAP Notes. Retrieved from www.ncbi.nlm.nih.gov/books/NBK482263/

Melzack, R., & Wall, P.D. (1965, November 19). Pain mechanisms: A new theory. *Science*, 150, 971–979.

Moayedi, M., & Davis, K.D. (2013). Theories of pain: From specificity to gate control. *Journal of Neurophysiology*, 109, 5–12.

National Institute on Drug Abuse. (2014). Research report series: Prescription drug abuse. Retrieved from www.drugabuse.gov/sites/default/files/rxreportfinalprint.pdf

Oakman, J., Kinsman, N., & Briggs, A.M. (2017). Working with persistent pain: An exploration of strategies utilized to stay productive at work. *Journal of Occupational Rehabilitation*, 27, 4–14.

Sezgin, M., Hasanefendioglu, E.Z., Sungur, M.A., Incel, N.A., Cimen, O.B., Kanik, A., & Sahin, G. (2015). Sleep quality in patients with chronic low back pain: A cross-sectional study assessing its relations with pain, functional status and quality of life. *Journal of Back and Musculoskeletal Rehabilitation*, 28, 433–441.

Smith, S.M., Paillard, F., McKeown, A., Burke, L.B., Edwards, R.R., Katz, N.P., ... Dworkin, R.H. (2015, May). Instruments to identify prescription medication misuse, abuse, and related events in clinical trials: An ACTION systematic review. *The Journal of Pain*, 16, 389–411.

Tang, N.K., & Crane, C. (2006, May). Suicidality in chronic pain: A review of the prevalence, risk factors, and psychological links. *Psychological Medicine*, 36(5), 575–586.

Volkow, N.D., & McLellan, A.T. (2016, March 31). Opioid abuse in chronic pain – Misconceptions and mitigation strategies. *The New England Journal of Medicine*, 374(13), 1253–1263.

Ultra-Brief Interventions with Sleep Problems   **8**

This chapter describes insomnia, the most common sleep condition to present in integrated settings. Included is an overview of the functional assessment and common interventions for insomnia. A case example is illustrated through four transcriptions with commentary. As with other mental health conditions seen in these settings, the behavioral health provider's role is primarily to complete a functional assessment and implement brief interventions, rather than complete a full diagnostic evaluation.

Sleep Problems

Sleep problems, like insomnia and sleep apnea, frequently present in integrated care and mental health care settings, leading to a number of functional impairments and reduced quality of life. This chapter will focus on the assessment and treatment of insomnia.

Insomnia

Insomnia, or the inability to fall or stay asleep, is the most common sleep issue seen in integrated care and mental health settings. Insomnia is marked by an individual's insufficient sleep quality or quantity. The DSM-5 outlines three types of insomnia. Sleep-onset insomnia, or initial insomnia, is characterized by difficulty falling asleep. Sleep-maintenance insomnia, or middle insomnia, is characterized by awakening through the night with the inability to return to sleep, while late insomnia involves early awakening without being able to return to sleep (American Psychiatric Association, 2013).

Rates of insomnia being reported in these settings has increased, with roughly 19.2% of American adults struggling with this condition (Ford, Cunningham, Giles, & Croft, 2015). Significant increases in insomnia have been found among individuals with co-occurring medical problems, including diabetes, hypertension, joint pain, and breathing problems (Ford et al., 2015). Unfortunately, insomnia has a damaging effect on quality of life. This sleep issue leads to poorer work and academic performance and worsening of existing psychiatric and medical issues (Fortier-Brochu, Beaulieu-Bonneau, Ivers, & Morin, 2012; Kraus & Rabin, 2012). Rates of insomnia are attributed to individual lifestyle habits, societal trends and occupational demands, and increased use of electronic devices (Ford et al., 2015).

Assessment and Screening Instruments

While clients presenting with sleep disorders often meet DSM-5 criteria for insomnia, and possibly other sleep disorders, the assessment of sleep issues in integrated care settings primarily focuses on the sleep problem's impact on the individual's daily functioning. Sleep hygiene, and associated habits and behaviors are assessed. Finally, in cases where a client relies on sleeping medications, a medication misuse assessment may be indicated.

Functional Assessment

The functional assessment for insomnia includes gathering information about the history of the presenting problem as well as any contributing factors like behaviors and sleeping environment. Behaviors include use of substances and technology, spending time in bed, napping, etc. The behavioral health provider determines if the insomnia is early, middle, or late insomnia. Related issues like sleep apnea and restless leg syndrome are also addressed. Finally, the consequences of insomnia should be assessed, including daytime sleepiness, ability to concentrate, and mood. A standardized instrument such as the Insomnia Severity Index can provide information on the client's sleep patterns and can be used for continuous monitoring. As with other functional assessments, primarily focused, closed-ended questions are used. Co-occurring psychiatric conditions, like depression and anxiety, are ruled in or out when indicated. Table 8.1 outlines questions commonly asked in a functional assessment of insomnia.

Table 8.1　Functional Assessment of Insomnia

Presenting Problem	Your primary care physician stated you have had some difficulty sleeping lately. Is that correct?
Duration	How long have you had this difficulty sleeping? When did you first have difficulty with sleep?
Frequency	How many times a week do you experience this?
Triggers	Did anything occur that led to your trouble with sleep?
Sleep Environment	Is your bedroom conducive to sleep, i.e., quiet, dark, comfortable, free of disturbances?
	Does anything routinely wake you up during the night, e.g. spouse, children, pets?
	Do you share a bed with someone who disturbs your sleep?
Use of Sedatives	Do you use any substances to help you fall asleep, i.e., sleeping medications, alcohol?
Use of Substances	Do you use tobacco products? If so, how long before you go to bed do you use them?
	Do you consume caffeine in any form? If so, how long before you go to bed do you use caffeine?
Exercise	What time of day do you exercise?
Bedtime Behaviors	What time do you usually go to bed? Is it the same time every day?
	How long does it typically take you to fall asleep?
	Do you wake up through the night? If so, how often? How long are you awake? What do you do when you are awake?
	How long before you go to bed do you stop using electronic devices?

(continued)

Table 8.1 *(Cont.)*

Other Behaviors	What time do you wake up? Is that before or after you need to wake up?
	Do you wake up at the same time every day?
	Do you take naps? How often, how long, and what time?
	Do you do other things in bed like eat, read, watch TV, or use electronic devices?
Consequences	Do you feel tired when you get up?
	Do you feel tired throughout the day?
	Have you ever fallen asleep in inappropriate places like work?
	Have you had difficulty concentrating?
	Do you worry about not being able to sleep?
	How else has your lack of sleep affected your daily functioning?
Related Conditions	Do you snore or wake up gasping for air while you sleep? (sleep apnea)
	Do your legs jerk and wake you or your partner? (periodic limb movements)
	Do you have sensations like burning or tingling in your legs that keep you from falling asleep? (restless leg syndrome)
	Do you ever suddenly fall asleep at inopportune times? (narcolepsy)
	Do you grind your teeth while you sleep? (bruxism)
Open-Ended Questions	Is there anything I have not asked you about that you would like me to know?

Medication Misuse Assessment

In some cases, clients may be prescribed sleeping medications and use those medications differently than intended. If the behavioral health provider suspects the client may be using medications incorrectly, the provider should assess how the client uses the medication, whether the client hoards medication, or is medication seeking. The provider can use a screener like the Drug Abuse Screening Test (DAST) to evaluate substance misuse.

Screening Instruments

The Insomnia Severity Index. The Insomnia Severity Index (ISI) is a 7-item questionnaire that corresponds to the DSM-5 criteria for insomnia. Each question is rated on a 5-point scale from 0–4 where 0 = none, 1 = mild, 2 = moderate, 3 = severe, and 4 = very severe. Questions assess difficulty falling and staying asleep, as well as implications for mood and daily functioning. The scoring for the ISI is as follows: 0–7 = no clinically significant insomnia, 8–14 = subthreshold insomnia, 15–21 = clinical insomnia (moderate severity), and 22–28 = clinical insomnia (severe).

The Drug Abuse Screening Test. The Drug Abuse Screening Test (DAST) is a 28-item forced choice (yes or no) self-report questionnaire that assesses problem drug use and its associated consequences. The DAST inquires about use of prescribed and over-the-counter drugs in excess of directions and the nonmedical use of drugs.

Ultra-Brief Interventions

After completing the functional assessment, the client and behavioral health provider must agree on treatment goals. The behavioral health provider provides psychoeducation about insomnia that addresses the client's primary concerns. For example, if the client consumes caffeine, the provider can inform the client that too much caffeine too late in the day can contribute to insomnia. The client may not know that certain foods and beverages contain caffeine and can explore this with the provider. Treatment focuses on improving sleep hygiene and stimulus control. Stress management techniques like progressive muscle relaxation and controlled breathing can be used to help clients relax. Pattern-focused therapy is used to treat underlying personality factors that contribute to the client's sleep problems. In some cases, sleeping medication may be used in conjunction with ultra-brief interventions.

Insomnia Psychoeducation

The provider provides psychoeducation tailored to the responses from the functional assessment. Psychoeducation about sleep hygiene can include a discussion of the adverse effects of caffeine, nicotine, and alcohol on sleep. The client should be advised not to take naps too late in the day and to go to sleep and wake up at the same time each day. The provider can help the client decide on ways to make the sleep environment more comfortable and eliminate distractions, as well as help the client make a plan for unwinding before bed each night. The client should be advised to stop using electronic devices at least an hour before bedtime. The provider should explain how these factors influence sleep.

Stimulus Control

Stimulus control for insomnia includes getting out of bed when unable to fall asleep, going to bed only when sleepy as to avoid tossing and turning, and avoiding activities other than sleep or sex in the bed. The provider should explain how controlling these stimuli help the client associate the bed with sleeping instead of being awake. Table 8.2, below, outlines instructions for proper sleep hygiene and stimulus control.

Progressive Muscle Relaxation

Progressive muscle relaxation is used to teach clients how to relax by demonstrating the difference between tensed and relaxed sensations in the body. The behavioral health provider instructs the client to tense one part of the body at a time and then release that body part, noticing the sensations before moving to the next. Clients can easily apply progressive muscle relaxation at home to relax before sleep and throughout the day for stress management.

Interventions with Sleep Problems **217**

Table 8.2 Sleep Hygiene and Stimulus Control

Sleep Environment	Making sure the bed is comfortable.
	Dark, quiet, cold.
	Minimize disturbances.
	Use of white noise, sleep masks, blackout curtains, or other helpful items.
Behaviors	Cease use of blue light devices at least one hour before bed.
	Limit naps to 30-minutes and not close to bedtime.
	Exercising regularly but avoiding exercise too close to bedtime.
	Getting natural light on a regular basis.
	Avoid foods that can disturb sleep (i.e., acidic or spicy foods).
Substances	Caffeine, nicotine, alcohol, and other substances can disturb sleep.
Bedtime Routine	Establish a calming bedtime routine. (e.g., a warm shower, drinking caffeine-free tea, reading, etc.) Going to bed and waking up at the same times every day.
Stimulus Control	Do not toss and turn in bed. Get out of bed.
	Do not use the bedroom for any activities other than sleep or sex (i.e., no television, eating, working, etc., in bed).

*Adapted from National Sleep Foundation

Pattern-Focused Therapy

Pattern-Focused Therapy is used to address the client's personality dynamics that contribute to insomnia. The client's personality pattern not only maintains the presenting problem but can lead to relapse after treatment, when triggered. Using Pattern-Focused Therapy facilitates the implementation of sleep hygiene and stimulus control, and increases the likelihood that the client will maintain treatment gains. For example, in the Case of Michael (outlined below), Michael's pattern of perfectionism drives him to work excessively. As a result, he consumes too much caffeine too late in the day, does not adhere to a sleep schedule, and often works late into the night. The provider helps Michael identify his pattern and work as his primary trigger. Through Pattern-Focused Therapy, Michael is able to move towards a more adaptive

218 Application of Ultra-Brief Interventions

pattern of being productive while maintaining his personal life and attending to his sleep hygiene.

Combined Medication Treatment

For some clients, short-term medication treatment may be necessary. The client should be informed that cognitive behavioral interventions for insomnia have been found to be effective for long-term treatment while sleep medications are more useful short-term. Morin et al. (2009) found that patients with persistent insomnia improved with a combination treatment of sleeping medication and CBT but that long-term outcomes improved when the medication was discontinued. If needed, the provider should arrange a meeting with the client and primary care physician to discuss a medication plan.

Progress Monitoring and Record Keeping

Progress Monitoring

Progress monitoring in the case of sleep problems involves assessing not only frequency and severity of these issues, but also their effect on the client's mood and daily functioning. Use of standardized instruments, like the Insomnia Severity Index, is helpful for progress monitoring, and should be administered prior to each session. Client self-reports and journals or logs can be used to help monitor symptoms and compliance with homework.

Record Keeping

When treating sleep problems, the behavioral health provider should use the structured SOAP note format for record keeping, with SOAP standing for the Subjective, Objective, Assessment, and Plan. The Subjective heading describes the client's subjective experience, including presenting symptoms, subjective ratings of intensity, and other relevant concerns. The Objective heading includes any objective ratings, like those obtained from standardized instruments or medical exams. The Assessment heading includes whether the client meets criteria for a DSM-5 diagnosis as well as the client's personality style. The client may meet the diagnosis for insomnia, and possibly a co-occurring mental health disorder and/or other sleep disorder. Items in this

Interventions with Sleep Problems **219**

category should be listed in order of importance. Finally, the Plan heading includes the next steps to be completed in the treatment plan, goals for the next session, and any necessary referrals.

Case of Michael Transcriptions

Case of Michael: Session 1

Michael is a 36-year-old African-American male referred to counseling by his primary care physician for insomnia. He works as a financial analyst and is married with two children. Michael was administered the Insomnia Severity Index, on which he scored 17, indicating clinical insomnia with moderate severity. This session will include a functional assessment of Michael's symptoms and psychoeducation on insomnia.

PROVIDER: Hi Michael, it's nice to meet you. I really enjoy working with Dr. Hakim's patients. I am going to start by asking you some questions so I can get a better idea of some of the symptoms you have been dealing with and how they have been affecting you. How does that sound?

MICHAEL: That sounds fine, thanks.

PROVIDER: Ok, when did you first start having difficulty with your sleep?

MICHAEL: It started almost a year ago. It's hard to believe it's been that long.

PROVIDER: Ok, did anything happen that triggered your sleep problem?

MICHAEL: I don't know. There's a lot going on at work. We got some big accounts at my firm and that's been very stressful. I've been working a lot more and I think that has something to do with it.

PROVIDER: How many nights of the week do you have difficulty sleeping?

MICHAEL: About four.

PROVIDER: Ok, and how has this been affecting you?

MICHAEL: Well, I feel really tired all the time. When I wake up, I feel terrible. Exhausted.

PROVIDER: Do you feel sleepy throughout the day?

MICHAEL: Yes, definitely. I feel tired a lot.

PROVIDER: Have you fallen asleep in inappropriate places, like in your car or at work?

MICHAEL: That usually doesn't happen. There are times when I feel like I could fall asleep but I don't.

220 Application of Ultra-Brief Interventions

PROVIDER: Do you have difficulty concentrating?

MICHAEL: It can be hard to focus. I have to drink coffee to get my work done.

PROVIDER: Do you nap?

MICHAEL: No, I'm afraid I don't have time to nap.

PROVIDER: What are some ways your sleep affects your daily life?

MICHAEL: Well, like I said I'm tired a lot and it's hard to focus. It's also really hard to play with my kids. Sometimes they want to go outside with me when I get home from work and I'm just ready to fall asleep. Plus, I usually have some work I have to do when I get home. That's really hard.

PROVIDER: Is there anything else?

MICHAEL: Yeah, my wife is upset with me. I can't remember the last time we had a date. If I'm not working, I usually want to crash on the couch because I'm so tired.

PROVIDER: Ok, has your wife ever told you that you kick at night or move your legs around?

MICHAEL: No.

PROVIDER: What about any uncomfortable sensations in your legs like burning, itching, or crawling sensations that make it difficult to fall asleep?

MICHAEL: No I don't.

PROVIDER: Do you ever have difficulty speaking or moving when you wake up?

MICHAEL: No, that hasn't happened to me.

PROVIDER: Do you grind your teeth at night or wake up with a headache?

MICHAEL: I sometimes wake up with headaches but my dentist hasn't mentioned that I grind my teeth.

PROVIDER: Ok, and how has your mood been lately?

MICHAEL: Well, I feel cranky. Sometimes I don't feel like doing much. But I think that's mostly because I'm tired. When I'm not tired, I don't feel that way.

PROVIDER: Would you consider yourself a nervous person?

MICHAEL: I'm stressed. I have a lot on my mind but I am not nervous.

PROVIDER: Have you had any frightening or stressful experiences lately?

MICHAEL: Just the day-to-day stress from my job.

PROVIDER: And do you use any substances?

MICHAEL: I drink occasionally but that's about it.

PROVIDER: Ok, thank you for answering these questions. It is very helpful for me to get an accurate idea of your insomnia and how it has been

Interventions with Sleep Problems **221**

affecting you. We often find that a person's environment and sleep habits have a lot to do with quality of sleep. So, I'm going to ask you some questions now about your sleep environment and behaviors. Is that ok?

MICHAEL: Sure.

PROVIDER: Ok, is your bedroom generally quiet and comfortable?

MICHAEL: It's pretty quiet and comfortable. Maybe I could use a new pillow.

PROVIDER: Ok, that is definitely something to consider. What about any light in your bedroom after you lie down to sleep?

MICHAEL: My wife usually stays up reading with the lights on. That can be distracting for me.

PROVIDER: Ok, is there anything that wakes you up during the night like noises, children, or pets?

MICHAEL: Yes, my kids will wake up sometimes. Not as much as when they were younger but they still do and sometimes they will come into our room.

PROVIDER: You mentioned your wife keeps the light on while she is reading. Is there any other way she affects your sleep?

MICHAEL: She gets up to go to the bathroom a lot. If I'm asleep I can usually sleep through it, but if I'm trying to fall asleep, it disturbs me.

PROVIDER: Do you take or use anything to help you fall asleep, including alcohol or sleeping medication?

MICHAEL: I haven't. I just got a prescription for sleeping pills from the doctor that I'm going to try.

PROVIDER: What time of day do you exercise?

MICHAEL: I like exercising in the morning but I haven't been able to because I fall asleep so late.

PROVIDER: You mentioned you have to drink coffee to get your work done. How much caffeine do you consume?

MICHAEL: Probably 4 or 5 cups of coffee a day.

PROVIDER: What about caffeinated teas or sodas?

MICHAEL: I don't really drink tea or soda.

PROVIDER: And what about chocolate treats?

MICHAEL: No, I don't like chocolate.

PROVIDER: Ok. What is the latest time you have any coffee before getting into bed?

MICHAEL: I drink coffee until probably about 6 p.m.

PROVIDER: And what time do you go to bed?

222 Application of Ultra-Brief Interventions

MICHAEL: I try to go to bed at 11:30 or 12 but sometimes I don't until about 1.

PROVIDER: How long does it take you to fall asleep once you are in bed?

MICHAEL: It can be between half an hour and forever! Sometimes it's four hours, sometimes I don't fall asleep at all.

PROVIDER: How many times do you wake up throughout the night?

MICHAEL: If I fall asleep, I might wake up two times. Sometimes I can fall back asleep within an hour and sometimes I can't fall back asleep.

PROVIDER: What do you do when you wake up?

MICHAEL: I just toss and turn. Close my eyes and try to fall asleep.

PROVIDER: Do you worry about not being able to sleep?

MICHAEL: Oh yeah! I get upset that I'm up and think about how tired I'm going to be or how I won't be able to focus.

PROVIDER: What time do you wake up?

MICHAEL: I usually wake up with my alarm at 7:30 if I fall asleep.

PROVIDER: When you are awake in bed, do you watch TV, read, or eat?

MICHAEL: I watch TV.

PROVIDER: Do you use any other electronic devices before going to sleep?

MICHAEL: Yes, I use my phone and my tablet. I usually am answering emails and stuff, even until I go to bed.

PROVIDER: So, you work a lot?

MICHAEL: Oh yes. Sometimes my wife complains.

PROVIDER: How does it affect you?

MICHAEL: Well it stresses me out, keeps me from getting rest. And it strains my marriage.

PROVIDER: Would you say you have a pattern of overworking even when it interferes with other important things in your life?

MICHAEL: You could definitely say that.

Commentary. Michael's symptoms are consistent with his score of clinical insomnia with moderate severity on the Insomnia Severity Index. Additionally, he displayed an obsessive-compulsive personality style, with a pattern of overworking even when it interferes with other important things in his life.

PROVIDER: Ok, Michael, there are some things you can do to help you with your sleep. I can explain them to you and how they work and then we can discuss if you would like to try them.

MICHAEL: Ok.

PROVIDER: If you go to bed when you are not sleepy and then toss and turn, that can make your sleep problem worse. Staying in bed when

Interventions with Sleep Problems **223**

you cannot sleep makes your brain associate the bed with being awake. We want the bed to be a signal to your brain that it is time to go to sleep.

MICHAEL: That makes sense.

PROVIDER: You mentioned you watch TV in bed and I suggest you stop doing that as well. Watching TV also helps you associate your bed with being awake. I also suggest you stop using your other devices for at least an hour before you go to sleep. Not only can the emails and other content be potentially stressful, but the light from the device helps signal to your brain that it's time to be awake. Another issue is your wife reading with the light on. Do you think she may be open to reading in another room once you have gone to bed?

MICHAEL: I think that would be ok. She wants me to get help with my sleep.

PROVIDER: Ok, now I know it can be tempting to drink more coffee to help get work done, but unfortunately that can turn into a self-perpetuating cycle that only serves to keep you up. You may want to limit your caffeine intake and have your last caffeinated beverage earlier in the day. And you also mentioned stress from your job. Stress and worry are likely to worsen your sleep problem. When you lie in bed feeling stressed and worrying, your bed becomes a trigger for your stress. We can go over some relaxation strategies to help you deal with your stress and keep your bed a place for sleep. What do you think about these recommendations?

MICHAEL: I think I can do them. The coffee will be hard because I need it to focus. But I do agree it probably keeps me up.

PROVIDER: That's good. On a scale from 0 to 10, where 0 is not at all and 10 is the most it could be, how important is it to you to try these recommendations?

MICHAEL: I would say 10. I am willing to try anything.

PROVIDER: That's excellent. On the same scale, how confident are you that you can implement these recommendations?

MICHAEL: Oh, I think only a 6.

PROVIDER: Ok, so that's more than halfway. That's good. What do you think it would take to move that to a 7 or 8?

MICHAEL: Um, maybe if I move the TV out of the bedroom, I'll feel like I'm really getting started.

PROVIDER: Ok, I agree that's a good start. Why don't you start trying these recommendations and next time we can go over some relaxation strategies?

MICHAEL: I will. Thank you.

PROVIDER: Ok, good. I look forward to working with you.

224 Application of Ultra-Brief Interventions

Commentary. S – Michael presents with moderate insomnia, with difficulty falling asleep approximately four nights per week.

O – He scored 17 on the Insomnia Severity Index, indicating clinical insomnia with moderate severity.

A – His insomnia appears to interfere with his daily functioning and social relationships. His poor sleep hygiene and caffeine consumptions likely contribute to his symptoms. Additionally, he displayed an obsessive-compulsive personality style, with a pattern of overworking, even when it interferes with his life.

P – Future sessions will focus on relaxation techniques and sleep hygiene. He will reduce his caffeine intake, remove his television from his bedroom, and go to bed only when he feels sleepy. The Insomnia Severity Index will be administered at each session.

Case of Michael: Session 2

Background. Michael was administered the Insomnia Severity Index and scored 14, indicating subthreshold insomnia. In this session, the provider will introduce Michael to the progressive muscle relaxation strategy to help him manage his stress and, in turn, his insomnia symptoms.

PROVIDER: Hi Michael, I see from your score on the Insomnia Severity Index that you are having some improved sleep. How has that been?

MICHAEL: Yes, it's been better. I did get to sleep more this last week.

PROVIDER: Can you give me an update on some of the recommendations we discussed during the last session?

MICHAEL: Yes, I did move the TV out of the bedroom. The kids are really excited because we're making a TV game room now.

PROVIDER: That's a great idea.

MICHAEL: Yes, also I stopped drinking coffee at 4 p.m. It was 6 before, sometimes later.

PROVIDER: How has that time been working for you?

MICHAEL: It's been better. Maybe it's still a little too late. But it's better.

PROVIDER: Is there anything else?

MICHAEL: Yes, well I couldn't do this every day last week but I did stop using my phone and sending emails at around 10 p.m. a few days.

Interventions with Sleep Problems **225**

PROVIDER: That's great. I'm very pleased to hear you are so enthusiastic about implementing these changes. I was thinking for this session we can explore some relaxation strategies to help you with stress.

MICHAEL: Yes, that would be good. I spend a lot of time thinking about my work and how I'm going to be tired at work. It definitely makes things worse.

PROVIDER: Ok. So, have you heard of a technique called progressive muscle relaxation?

MICHAEL: I've heard of that. I don't really know much about it.

PROVIDER: It is an effective way to relax, to relax your muscles, and to tune in to your body more so you can know the difference between when your muscles are tense and when they are relaxed. Often when we are stressed, we become unaware of how tense our muscles are.

MICHAEL: That is true. I can attest to that. I sometimes notice my shoulders are tense, then I wonder how long I've been tensing them without realizing.

PROVIDER: That is a very good example. So, with this exercise, you tense a part of your body and hold it tense for a few seconds and then release. Focus on the sensations both when you tense and when you release. You can start from your head and work your way down or the other way around. Let's start with your feet and work our way up. Start by closing your eyes and scrunch up your toes as hard as you can.

MICHAEL: Ok, I'm doing it.

PROVIDER: Ok, I want you to concentrate for a moment about how tense your muscles feel.

MICHAEL: Ok.

PROVIDER: Ok, now go ahead and relax your toes and notice the difference in the sensation. Now moving up, you can flex your feet and feel the backs of your legs tense up.

MICHAEL: Yes, I feel that. They feel very tight.

PROVIDER: Ok, now release them.

MICHAEL: Yeah, that feels nice.

Commentary. The provider continues guiding Michael through the exercise.

PROVIDER: Ok, Michael, now that we have completed the full muscle relaxation exercise, how do you feel?

MICHAEL: Wow, I feel a lot more relaxed. I actually feel more present and focused.

226 Application of Ultra-Brief Interventions

PROVIDER: That is great to hear. Many people find great relief from these exercises. Do you think this is something you would like to try to help with your stress and insomnia?

MICHAEL: Yes, definitely.

PROVIDER: Ok, good. I want you to complete the exercise twice a day. I'm going to give you this log so you can note when you do the progressive muscle relaxation.

MICHAEL: Ok, thank you.

PROVIDER: I look forward to hearing about how it goes.

Commentary. S – Michael reports decreased insomnia symptoms.

O – He scored 14 on the Insomnia Severity Index, indicating subthreshold insomnia.

A – He appears motivated to change his behaviors, as he was compliant with sleep hygiene suggestions and the progressive muscle relaxation.

P – He will continue sleep hygiene changes and practice progressive muscle relaxation twice per day. Future sessions will focus on progress monitoring and Pattern-Focused Therapy.

Case of Michael: Session 3

Michael was administered the Insomnia Severity Index and scored 10, indicating subclinical insomnia. For this session, the provider will start with progress monitoring, then use Pattern-Focused Therapy, focusing on Michael's obsessive-compulsive pattern.

PROVIDER: Hi Michael, nice to see you again. Why don't we start out by reviewing your log of progressive muscle relaxation exercises?

MICHAEL: Sure, I have it right here.

PROVIDER: How did you find this exercise?

MICHAEL: I really liked it. You can definitely feel your whole body relaxed. I even showed my wife how to do it. She likes it too.

PROVIDER: That's great! I see you did it most days, which is great. You did it twice on only one day.

MICHAEL: Yeah, it's hard to fit it in twice a day.

PROVIDER: I'm sure. Hopefully this week you can get in a few more times.

MICHAEL: Yes, I would actually like that.

Interventions with Sleep Problems **227**

PROVIDER: Good. Well, we were discussing your pattern of overworking, even when it gets in the way of other things.

MICHAEL: Yeah, like sending emails late at night.

PROVIDER: Right. Was there a situation where that happened recently?

MICHAEL: Yes. The other night. My wife got upset, actually.

PROVIDER: Can you tell me what happened?

MICHAEL: Sure, we have this big case we are working on at my job. We had a special meeting about it and everyone agreed we need to do a lot more research about this particular subject area. The boss said everyone should look into it and tell her what we find. I wanted to be the first to get something to her, and I wanted to find some good information. Something that would really help us. So I worked all day and continued working through dinner and then didn't go to bed until late.

PROVIDER: You mentioned your wife was upset. What happened with that?

MICHAEL: She was mad that I wouldn't come down for dinner and spend time with the family and she was mad that I was staying up because she said I was just getting better with my sleep and I need to stay on the schedule.

PROVIDER: Ok. Is that all of what happened?

MICHAEL: Pretty much. We got into an argument. Then I was stressed about that and work.

PROVIDER: Ok, so you were really excited to get some research to send to your boss and so you worked through dinner and went to bed late and ended up getting into an argument with your wife. Is that right?

MICHAEL: Yes.

PROVIDER: Ok, so what were you thinking at the time when your wife asked you to dinner?

MICHAEL: I was thinking doesn't she know how important this is to me?

PROVIDER: Ok, so you didn't like her asking?

MICHAEL: No.

PROVIDER: What else were you thinking?

MICHAEL: I thought I have to get this work done so the boss knows I'm the best.

PROVIDER: Ok, anything else?

MICHAEL: Umm, I thought whatever I had already found wasn't good enough.

PROVIDER: Ok, so you thought your wife doesn't realize how important your work is, that you have to get your work in so your boss knows you're the best, and that what you had already done was not good enough. Is that correct?

228 Application of Ultra-Brief Interventions

MICHAEL: Yes.

PROVIDER: And what were some of your behaviors? What did you do?

MICHAEL: Um, I told my wife to stop bothering me.

PROVIDER: Ok, what else?

MICHAEL: I kept working and didn't have dinner.

PROVIDER: Ok, so you told your wife to stop bothering you and you kept working. Did you do anything else?

MICHAEL: Yes, I stayed up late and got barely any sleep.

PROVIDER: Ok, well what did you want to get out of this situation?

MICHAEL: Well, really I was hoping to get my stress under control.

PROVIDER: And what actually happened?

MICHAEL: Well, I got in a fight with my wife, missed dinner, and went to bed late.

PROVIDER: So would you say you got what you wanted?

MICHAEL: No, definitely not.

PROVIDER: So would you like to take a look at this situation again to see how it may have turned out differently?

MICHAEL: Sure.

PROVIDER: Ok, so you said your first thought during this situation was about your wife, doesn't she know how important this is to me. Do you think that thought hurt you or helped you get what you wanted, which was getting your stress under control?

MICHAEL: It didn't help. It was a distraction and then the argument with my wife took time.

PROVIDER: Ok, what would have been an alternative thought?

MICHAEL: Well, my wife wants what's best for me. She's concerned about me.

PROVIDER: Ok, so she wants what's best and she's concerned about me. How do you think that thought would have helped?

MICHAEL: I think it would have helped me stay calm and maybe even reminded me I should be watching the time and think about going to bed.

PROVIDER: Ok, so it would have been a reminder to take care of yourself as well.

MICHAEL: Yes.

PROVIDER: That's good. Your second thought was I have to get this work done so the boss knows I'm the best. Did that thought help you or hurt you in coping with your stress?

MICHAEL: It hurt.

PROVIDER: How is that?

MICHAEL: That put a lot of pressure on me. A lot more stress.

Interventions with Sleep Problems **229**

PROVIDER: More stress. And what could have been an alternative thought?

MICHAEL: I'm just going to do my best. I always do a good job.

PROVIDER: That's great. I'm just going to do my best. And reminding yourself that you always do a good job. How would that thought have helped?

MICHAEL: It would have calmed me down. Given me permission to just do my best.

PROVIDER: Ok, and your third thought was that what you found in your research so far wasn't good enough. Was that thought helpful or hurtful in getting what you wanted?

MICHAEL: It was hurtful like the last one.

PROVIDER: What would have been a more helpful thought?

MICHAEL: I'm being too hard on myself. I'm doing my best.

PROVIDER: Good! You are very good at this. How do you think that thought would help?

MICHAEL: Maybe if I wasn't so uptight about the work, I could actually get to bed earlier or at least have dinner with my family.

PROVIDER: Right. Now moving on to your behaviors. You said your first behavior was to tell your wife to leave you alone. Was that behavior helpful or hurtful in coping with your stress?

MICHAEL: It hurt because she got mad and we got into an argument.

PROVIDER: What would have been a more helpful behavior?

MICHAEL: I could have explained to her that I was under a lot of stress.

PROVIDER: Ok, you could have explained yourself. How would that be more helpful?

MICHAEL: I think it would have prevented the argument.

PROVIDER: Ok. Your second behavior was to continue working and skip dinner. Do you think that behavior helped you or hurt you in getting your stress under control?

MICHAEL: It hurt. Obviously I was hungry and didn't feel too well skipping dinner. Then I ate junk food.

PROVIDER: So what could you have done that could have helped you get what you wanted?

MICHAEL: I could have put the work aside and come to dinner.

PROVIDER: And that would have been enjoyable for you and your family?

MICHAEL: Yes.

PROVIDER: And your final behavior was that you stayed up late. Did that help or hurt you in getting your stress under control?

MICHAEL: It hurt. I am just starting to get back on a good sleeping schedule and I can't mess that up now.

230 Application of Ultra-Brief Interventions

PROVIDER: So what could you have done that would have been more helpful?

MICHAEL: I think if I set a time limit on when I would stop my work.

PROVIDER: Ok, that's a great idea. How do you see that helping you?

MICHAEL: It would remind me to stop and take care of myself. Attend to other things.

PROVIDER: That's great. You can also set an alarm on your phone for the time you've chosen so you can stay on track.

MICHAEL: That's a good idea.

PROVIDER: Well you have come up with some great alternatives. On a scale from 0 to 10, how important is it for you to change this pattern of overworking? Where 0 is not at all and 10 is the most.

MICHAEL: I would say 9. I really want to balance my work and personal life better to deal with my stress.

PROVIDER: Ok, that's great. Now, on the same 0 to 10 scale, how confident are you that you can change that pattern?

MICHAEL: Um, I think 6.

PROVIDER: Ok, what do you think it would take to move that to 7 or 8?

MICHAEL: Maybe if I can try that thing with the timer – cutting off my work at a certain time.

PROVIDER: I think that's a great idea. You have done very well today. I look forward to working with you again and seeing you progress.

Commentary. S – Michael reports decreased insomnia symptoms.

O – He scored 10 on the Insomnia Severity Index, indicating subthreshold insomnia.

A – He was able to generate alternatives to address his pattern in Pattern-Focused Therapy.

P – He will continue sleep hygiene changes and practice progressive muscle relaxation twice per day. Future sessions will focus on progress monitoring. He will be administered the Insomnia Severity Index at each session.

Case of Michael: Session 4

Michael was administered the Insomnia Severity Index, on which he scored 9, indicating subthreshold insomnia. Michael has been prescribed a sleeping medication to be used as needed, up to three nights a week, until Michael can

Interventions with Sleep Problems   **231**

get his sleep back on track. During this session, Michael reveals he has been struggling to manage his prescribed medication.

PROVIDER: Hi Michael. I would like to start by checking in to see how you have been sleeping.

MICHAEL: I've actually been a lot better.

PROVIDER: Good. How do you feel at work and doing your daily tasks?

MICHAEL: Better. I definitely have more energy. It's still difficult to concentrate at times though.

PROVIDER: I see. I am glad to hear you have more energy. How has the medication the doctor prescribed been helping?

MICHAEL: It's good. It really helps me get to sleep.

PROVIDER: Ok. And how often have you been taking it?

MICHAEL: Well at first I took it every few days. This last week or so I have been taking it every day.

PROVIDER: Yes, you said every few days at first. Is that what your prescription indicates?

MICHAEL: Yes, that's how it says I should take it. But it is as needed and I have to be honest it was so nice being able to finally sleep. I just didn't want to risk being tired the next day when I had a big meeting and then I found a reason every night.

PROVIDER: Yes, it's always easy to think of something else there is to do or to feel awake for.

MICHAEL: Yes. And when I worry about if I'm going to get enough sleep, it's very stressful. This makes it much less stressful.

PROVIDER: I understand how that can be stressful. Do you use any other substances?

MICHAEL: I have a drink once in a while. I don't mix the pills with that though. There was just one night, my wife and I went to a work function and I had a couple of drinks then took the pill later that night.

PROVIDER: About how many drinks did you have?

MICHAEL: Two or three.

PROVIDER: In the past year, have you used any illegal drugs?

MICHAEL: Oh no, I would never do that.

PROVIDER: What about any prescription drugs for nonmedical reasons?

MICHAEL: No, just the ones prescribed to me.

PROVIDER: Have you ever used illegal drugs or misused prescription drugs?

MICHAEL: No, I haven't.

232 Application of Ultra-Brief Interventions

PROVIDER: What about anyone in your family? Does anyone in your family have a history of misusing alcohol, prescription drugs, or illegal drugs?

MICHAEL: No one in my family does that.

PROVIDER: Ok, thank you for being patient with my questions. I would like to get an accurate idea of what is going on so I can help you correctly.

MICHAEL: No problem.

PROVIDER: Ok, how do you think the medication has been affecting your daily functioning?

MICHAEL: I do feel better. I feel rested.

PROVIDER: You mentioned you still had difficulty concentrating. Do you think that may be related?

MICHAEL: Yes, now that you mention it. I think it might be contributing.

PROVIDER: I understand that you are concerned about falling asleep and feeling rested for your busy and demanding days. But I am concerned about the way you are using your medication and that you've been experiencing some difficulty using it as it was designed to be used. I am concerned about both the short-term and long-term consequences of medication misuse which can include addiction, liver problems, and tolerance so that the medication does not work for you any more.

MICHAEL: Yes, I certainly don't need that.

PROVIDER: Remember, as we discussed, there are many tools you can learn in these sessions that can help you manage your stress, and improve your sleep environment and behaviors to alleviate your symptoms and help you get rest without medication.

MICHAEL: I have been enjoying the muscle relaxation.

PROVIDER: That's great! There are more strategies like that that we can continue to employ. I would like for us to have a medication agreement, between you, me, and Dr. Hakim. It will outline how and when you will use the prescribed medication. How does that sound?

MICHAEL: Ok, we can do that. Thank you.

PROVIDER: Ok, this is something we will come up with together, that will suit your needs, while helping you protect yourself from some of those ill effects of using this medication incorrectly.

MICHAEL: Ok. I'm willing to do that.

Commentary. S – Michael reports he has been misusing his sleeping medication.

O – He scored 9 on the Insomnia Severity Index, indicating subthreshold insomnia.

A – His prescription indicates he is to take one pill as needed, up to three times per week. He reports he has been taking a pill every night. He has no personal or family history of substance abuse. He displays an obsessive-compulsive personality style.

P – A meeting will be arranged with the client, the primary care physician, and myself to draft a medication agreement. The agreement will specify the amount of medication Michael may take, as well as when and how often he will take it. The primary care physician will also create a flow chart to monitor Michael's medication refills.

Concluding Note

Sleep disorders, especially insomnia, are commonly seen in integrated care and mental health care settings. These problems can cause severe impairments in functioning and contribute to a range of other issues. When assessing insomnia, the behavioral health provider should complete a functional assessment that evaluates the duration and intensity of symptoms, the client's sleep hygiene and associated behaviors, and other factors that might contribute to the sleep problem. Interventions include relaxation exercises, improving sleep hygiene, stimulus control, and pattern-focused therapy.

References

American Psychiatric Association (2013). *Diagnostic and statistical manual of mental disorders* (5th ed.). Washington, DC: American Psychiatric Association.

Ford, E.S., Cunningham, T.J., Giles, W.H., & Croft, J.B. (2015, March). Trends in insomnia and excessive daytime sleepiness among US adults from 2002 to 2012. *Sleep Medicine Review*, 16(3), 372–378. http://dx.doi.org/10.1016/j.sleep.2014.12.008

Fortier-Brochu E., Beaulieu-Bonneau S., Ivers H., & Morin C.M. (2012). Insomnia and day-time cognitive performance: A meta-analysis. *Sleep Medicine Review*, 16(1), 83–94.

Kraus S.S., & Rabin L.A. (2012). Sleep America: Managing the crisis of adult chronic insomnia and associated conditions. *Journal of Affective Disorders*, 138(3), 192–212.

Lew, V., & Ghassemzadeh, S. (2018). SOAP Notes. Retrieved from www.ncbi.nlm.nih.gov/books/NBK482263/

Morin, C.M., Vallieres, A., Guay, B., Ivers, H., Savard, J., Merette, C., … Baillargeon, L. (2009, May 20). Cognitive behavioral therapy, singly and combined with medication, for persistent insomnia. *Journal of the American Medical Association*, 301(19), 2005–2016. Retrieved from https://jamanetwork.com/journals/jama/fullarticle/183931

National Sleep Foundation. (n.d.). Sleep Hygiene. Retrieved from www.sleepfoundation.org/sleep-topics/sleep-hygiene

Wong, M.L., Ting Lau, K.N., Espie, C.A., Luik, A.I., Kyle, S.D., & Ying Lau, E.Y. (2017). Psychometric properties of the Sleep Condition Indicator and Insomnia Severity Index in the evaluation of insomnia disorder. *Sleep Medicine, 33,* 76–81.

Ultra-Brief Interventions for Weight Problems   9

This chapter provides an overview of weight management issues as they commonly present in integrated care and mental health care settings. The evaluation includes primarily a functional assessment and can include a mental health diagnostic assessment, if indicated. This chapter provides a detailed format for the assessment and reviews common treatment interventions. A case example is illustrated through four transcriptions with commentary.

Weight Management Issues

Problems of being overweight or obese commonly present in integrated settings. Overweight or obese is defined as weight that is greater than the accepted healthy weight for an individual's height (CDC). This is commonly measured using Body Mass Index (BMI). The Center for Disease Control provides a chart for calculating BMI and corresponding weight category including underweight, healthy weight, overweight, obese, or class three obese. Class three obesity is considered to be severe obesity. The prevalence of obesity among American adults was 39.8% between 2011–2014 (NCHS, 2015).

Obesity is believed to result from an interaction of biological, behavioral, and social factors. While the CDC does not attribute genetics to the rise in obesity, it does state that biological inclinations towards certain eating and physical behaviors can influence weight gain. Living in a community that does not provide access to healthy foods or opportunities to walk or bike, can contribute to obesity. Finally, poor eating behaviors, lack of physical activity,

236 Application of Ultra-Brief Interventions

and use of certain medications can all contribute to obesity (CDC). Obesity is related to a lower quality of life, increase in medical conditions like heart disease and diabetes, and mental health conditions (CDC).

Assessment and Screening Instruments

Assessment of overweight and obesity begins with determining how overweight the client is and the effect this has had on the client's quality of life. Factors that contribute to eating can include low self-efficacy, personality dynamics, environmental factors, misinformation about food, and poor coping mechanisms. In some cases, a mental health condition like depression or binge eating disorder may be present. Standardized screening tools can help the behavioral health provider accurately assess the client.

Functional Assessment

While Body Mass Index (BMI) is useful for determining if an individual is in the overweight or obese range, the behavioral health provider must obtain information about the client's weight history, weight loss attempts, level of physical activity, and eating habits. The behavioral health provider should also explore the client's thoughts related to weight, including perceived self-efficacy and control over eating and weight. The client should be screened for eating disorders and comorbid conditions including depression and anxiety. The Weight-Related Eating Questionnaire (WREQ) can be used to assess eating and weight-related behaviors and to monitor progress. The functional assessment is comprised of mostly focused, closed-ended questions intended to obtain all necessary information in a short time. Relevant medical information can also be obtained from the client's electronic health record. Weight is often a sensitive topic so the behavioral health provider must obtain client permission to discuss weight loss and eating behaviors. Motivational Interviewing is a useful technique for obtaining permission, particularly for resistant clients. Table 9.1 outlines questions commonly asked in a functional assessment of overweight and obesity.

Table 9.1 Functional Assessment of Overweight and Obesity

Weight History	What is the most you have weighed as an adult?
	What is the least you have weighed as an adult?
Past Weight Loss Attempts	Have you tried losing weight before? Were you successful? Did you use a diet or program?
	Have you ever tried counting calories or exercising to lose weight?
Recent Weight History	Has your weight fluctuated in the last year?
Self-Efficacy	Do you believe you have control over your weight?
Weight-Related Beliefs	Do you worry about your weight? About gaining more weight?
	Do you worry about your appearance?
Effects on Health	Has your weight had an effect on your health?
Eating Habits	Do you eat while you are doing other things, e.g., reading or watching TV?
	Do you eat three meals a day?
	Do you snack during the day?
	Do you snack at night?
	Do you eat more when you feel stressed?
	Do you eat more when you are sad or upset?
	Do you eat out? How often?
Depression and Anxiety	How has your mood been?
	Have you been experiencing nervousness or tension?

(continued)

238 Application of Ultra-Brief Interventions

Table 9.1 (*Cont.*)

Binge Eating and Bulimia	Have you ever eaten a large amount of food in one sitting where you felt you had no control over your eating?
	If so, how often?
	Have you ever tried to compensate after a binge by making yourself throw up, exercising, or taking laxatives?
	How do you feel after you binge?
	Does anyone know about the bingeing?
Open-Ended Questions	Is there anything I have not asked you about that you would like me to know?

Diagnostic Assessment

In some cases, a diagnostic assessment for related mental health conditions is indicated. The behavioral health provider should screen for symptoms and disorders that commonly co-occur with obesity, including depression, anxiety, bulimia, and binge eating disorder. If the client indicates these symptoms, the provider should rule in or out any relevant disorders and complete a risk assessment if needed.

Assessment of Contributing Factors

Clients who struggle with weight often present with varying reasons why keeping their weight or eating under control has been challenging. Personality dynamics affect weight-related behaviors in several ways. A client who has a dependent personality style may be more likely to eat unhealthy foods if that is what friends or family members prefer, whereas an avoidant client may use food as a self-soothing tool to deal with social anxieties. The provider must understand both the client's personality style as well as how it contributes to and maintains weight issues. Clients with low self-efficacy and negative cognitions about eating are also more likely to behave in ways that hinder their ability to lose weight. Sometimes, poor weight-related habits are a result of misinformation, like eating so-called "health foods" without being mindful of calories, ingredients, or serving sizes. Clients may be resistant because they feel embarrassed about their weight or their doctors' admonitions about their weight. They may be skeptical of treatment plans or worry that if they begin exercising, they will hurt themselves, in addition to many other possible faulty cognitions. Finally, clients may have pressures from family, friends, or coworkers, or may live in a neighborhood where healthier, lower calorie food is not readily available. The behavioral health provider should be aware that one or more of these factors may be present and that they often interact with one another as a hindrance to the client achieving and maintaining a healthy weight.

Screening Instruments

The Weight-Related Eating Questionnaire. The Weight-Related Eating Questionnaire (WREQ) is a 16-item questionnaire that assesses theory-based eating behaviors. Each question is rated on a 5-point scale from 1–5 where 1 = not at all, 2 = slightly, 3 = more or less, 4 = pretty well, and 5 = completely. Questions assess common eating behaviors including eating more during heightened stress, craving food when others are eating it, difficulty resisting cravings, etc. The WREQ yields scores for four subscales: routine restraint, compensatory restraint, susceptibility to external cues, and emotional eating.

Body Mass Index. Body Mass Index (BMI) is a useful tool for determining if a person is within the range of healthy weight, underweight, or overweight, and to what degree. BMI is not intended to diagnose a person with obesity or any other condition, but to be used as a screening tool and indicator that a person must make changes to his/her weight. BMI is calculated by dividing a person's weight in pounds by the square of the person's height in inches. The resulting score is tracked on a chart to determine the weight category. Categories include below 18.5 = underweight, 18.5–24.9 = normal or healthy weight, 25–29.9 = overweight, 30.0 and above = obese. Some people may have more body fat than others with the same BMI. Despite these variations, BMI is still a strong indicator of fatness. Many BMI charts and calculators are readily available online and easy to use.

240 Application of Ultra-Brief Interventions

Ultra-Brief Interventions

Motivational interviewing is a key intervention for overweight and obese clients. Though clients likely are aware that they need to lose weight, the subject can be a source of shame or embarrassment. It is imperative that the counselor uses motivational interviewing and asks permission to discuss these topics and ask certain questions. Ultra-brief interventions for weight loss include goal setting and self-monitoring. Psychoeducation helps clients understand their weight problems and what they need to do to lose weight. Many clients may have misunderstandings about weight loss, or have tried fad diets in the past. The counselor should explain that weight loss is best as a slow and steady process. Pattern-focused therapy is useful to address client personality patterns that help maintain the presenting problem.

Motivational Interviewing

Motivational interviewing (MI) is useful for helping clients become more motivated to change a behavior. Many clients are resistant to change, particularly regarding a sensitive subject like weight loss. They may have low self-efficacy, negative cognitions about change, and/or a personality style that is more likely to be resistant to suggestions. The behavioral health provider should use the MI skill OARS: Open-ended questions, Affirmations of the client, Reflective listening, and Summarizing. Conversing with the client in this way facilitates change talk from the client (Miller & Rollnick, 2002). Asking the client permission to discuss a topic is key to reducing client resistance. Using scaling questions and helping the client list pros and cons of change can help motivate the client to make change without being directed or lectured by the provider.

Goal Setting

The behavioral health provider should work with the client to set concrete goals that are both achievable in small increments, and focus on long-term behavioral changes. These include changing eating habits and incorporating an exercise routine. Goals for weight loss and target number of calories should be determined, with the physician, based on the client's current weight, daily activity level, and other relevant physical factors. Goals should be reasonable,

Interventions for Weight Problems **241**

achievable, and measurable and pertain to the client's medical needs. The client is asked to monitor progress towards these goals in a log or journal.

Psychoeducation

Psychoeducation is critical for clients trying to lose weight because of commonly held misconceptions about weight loss and dieting. As the provider informs the client of ways to lose weight, the client and provider can set goals together. Goals should be reasonable, achievable, and measurable. The behavioral health provider should inform the client that reducing calorie intake is the most effective way to lose weight and that the client should aim for a calorie deficit that facilitates the loss of one to two pounds per week. The provider can help the client identify the target number of calories to be consumed per day based on the client's weight, height, BMI, and activity level. The behavioral health provider should provide the client with useful handouts about how to choose lower calorie foods instead of higher calorie foods. Handouts like the DIMES (Decrease, Increase, Modify, Exclude, Swap) help clients plan which foods they should remove from their diet, which to reduce, and what alternatives to substitute. The client should be given a food journal to keep track of meals and snacks and help identify areas to change.

Areas of concern identified in the assessment process should also be addressed. These may include the client's triggers for overeating, mindless eating, and environmental factors. The behavioral health provider can explain these issues to the client and help the client make a plan to manage these factors. Physical activity should also be discussed and the client encouraged to increase activity slowly. The client can use an electronic fitness tracker to track progress. The ultimate goal should be 30 minutes of physical activity daily, and the counselor can help the client identify ways to add physical activity into a daily routine. Table 9.2 outlines common psychoeducation points for clients trying to meet weight loss goals.

Pattern-Focused Therapy

Pattern-focused therapy is key to helping overweight and obese clients reach their weight loss goals and maintain a healthy weight. Personality factors affect client behaviors and the way the client interacts with the environment, helping to maintain the presenting problem. Ameliorating a client's maladaptive pattern can help resolve the presenting problem and maintain treatment gains.

242 Application of Ultra-Brief Interventions

Table 9.2 Psychoeducation for Weight Loss

Goal	Psychoeducation
Healthy Eating Habits	☐ Some foods may be marketed as healthy but are high in calories, e.g., granola, restaurant salads. Clients should read labels for calorie and fat count.
	☐ Clients often consume too many calories through drinks like juice, coffee drinks, and alcohol.
	☐ Clients can cut down on certain unhealthy foods and eliminate others, while adding healthier foods into their diet.
	☐ Some foods have more calories than clients expect, e.g., salad dressings. Teach clients to read labels.
	☐ Clients should avoid drastic or fad diets.
Exercise	☐ Clients should aim for 30 minutes of exercise per day.
	☐ Clients should take about 10,000 steps per day.
	☐ Clients should refrain from drinking sports drinks and shakes after exercise, as these can contain a lot of calories and sugar.
	☐ Clients can exercise with a partner to keep them accountable.
Weight Loss	☐ Clients should aim to lose between one and two pounds a week and understand this is a healthier and more sustainable plan than drastic weight loss.
	☐ Clients should learn about Body Mass Index (BMI) so they can track their own progress.
	☐ The client should learn about personal triggers, environmental factors, and mindless eating that contribute to poor eating and exercise habits.

For example, in the exemplar Case of Kassandra, below, Kassandra's pattern is to please others even at her own expense. This leads her to eat unhealthy foods to appease her family and coworkers. She cooks unhealthy foods for others and does not turn down foods so as to not offend anyone. Using pattern-focused therapy, Kassandra is able to move towards a more adaptive pattern

Interventions for Weight Problems **243**

of connecting with others while meeting her own needs. This helps her make healthier choices despite others' demands.

Progress Monitoring and Record Keeping

Progress Monitoring

Progress monitoring for weight loss encompasses not only monitoring weight loss and progress towards goals, but also tracking adherence to treatment plans and other factors that relate to weight management. This might be family relationships, negative cognitions about food and weight loss, level of client self-efficacy. The provider and client should review progress towards weight loss goals and the client's behaviors at every session. This may include tracking the client's adherence to diet and exercise plans, the client's average steps per day, and other agreed upon activities. The behavioral health provider should also monitor changes in the client's personality style and its effect on the client's behaviors as they pertain to weight loss. Finally, any co-occurring mental health disorders should be monitored as well. Standardized instruments like the Weight-Related Eating Questionnaire should be administered regularly and responses discussed with the client. Client self-reports, journals, and logs are also useful in progress monitoring.

Record Keeping

As with other presentations, the SOAP note model is the preferred way of record keeping for weight loss treatment in an integrated care setting. SOAP represents the categories Subjective, Objective, Assessment, and Plan. Presenting symptoms, subjective ratings of intensity, and associated complaints are recorded under the Subjective category. Objective ratings, like those obtained from standardized instruments, like the Weight-Related Eating Questionnaire, or medical exams are recorded in the Objective category. The Assessment heading includes whether the client meets criteria for a DSM-5 diagnosis as well as the client's personality style. Items in this category are listed in order of importance. Finally, the Plan includes the next steps to be completed in the treatment plan, directives for the next session, and referrals as needed.

244 Application of Ultra-Brief Interventions

Case of Kassandra Transcriptions

Case of Kassandra: Session 1

Background. Kassandra is a 38-year-old African-American female. She is a married mother of two who works. She was referred to counseling for weight management by her primary care physician, Dr. Ortiz. Kassandra's BMI was 26, indicating she is in the overweight range. Kassandra is 5'2" and weighs 152 pounds. Additionally, Kassandra was administered the Weight-Related Eating Questionnaire.

PROVIDER: Hi Kassandra, I'm glad to meet you as I really enjoy working with Dr. Ortiz's patients. I understand you would like help managing your weight.

KASSANDRA: Yes, it's been very hard for me but I would like to lose some weight. It seems like I try but nothing happens and then I gain more.

PROVIDER: That does sound frustrating.

KASSANDRA: Yes, it really is.

PROVIDER: Ok, I would like to start out by asking you some questions so I can get a better idea of how we can help you. Is that ok?

KASSANDRA: Yes.

PROVIDER: Alright, what is the most you have ever weighed as an adult?

KASSANDRA: Um, I'm about 152 now. The most I've weighed is 155.

PROVIDER: And what was the least you have weighed?

KASSANDRA: Oh, when I was in college I was about 130. I wish I could go back to that.

PROVIDER: So, you have lost weight though, if you went from 155 to 152 now?

KASSANDRA: Yes, I did lose actually a few pounds. But I've been gaining it back.

PROVIDER: How did you lose that weight?

KASSANDRA: I started cutting back on stuff, like how often I go out to eat. I started bringing my own lunch to work.

PROVIDER: That's great. So, you definitely already have some skills that can help us with your weight loss. Did you use a special program?

KASSANDRA: Yes, I used a program that comes with containers so you can measure your food. It really helped to see it.

PROVIDER: Have you tried monitoring calories or increasing your exercise?

KASSANDRA: I never counted the calories. I did start going to the gym but that lasted about a week. I just got too busy and too tired.

PROVIDER: What has been your weight pattern over the past year?

Interventions for Weight Problems **245**

KASSANDRA: Well, I lost that bit of weight and recently I've been gaining. It was steady for a while, now I'm gaining weight again. I haven't been able to stick with the food portions as well.

PROVIDER: Do you feel like you have control over your weight?

KASSANDRA: Not really. I did for a little while but it seems if I slip up even a little I gain a bunch of weight. And working out doesn't really help at all.

PROVIDER: Do you worry about your weight or about gaining weight?

KASSANDRA: Yes, absolutely. I worry I'm going to keep gaining until I'm like one of those people that can't leave their house.

PROVIDER: What effects has your weight had on your health?

KASSANDRA: Um, I think it slows me down. I feel really tired. I can't take the stairs. When I go somewhere and there's no elevator, I feel really anxious. Also, the doctor said I have metabolic syndrome.

PROVIDER: I understand. What are your thoughts about that diagnosis?

KASSANDRA: It is very upsetting. I am very worried about developing diabetes. My mother had diabetes. She now has some neuropathy and she is starting to lose her vision. It is very scary. I definitely do not want to go through what my mother deals with.

PROVIDER: I understand your concerns. How often do you find yourself worrying about this?

KASSANDRA: Oh, all the time. It's really hard to deal with sometimes.

PROVIDER: Would you consider yourself a nervous person in general?

KASSANDRA: No, not really. There are just things connected to my weight that are very upsetting to me.

PROVIDER: I understand. What about your mood? How has your mood been lately?

KASSANDRA: It's been ok. Sometimes I feel self-conscious that people are looking at me like, "oh look how fat she is." That makes me sad. But otherwise I think my mood has been fine.

PROVIDER: I can see how that is upsetting. Are there other things you feel self-conscious about or wonder if people are thinking about you?

KASSANDRA: No. It's really just about my weight. Like if my clothes are tight, I think people notice that.

PROVIDER: How would you describe your relationships with others?

KASSANDRA: I have pretty good relationships. I take care of my family and even my friends and extended family know they can count on me. I guess that's part of the weight issue. I'm always cooking for people and they want fatty foods. Or I have to bring cake for a party or something like that. It's hard to resist and not to snack along the way.

246 Application of Ultra-Brief Interventions

PROVIDER: Yes, I understand how that can be difficult. Have you ever volunteered to bring something else to a party, say instead of cake?

KASSANDRA: Oh no! Everybody loves my cakes and cupcakes. I could never let everyone down like that.

PROVIDER: Do you find yourself often pleasing others?

KASSANDRA: Yes, I would agree with that. Sometimes even when it's not that good for me.

PROVIDER: Would you say that is a pattern for you?

KASSANDRA: Yes, I would say so.

Commentary. Kassandra's responses indicate a dependent personality style with a pattern of pleasing others and neglecting herself.

PROVIDER: Ok, I see how it can be easy to snack on some of those foods you mentioned. Do you ever eat while you are doing other things, like watching TV?

KASSANDRA: Yes, I can go through a whole bag of chips. You know how that is.

PROVIDER: Yes, that can be very easy to do when we are distracted. How often do you go out to eat?

KASSANDRA: I don't go out much but we get takeout a lot. Pizza, wings, things like that.

PROVIDER: Do you eat three meals a day – breakfast, lunch, and dinner?

KASSANDRA: Mostly. But I snack a lot too. Sometimes when I'm busy it feels like I graze all day. Oh, when I'm at work, I usually go out to lunch too.

PROVIDER: Do you feel you are more likely to eat when you are stressed out or upset?

KASSANDRA: Oh, definitely. They call it comfort food for a reason.

PROVIDER: Yes, that is true. What about do you ever eat large amounts of food at once, perhaps where you feel your eating is out of control?

KASSANDRA: No, I never eat a ton like that all at once. I just eat like normal. The three meals, like you said, and then snacks and stuff. People are always bringing things into the office, like donuts, cake for someone's birthday, things like that.

PROVIDER: Have you ever done anything to try to make up for what you ate, like exercise a lot, take laxatives, or make yourself throw up?

KASSANDRA: No, I would never do something like that.

PROVIDER: Ok, well you have been very cooperative and given me a lot of information so that I can better help you. As you know, we want to help you reach your weight loss goals. That is something that can be very difficult to tackle on your own and without the right information. I'd like to give you some more information on weight loss that I think will be helpful to you. How does that sound?

KASSANDRA: Sounds good.

PROVIDER: Ok, great. To lose weight, and keep it off, we recommend a plan that helps you lose about one to two pounds a week.

KASSANDRA: That sounds like so little!

PROVIDER: I know it doesn't sound like much but it really adds up and it is a safer, healthier way that helps you not gain the weight back like you would with a crash diet.

KASSANDRA: That's true.

PROVIDER: Over the next six months or so on this plan, we hope you will lose about 5% to 10% of your weight. That will help stave off those negative health effects from your weight. It will be important that you check in with us on a regular basis so we can track your weight loss and continue to assist you.

KASSANDRA: What about if I did another diet like South Beach diet?

PROVIDER: Well, we have seen that some of those diets work but really more short-term. There isn't a lot of information about people being able to keep that weight off like they can with a structured plan tailored to them. What may be helpful is if you use that plan along with ours. It may be a good place to find healthier, leaner recipes.

KASSANDRA: Yeah, new recipes would be good. I guess I need to tell my family we are going to cut back on the pizza. That won't be easy, especially with my kids.

PROVIDER: That's a good plan. I really admire your effort and commitment. I can hear that you have been struggling with your weight for a while. I understand it is frustrating that although you were able to lose some weight, you gained it back. Now that Dr. Ortiz has told you your weight can affect your health, you have decided to do something about it. Are you interested in continuing to work with me to make a plan that will help you lose and keep off the weight?

KASSANDRA: Yes, absolutely.

PROVIDER: Ok, so first let's set a goal. Do you think it is realistic for you to lose one to two pounds a week over the next six months?

KASSANDRA: Yes, it seems like really gradual and not so daunting.

248 Application of Ultra-Brief Interventions

PROVIDER: Ok so how much exercise do you think you get a week?

KASSANDRA: Oh, not much at all.

PROVIDER: Would you consider yourself sedentary, moderately active?

KASSANDRA: Really more sedentary.

PROVIDER: Ok, we will want to increase your activity. But first let's concentrate on your calories. So, at your current weight, you would need to eat about 1,500 calories a day to lose about a pound a week. I suggest you don't go any lower than about 1,300 calories a day without speaking to Dr. Ortiz first because we want you to be safe. I am going to give you this handout to help you set goals for your weight loss. There are many resources online as well as apps that can help you figure out how many calories are in your food. Some apps can help you track your calorie intake as well. You can start by making small changes, like swapping unhealthy snacks for healthy ones. Like some fruit instead of chips.

KASSANDRA: Yeah, I can do that.

PROVIDER: So here is a handout on a method we call DIMES. That stands for decrease, increase, modify, exclude, and swap. This can help you track what you eat and which foods you would like to eliminate or cut back on and which foods you can substitute for them.

KASSANDRA: Ok.

PROVIDER: I am also going to give you this handout on modifying eating habits. It gives some great tips on how to eat healthy. For example, we know salads are healthy but often the amount of fat and calories in the dressing defeats the purpose of choosing a salad over, say, a burger.

KASSANDRA: I have heard that before.

PROVIDER: Another good tip is to watch your portions. I have a helpful handout on portion control. Many people find they can do this even when they eat out, by only eating half their meal and taking the other half to go for another meal.

KASSANDRA: Yeah, they sure do give you a lot at lots of those restaurants.

PROVIDER: Right. Finally, I'm going to give you this personal food journal handout. What you do is write the time of day you eat, what you ate and the size of the serving, as well as any comments you may have about your eating, like if you were stressed or upset. There is also space for you to track your physical activity. I suggest starting small, even just a 10-minute walk. Starting small will give you great benefits without making you feel so overwhelmed that you give up the physical activity.

KASSANDRA: Ok, yeah, I can't handle that much at first. Ten minutes sounds very doable.

PROVIDER: Great, eventually as you feel more energized, we can increase your activity. I think you will find that as you get some exercise you will want to do more.

KASSANDRA: Ok, this is a lot to take in but I feel really hopeful about it.

PROVIDER: I'm glad. On a scale of 0 to 10 with 0 being not at all and 10 being the most, how important is it to you to start making these changes?

KASSANDRA: Definitely a 10.

PROVIDER: Good, I can tell this is very important to you and that is half the battle. On the same 0 to 10 scale, how confident are you that you can make these changes?

KASSANDRA: Probably 7.

PROVIDER: Ok that's great. You're almost at 10. What do you think it would take for that to move to an 8?

KASSANDRA: Well, if I can bring a healthy lunch to work instead of eating out, that would be a big deal.

PROVIDER: Great. I am confident you will be able to do that and I look forward to hearing about it.

Commentary. S – Kassandra reports concerns about her weight, a recent diagnosis of metabolic syndrome, and associated sadness and anxiety.

O – Her BMI is 26, in the overweight range, and her functional interview reveals poor eating habits and a lack of physical activity. On a 0–10 scale, she rated her motivation for weight management changes as 10 and her confidence as 7.

A – She seems motivated to lose weight and is open to suggestions. She experiences fatigue and has metabolic syndrome. Although she reports some sadness, self-consciousness, and anxiety associated with her weight, she does not meet any DSM-5 diagnoses. She demonstrated a dependent personality style.

P – Future sessions will concentrate on monitoring Kassandra's progress and addressing her pattern's role in maintaining her weight. The Three Factor Eating Questionnaire will be administered again in 12 weeks.

250 Application of Ultra-Brief Interventions

Case of Kassandra: Session 2

Background. In this session, the provider will review Kassandra's progress with her and discuss her physical activity and ways Kassandra can increase and monitor it.

> PROVIDER: Hi Kassandra. Why don't we start out by looking at the personal food journal that you have been keeping since the last time we met?
>
> KASSANDRA: Ok, here is the log I kept on the form you gave me.
>
> PROVIDER: Ok, I see you did well monitoring everything. This looks pretty comprehensive.
>
> KASSANDRA: It is. I wrote everything I ate in there.
>
> PROVIDER: So, I see you had some snacks several times a day and late at night. You wrote that you felt stressed out when you were eating?
>
> KASSANDRA: Yeah, I guess that's become my go-to thing, eating when I feel stressed. I did not realize how much I was doing that until I started keeping this log.
>
> PROVIDER: Yes, that's a major advantage of tracking these things. Sometimes we are unaware of our habits and things associated with them.
>
> KASSANDRA: Yes. I also did not realize how many calories some of these foods have. At some restaurants, they tell you how many calories there are. I never paid attention to that until I had to keep track. The other day I was having lunch out and I saw that my lunch basically had 700 calories. That is about half of my daily calories.
>
> PROVIDER: That is true. There is also a lot of hidden sodium and sugar in restaurant food.
>
> KASSANDRA: I couldn't believe it. I also realized some healthy foods have a lot of calories. My friend told me to eat more nuts because they're healthy but more than just a handful can start to add up.
>
> PROVIDER: Yes, taking a closer look at these things can be surprising but also a good first step in helping you gain control and make decisions about what you want to eat.
>
> KASSANDRA: That is true. Like they say, knowledge is power.
>
> PROVIDER: So, I also gave you the DIMES worksheet. How did you do with that?
>
> KASSANDRA: Well, I didn't eat so well recently but I did make a plan to start bringing my own lunch and changing my snacks up. The first thing

I wrote on the DIMES is that I was putting a lot of sugar and cream in my coffee. So, I decided to cut the sugar and eliminate the cream. I don't mind my coffee black but I need it a little sweet. So, I wrote I was putting three packets in a cup and I'm going to start putting just one packet.

PROVIDER: I think that's a great idea. I think you will find that some of these things just take a little getting used to and then they don't seem as drastic and overwhelming as they do at first.

KASSANDRA: So, next I wrote I love to have chips and popcorn while I am watching TV. So, I'm going to cut back on the popcorn since it isn't so bad calorie-wise. I found they make these small single serve bags of popcorn. I'm going to have those instead of the big bag. Then I'm eliminating the chips and substituting some fruit or a couple of rice cakes. Those are salty and satisfy that craving with a lot less fat and calories.

PROVIDER: It sounds like you have made great progress. I'm very proud of the effort and attention you have put into this. I was hoping today we could address adding in the physical exercise component.

KASSANDRA: Yes, I know that needs to be a part of it.

PROVIDER: Right. I suggest purchasing an activity monitor and aiming for 10,000 steps per day. There are a number of ways you can achieve that. Are there some exercises you would like to add into your routine?

KASSANDRA: Yes, I would like to take more walks. Walk with my dog. I think it would be nice to get some fresh air.

PROVIDER: That sounds like a great idea. There are also small things you can do to add that activity into your daily life as well. You can opt for the stairs instead of the elevator. You can park your car further away from where you are going so you have to walk. That can help you get in more steps during your day.

KASSANDRA: Yes, I can do both of those things.

PROVIDER: I'm glad to hear that. You have made great progress. On a scale from 0 to 10, where 0 is not at all and 10 is the most, how important is it for you to begin adding physical activity into your schedule?

KASSANDRA: Oh, I would say a 10. I really would like to lose this weight and start feeling better.

PROVIDER: That's really good. Now, on the same scale, from 0 to 10, how confident are you that you can add in the physical activity?

KASSANDRA: Um I think just a 6. I am scared that I will get tired and not want to do it anymore.

252 Application of Ultra-Brief Interventions

PROVIDER: That is a valid concern. And it is possible that you will feel tired at first, but the more you do, the more energy you will have and it will become easier.

KASSANDRA: That's true. It can become easier with time.

PROVIDER: And as you get stronger and healthier. What do you think it would take to move your confidence level from 6 to say 7 or 8?

KASSANDRA: Well, if I could take a couple of walks with my dog this week, I think that would help.

PROVIDER: Ok, great. I agree. So, the next time we meet, we can discuss your progress. Be sure to bring your food and activity logs.

Commentary. S – Kassandra reports she has been monitoring her food intake and understanding how many calories she is consuming.

O – Her functional assessment revealed she lacked physical activity.

A – On a scale from 0–10, her motivation for increasing physical activity was 10 and her confidence was 6.

P – Future sessions will concentrate on monitoring her progress and addressing her pattern's role in maintaining her weight. She will purchase an activity monitor and walk for 10,000 steps per day.

Case of Kassandra: Session 3

Background. Kassandra indicated that she lost 10 pounds within the last two weeks, and now weighs 142 pounds. Her average number of steps per day is 9,200 according to her activity monitor. In this session, the counselor will evaluate Kassandra's progress through reviewing her eating and physical activity logs.

PROVIDER: Hi Kassandra, how are you today?

KASSANDRA: I am feeling great. I lost ten pounds. I couldn't believe it.

PROVIDER: Well that's great news. You are pleased with that?

KASSANDRA: Oh yes. I feel better too.

PROVIDER: I am glad to hear that. For today's session, I was thinking we could look over your eating and activity logs to see how you have been progressing. How does that sound?

KASSANDRA: Good, I am eager to look them over with you, especially because I am seeing results.

PROVIDER: Ok, let's take a look at your eating log first.

Interventions for Weight Problems 253

KASSANDRA: Alright. I have been bringing my own lunch to work pretty much every day. I can't say I cut out all eating out though. We ate out three times in these last two weeks.

PROVIDER: Well, that's not much at all. I remember you were eating out a lot more. I also see you have some healthy snacks in here – carrot sticks, almonds, frozen grapes.

KASSANDRA: Yes, I've been eating some of those things in place of dessert or just when I'm hungry. Usually I would grab a candy bar or something like that.

PROVIDER: Yes, replacing some of those was one of your goals. On a scale from 0 to 10, how much do you feel you have met that goal?

KASSANDRA: I think about an 8.

PROVIDER: Wow, very high.

KASSANDRA: Yes. I did have some chocolate at work and a couple of things like that but nothing too bad.

PROVIDER: Great. One of your other goals was to add physical activity back into your schedule. You were hoping to start by walking with the dog twice a week. On a scale from 0 to 10, how much do you feel you have met that goal?

KASSANDRA: 10!

PROVIDER: That's wonderful.

KASSANDRA: Yes, I was able to walk the dog a few times a week both weeks. It was actually really nice. I got some fresh air and I got to see some of the neighbors. It was a nice change from being cooped up inside.

PROVIDER: That does sound lovely. How many steps per day did you average?

KASSANDRA: Well, according to my activity monitor, it's about 9,200 a day.

PROVIDER: That is a great accomplishment. And it seems you got an added bonus being able to connect with your neighbors. Are you proud of yourself for all the progress you have made?

KASSANDRA: Oh yes. I definitely am. There was part of me that thought I couldn't do it but I realized I am more capable at this than I thought.

PROVIDER: I'm glad to hear that because I am very pleased with your progress. Is there something you would enjoy as a reward for all your hard work?

KASSANDRA: Well, I have been wanting to get my nails done. It has been a while since I've done that.

PROVIDER: That sounds like a great idea. When could you do that?

KASSANDRA: I can go this weekend. Maybe my friend can go with me.

254 Application of Ultra-Brief Interventions

PROVIDER: That would be a well-deserved reward for you. So, given your weight loss, you are very close to your target weight. So, I suggest to continue with the reduced calories and the activity, as you have been.

KASSANDRA: Yes, I can do that.

PROVIDER: How important is it for you, on a scale of 0 to 10, to continue with your plan and self-monitoring?

KASSANDRA: Definitely a 10. Now that I have lost some weight, I want to continue.

PROVIDER: Great. On the same scale, how confident are you that you can continue?

KASSANDRA: Maybe 9. If I could lose another 3 pounds and be that much closer. I think that would help.

PROVIDER: I agree with you. Again, I think you're doing very well and I am pleased with your progress.

Commentary. S – Kassandra reports making progress with her eating and physical activity plan.

O – She has lost 10 pounds in two weeks. Her current weight is 142. Her average number of steps per day was 9,200.

A – She seems motivated to stick to her plan and has made progress towards achieving her goals. She has decreased her calorie intake and increased her physical activity.

P – Future sessions will concentrate on monitoring Kassandra's progress and addressing her pattern's role in maintaining her weight. I encouraged Kassandra to reward herself for her hard work as an incentive for continuing her weight loss plan.

Case of Kassandra: Session 4

Background. Kassandra has been compliant with her weight loss plan. She has lost an additional 4 pounds. Her current weight is 138. According to her activity monitor, her average number of steps per day is 9,500. During this session, the counselor will use Pattern-Focused Therapy to address her dependent personality style.

PROVIDER: Hi Kassandra, it is great to see you again.

KASSANDRA: Nice to see you too.

Interventions for Weight Problems **255**

PROVIDER: Why don't we start out by reviewing your progress with your eating log and physical activity log?

KASSANDRA: Ok.

PROVIDER: Let's start with the eating log. How did that go?

KASSANDRA: It went well, mostly. I did lose another 4 pounds.

PROVIDER: That is very good!

KASSANDRA: Yes, I am very happy with that. But you see I did have some extra snacks. It was a stressful week at work. Plus, I ate poorly at a work party.

PROVIDER: Ok, but I see you did continue to eat well the rest of the time. I notice you did continue to swap out several snacks with healthy options.

KASSANDRA: That is true.

PROVIDER: Ok, how about the physical activity log?

KASSANDRA: I did do well with that.

PROVIDER: Yes, I see you took several walks a week and you even went to the gym. How was that?

KASSANDRA: I did go to the gym. I didn't sign up but I went with my friend. She can get two free passes for a friend with her membership.

PROVIDER: That sounds like a great way to test it out.

KASSANDRA: Yeah, and we got in a little workout. I did the stationary bike. It was good.

PROVIDER: I am glad to see that you have not only been maintaining your hard work but that you have progressed even further.

KASSANDRA: Thank you. I am pleased with it.

PROVIDER: How many steps a day did you average?

KASSANDRA: My current average is 9,500 steps per day.

PROVIDER: Great! That is an improvement from before.

KASSANDRA: Yes, I am glad I kept it up and even increased it.

PROVIDER: So, remember we discussed your pattern of pleasing others even when it is at your own expense?

KASSANDRA: Yes, I do remember that.

PROVIDER: I was thinking we could address that pattern in today's session so we can help you manage certain situations more effectively. How does that sound?

KASSANDRA: Sounds good.

PROVIDER: Was there a situation recently where you saw that pattern come up?

KASSANDRA: Yes, of course it has to do with my eating.

PROVIDER: Ok, can you tell me what happened in detail?

256 Application of Ultra-Brief Interventions

KASSANDRA: Well, I have been doing pretty well with my eating like we went over. I've been bringing my own lunch. But then there's the work party I mentioned. Well we were planning an event for work and I was on the committee to plan the food. I suggested we order catering from this healthy place that makes great food. They have smoothies, really interesting sandwiches and salads, and some vegetarian dishes. Plus, they are affordable and really close to the office. So, I suggested that and everyone was like, "ew" and they all said they wanted pizza.

PROVIDER: Your idea does sound good. So, what ended up happening?

KASSANDRA: What ended up happening was that no one listened to me, as usual, and we got all this bad stuff. We had pizza, wings, fries, and dessert. And the worst part is, I ended up eating it because I didn't want to seem like I had a problem with it.

PROVIDER: Ok, so you were on the planning committee for this work event, and you suggested ordering from a nice healthy place you know and instead other people sort of took over and ordered some pretty unhealthy foods which you ended up eating. Is that right?

KASSANDRA: Yes.

PROVIDER: Is that all of what happened?

KASSANDRA: Yes.

PROVIDER: Can you tell me what you were thinking during the situation?

KASSANDRA: First I thought these people don't really care what I have to say.

PROVIDER: Ok, what else?

KASSANDRA: I thought maybe my idea was actually stupid. Who wants smoothies when they can have pizza?

PROVIDER: Ok, did you think anything else?

KASSANDRA: Yeah, I thought I better eat this food so they don't think I'm lame or a buzzkill or something.

PROVIDER: Ok, so your thoughts were that they didn't really want to hear what you had to say, that your idea was actually stupid, and that you better eat the food they ordered so they don't think you're lame. Did I get that right?

KASSANDRA: Yes.

PROVIDER: Good. What were some of your behaviors during the situation?

KASSANDRA: Well I kept quiet once they got to talking. I didn't speak up for what I wanted, which is typical. I just agreed with them.

PROVIDER: Ok, you kept quiet, you agreed with them. Was there anything else?

KASSANDRA: Yeah, I ate the unhealthy food.

PROVIDER: Ok, right. So, what were you hoping to get out of this situation?

Interventions for Weight Problems **257**

KASSANDRA: I wanted them to get what I wanted!

PROVIDER: Right. Do you think that is something that is within your control?

KASSANDRA: Well, I can't force them to do what I want. So, no.

PROVIDER: Ok, what is an outcome that you would have liked that is in your control?

KASSANDRA: Really I just wanted to eat healthier and not go back to eating bad foods.

PROVIDER: Ok, so what actually happened?

KASSANDRA: I did what I didn't want to do and I ate the unhealthy food.

PROVIDER: So, would you say you got what you wanted?

KASSANDRA: No I did not.

PROVIDER: Would you like to go over this situation again together to see how it may have turned out differently?

KASSANDRA: Yes, I would like that.

PROVIDER: Ok, so you said your first thought was that they didn't really want to hear what you had to say. Do you think that thought helped you or hurt you in getting what you wanted, which was to eat healthy?

KASSANDRA: It hurt.

PROVIDER: How so?

KASSANDRA: It made me feel really discouraged.

PROVIDER: What is a thought that you think may have been more helpful?

KASSANDRA: Well, they did ask me to be on the committee so they must want to know my opinion.

PROVIDER: That is true. You were invited on the committee. So how would that thought be more helpful?

KASSANDRA: I think it would have encouraged me to speak up.

PROVIDER: Ok, your second thought was that your idea was actually stupid. Did that thought hurt you or help you in eating healthy?

KASSANDRA: It hurt because again it was discouraging. I started to doubt myself.

PROVIDER: What would have been a more helpful thought?

KASSANDRA: Well, I've been to this place and I know it's good.

PROVIDER: How would that have helped you?

KASSANDRA: It would have made me more confident in my choice.

PROVIDER: I think so too. Your third thought was you have to eat the unhealthy food or people will think you're lame. Did that thought help you or hurt you in eating healthy?

KASSANDRA: It hurt. That was the worst one because that pressured me into eating the bad foods.

PROVIDER: So, what could have been a more helpful thought?

258 Application of Ultra-Brief Interventions

KASSANDRA: Um, it really doesn't matter what people think because this is my life and my personal goals.

PROVIDER: That's true. You are working on this for yourself. Now moving on to your behaviors. Your first behavior was that you kept quiet in the meeting and didn't speak up. Did that behavior help you or hurt you in eating healthy?

KASSANDRA: It hurt me because I didn't get to make a case for what I thought was a good idea.

PROVIDER: I agree. What do you think would have been more helpful?

KASSANDRA: Um, I think I should have persisted and told them why I thought my idea was good.

PROVIDER: Ok, how would that have been more helpful?

KASSANDRA: Well, maybe I could have convinced them. Or at least let them know that healthy eating is important to me.

PROVIDER: Ok, so telling them your point of view.

KASSANDRA: Yes.

PROVIDER: Your second behavior was that you agreed with them. Was that helpful or hurtful in getting what you wanted?

KASSANDRA: It hurt.

PROVIDER: How so?

KASSANDRA: Well, I sent the message that I agree with them when I actually don't. I misrepresented myself.

PROVIDER: What would have been a more helpful alternative?

KASSANDRA: I think if I made it clear that they can do what they want but I don't agree, then at least I could state my position. I think it would help me stick to what I really want.

PROVIDER: So, sort of a reminder to yourself as well?

KASSANDRA: Yes, exactly.

PROVIDER: Ok, then your last behavior was that you ate the unhealthy food. Did that help you or hurt you?

KASSANDRA: It hurt. Obviously, I did what I didn't want to do. I ate the unhealthy food.

PROVIDER: What would have been a better alternative?

KASSANDRA: I think even if they got the unhealthy food I could have brought my own. Or just ate before I got there. Then I could participate and not break my diet.

PROVIDER: I think that's a great idea. You have come up with some excellent alternatives in this session. Do those seem like things you can actually implement in your life?

KASSANDRA: Yes, I think so.

Interventions for Weight Problems **259**

PROVIDER: On a scale of 0 to 10, where 0 is not at all and 10 is the most, how important is it for you to change this pattern of pleasing others even when it hurts you?

KASSANDRA: I think an 8. I want to stick up for myself but of course I don't want to hurt or offend anyone.

PROVIDER: Yes, and I think you have found ways in this session that you can do just that. On the same 0 to 10 scale, how confident are you that you can change that pattern?

KASSANDRA: Probably a 6. I feel discouraged after what happened at the party.

PROVIDER: Ok, well that is still good, more than halfway there. What do you think it would take to bring that to a 7 or an 8?

KASSANDRA: I think if I can speak up for myself more when it's easier. Like it's easier to tell my kids we aren't having pizza for dinner than my coworkers.

PROVIDER: It can often be that way. I think you have done a great job today and overall. I'm looking forward to seeing you again and hearing about your progress.

Commentary. S – Kassandra reports progress with her eating and activity plans.

O – Kassandra has lost an additional 4 pounds, bringing her weight to 138. Her average number of steps per day was 9,500.

A – Kassandra seems motivated to stick to her plan and has made progress towards achieving her goals. She has decreased her calorie intake and increased her physical activity. She made some connections between her thoughts and behaviors and their consequences in pattern-focused therapy.

P – Future sessions will concentrate on monitoring Kassandra's progress and addressing her pattern's role in maintaining her weight.

Concluding Note

Weight problems are prevalent in all health care settings, with the rate of obesity in American adults at 39.8% between 2011–2014 (Hales et al., 2017). Weight problems can be difficult to treat because of the multitude of factors that contribute to and maintain them. Weight issues also contribute to other medical problems and are related to mental health disorders like depression and binge eating disorder. The first step for the behavioral health provider is to assess the client. This is accomplished through a functional assessment interview and use of standardized instruments. Primary interventions include psychoeducation, goal setting, motivational interviewing, and pattern-focused therapy. Because weight can be a triggering topic, the provider should focus on motivational interviewing skills like asking the client permission to discuss topics. Progress monitoring includes ongoing assessment of symptoms and goal achievement.

References

Centers for Disease Control and Prevention. (n.d.). About Adult BMI. Retrieved from www.cdc.gov/healthyweight/assessing/bmi/adult_bmi/index.html

Hales, C.M., Carrol, M.D., Fryar, C.D., & Ogden, C.L. (2017, October). Prevalence of obesity among adults and youth: United States, 2015-2016. National Center For Health Statistics. Retrieved from www.cdc.gov/nchs/products/databriefs/db288.htm

Lew, V., & Ghassemzadeh, S. (2018). SOAP Notes. Retrieved from www.ncbi.nlm.nih.gov/books/NBK482263/

Miller, W.R., & Rollnick, S. (2002). *Motivational interviewing: Preparing people for change* (2nd ed.). New York, NY: Guilford Press.

Schembre, S., Greene, G., & Melanson, K. (2009). Development and validation of a weight-related eating questionnaire. *Eating Behaviors, 10,* 119–124.

Ultra-Brief Interventions with Diabetes **10**

This chapter provides an overview of diabetes and how it commonly presents in integrated care and mental health care settings. The functional assessment addresses compliance with treatment plans and possible reasons for nonadherence. Brief interventions are reviewed, including self-monitoring and medication coordination. A case example is illustrated through four transcriptions with commentary.

Diabetes

Diabetes is a medical condition that occurs when the body does not make enough insulin to help cells process blood glucose, or blood sugar. Without the help of insulin, glucose stays in the blood and does not reach the cells, resulting in a number of symptoms and serious health concerns. There are three types of diabetes – Type 1, Type 2, and Gestational. In Type 1 diabetes, the immune system destroys insulin-producing cells in the pancreas. Though once thought to only appear in childhood, Type 1 diabetes can occur at any age. Type 2 diabetes is the most common and can appear at any age although it most commonly occurs in middle aged and older adults. Individuals with Type 2 diabetes cannot make or use insulin properly. Gestational diabetes occurs in pregnant women and typically goes away after birth but may lead to an increased possibility of developing Type 2 diabetes later in life (NIDDKD).

Diabetes is a common and costly problem in the United States. According to the CDC National Diabetes Statistic Report (2017), 30.3 million people in the US have diabetes, accounting for 9.4% of the population. The CDC

262 Application of Ultra-Brief Interventions

estimates that 7.2 million, or 23.8% of individuals with diabetes, are undiagnosed. Of those diagnosed with diabetes, roughly 5% have Type 1 diabetes, so it is likely that most cases presenting in integrated settings are individuals with Type 2 diabetes. Diabetes is associated with a number of comorbid conditions including cardiovascular disease and stroke (NDSR, 2017). Additionally, Golden et al. (2008) found a relationship between diabetes and depression. Type 2 diabetes was found to increase the risk of depression, and depression was found to increase the risk of Type 2 diabetes. Symptoms of diabetes include increased hunger and thirst, increased urination, fatigue, numbness and tingling in the extremities, vision loss, and sores that do not heal (NIDDKD). Diabetes-related complications can be fatal, and the disease was ranked as the seventh leading cause of death in the United States in 2015 (NDSR, 2017). It is estimated that the total cost of diabetes in the United States was $245 billion in 2012 (NDSR, 2017).

Managing diabetes requires a lifestyle change that includes eating habits, physical activity, and adherence to a medical routine. Individuals with diabetes must routinely check that their A1C levels are in a normal range as advised by their physician, and also check their blood pressure and cholesterol levels. Individuals are discouraged from smoking or use of tobacco products and include 30 minutes of physical activity into their daily routines. A diabetes meal plan should be high in fruits and vegetables, legumes, whole grains, and lean meats, and low on sugary or fatty foods. Additionally, it is important that individuals take any prescribed medication or recommended over-the-counter medications. This includes medication for diabetes and any related conditions like high cholesterol or aspirin to prevent heart attack or stroke (NIDDKD). Finally, clients with diabetes must check their blood glucose level daily. Target blood glucose levels are 80–130 mg/dL before a meal, and less than 180 mg/dL after a meal begins (NIDDKD). When blood glucose levels are too low, the individual can have life-threatening hypoglycemia.

Assessment and Screening Instruments

The assessment of diabetes in integrated settings includes an evaluation of the client's symptoms, adherence to medical plans, and related conditions. Clients who are resistant to medical treatment should be assessed for beliefs about their diagnosis or treatment that may be interfering with compliance.

Functional Assessment

The behavioral health provider will be able to obtain all relevant medical information including latest A1C levels, weight, history of hypoglycemia, and comorbid medical conditions, from the client's electronic health record. The assessment should focus on factors that inhibit effective treatment of diabetes. Factors may be behavioral, environmental, cognitive, or emotional. Behavioral factors include the client's adherence to a medical treatment plan, medication compliance, and other behaviors intended to manage diabetes. Environmental factors include family, friends, work, and social life. For example, a client may find it difficult to adhere to a diabetes-friendly meal plan if his social and family life centers around eating. Cognitive factors can include low self-efficacy, skepticism about the prescribed treatment plan, or worry about future outcomes. Emotional factors include depression, stress, and anxiety. Any of these factors can derail the client's treatment regimen and lead to adverse health effects. The behavioral health provider should determine which of these areas must be addressed with ultra-brief interventions. The Diabetes Distress Scale (DDS) can be used to assess the level of distress resulting from the diagnosis and treatment plan. The DDS assesses four areas: emotional burden, physician-related distress, regimen-related distress, and interpersonal distress. Any areas of distress indicated by the client should be further addressed during the interview. Eating behaviors, physical activity, and use of tobacco products and alcohol are also assessed. Questions are typically focused and closed-ended. Particularly with resistant clients, the provider should obtain the client's permission to discuss these topics. Table 10.1 outlines questions commonly asked in a functional assessment of diabetes.

Screening Instruments

The Diabetes Distress Scale. The Diabetes Distress Scale (DDS) is a 17-item instrument used to assess difficulties associated with living with diabetes. Each question is rated on a 6-point scale from 1–6 where 1 = not a problem, 2 = a slight problem, 3 = a moderate problem, 4 = a somewhat serious problem, 5 = a serious problem, and 6 = a very serious problem. Clients are asked to rate their diabetes-related problems for the past month. Questions explore potential client issues like feeling the physician is providing inadequate care; feeling angry, frustrated, tired, or like a failure; feeling that friends and family are not supportive enough; and worries about long-term complications. Self-defeating

Table 10.1 Functional Assessment of Diabetes

Eating and Weight	How would you describe your eating habits?
	What is the dietary plan the doctor gave you?
	Have you been able to follow the dietary plan the doctor gave you? If not, what interferes with following the dietary plan?
	How have you tried to manage your weight?
Physical Activity	How often do you exercise?
	How do you make sure your blood sugar is at a safe level during physical activity?
Tobacco Use	Do you smoke cigarettes or use any other tobacco products including electronic cigarettes? How much and how often?
Alcohol Use	How often do you drink alcohol? How much?
Behavioral Factors	Do you take your medications as prescribed?
	What interferes with you taking your medications?
	How often do you check your blood sugar?
	Do you know how often your doctor suggests that you check your blood sugar?
	When do you typically check your blood sugar?
	What interferes with you checking your blood sugar?
	Has your blood sugar ever become too low or too high? How did you respond to that?
	Have you noticed your blood sugar is lower or higher at different times? What is associated with that?
	How often do you attend your appointments with your physician?
	How often do you get an eye exam?
	How often do you check for sores or cracks in your feet?

Table 10.1 (Cont.)

Environmental Factors	How has your family supported your medication plan?
	How has your family supported your eating plan?
	Do your friends or family interfere with you maintaining your medication or eating plans?
	Have any work-related issues interfered with you maintaining your medication or eating plans?
Cognitive Factors	Emotions related to the treatment regimen, diagnosis, and physician, as indicated on the Diabetes Distress Scale, are explored further.
Emotional Factors	Thoughts related to the treatment regimen and diagnosis, as indicated on the Diabetes Distress Scale, are explored further.
Open-Ended Questions	Is there anything I have not asked you about that you would like me to know?

cognitions and behaviors are also assessed. The DDS yields a total score and four subscale scores: emotional burden, physician-related distress, regimen-related distress, and interpersonal distress. A score equal or greater than three on any subscale, or on the entire instrument, is considered to be worthy of clinical attention.

Ultra-Brief Interventions

Ultra-brief interventions for diabetes in integrated settings primarily include goal setting, psychoeducation, self-monitoring, and stimulus control. Clients often struggle to understand all the changes they must make to their lifestyle habits in order to effectively manage diabetes. Self-monitoring and stimulus control are easy interventions to help clients improve their eating habits and increase adherence to treatment regimens. Pattern-focused therapy is useful for correcting a client's maladaptive pattern that may serve to maintain the problem and interfere with treatment.

Goal Setting

The behavioral health provider should work with the client to set concrete dietary, exercise, and medical goals. Goals can include specific dietary plans, medication regimens, decreasing or eliminating problematic foods and behaviors, and getting blood sugar levels under control. Goals should be reasonable, achievable, and measurable and pertain to the client's medical needs. The client is asked to monitor progress towards these goals in a log or journal.

Psychoeducation

Though the client's primary care physician may have provided the client with information about eating plans and medication regimens, as well as the importance of properly managing diabetes, it is important that the behavioral health provider informs the client of how behavioral, cognitive, emotional, and environmental factors influence treatment. The counselor should address any areas of concern identified in the functional assessment and on the Diabetes Distress Scale. The client should be informed of the dangers of not checking blood sugar levels regularly and the importance of maintaining an eating and physical activity plan. Thoughts, emotions, and environmental triggers should be explored and the counselor can give psychoeducation accordingly. For example, a client with negative thoughts about the diabetes diagnosis and treatment regimen can be given information about how thoughts influence feelings and how to replace negative thoughts with more adaptive ones.

Motivational Interviewing

Behavioral health providers working with clients with diabetes often need to work with resistance. Motivational Interviewing is a helpful tool for client motivation to change a behavior. Clients with negative cognitions, low self-efficacy, and particularly resistant personalities may be more averse to change. The counselor must work with this resistance to increase motivation using the Motivational Interviewing OARS skill: Open-ended questions, Affirmations of the client, Reflective listening, and Summarizing (Miller & Rollnick, 2002). With the client's permission, the provider should ask about the pros and cons of adhering to the medical treatment plan and assess the client's willingness to comply using scaling questions.

Self-Monitoring

Self-monitoring is used to help the client become more aware of his/her behaviors. This technique can be employed in different ways with a client seeking help for diabetes. For example, the client can monitor the times in a day he/she checks blood sugar levels or takes medication. Monitoring can serve as a reminder and increase compliance. Monitoring can also help the client identify triggers and patterns that can then be managed through stimulus control.

Stimulus Control

Stimulus control helps clients become aware of the triggers associated with certain unwanted behaviors. Triggers can include thoughts, feelings, behaviors, and environmental factors, including other people. For example, a client with diabetes may find a trigger for smoking cigarettes, a contraindicated behavior, is stress from work. The client is encouraged to become more aware of these triggers by monitoring them and then identify ways to control the trigger. For example, the client who craves cigarettes when stressed over work, can employ relaxation techniques when noticing that trigger, rather than engaging in the unwanted behavior.

ABC Model

Negative beliefs about the client's diagnosis, treatment, and other diabetes-related concerns are addressed by teaching the client how thoughts affect emotions and behaviors. The ABC model teaches clients the relationship between activating events (A), the beliefs individuals have about those events (B), and the individual's behavioral and emotional consequences (C). The behavioral health provider teaches the client to identify negative or irrational beliefs about triggers and events, and how to change them to more effective thoughts.

Pattern-Focused Therapy

Pattern-focused therapy is useful to help diabetic clients address maladaptive patterns and personality dynamics that might be sabotaging how they manage their illness. Assisting the client in moving towards a more adaptive

268   Application of Ultra-Brief Interventions

pattern can help ensure the client makes and maintains necessary lifestyle changes. For example, in the exemplar Case of James, James' pattern of being distrustful of others in order to stay safe undermines his adherence to his diabetes treatment plan. He distrusts the doctor's suggestions and is hesitant to make lifestyle changes because he is skeptical of the doctor and the prescribed treatment. Moving towards a more adaptive pattern of feeling safe while trusting others helps James become more receptive to his treatment plan.

Progress Monitoring and Record Keeping

Progress Monitoring

Progress monitoring for diabetes includes continuous assessment of diabetes symptoms, compliance with medical treatment plans, and any associated conditions, like depression. Standardized instruments like the Diabetes Distress Scale should be administered prior to each session to monitor emotional and cognitive distress caused by the diagnosis. Clients can also self-report progress with diet, exercise, and medication plans using logs or journals.

Record Keeping

Efficient record keeping is especially important when treating a diagnosis like diabetes. Salient information must be transmitted efficiently between providers and other staff. The SOAP note is the recommended method for record keeping. SOAP stands for Subjective, Objective, Assessment, and Plan. The Subjective section includes the client's subjective experience, presenting symptoms, subjective ratings of intensity, and associated complaints. The Objective heading includes any objective ratings, like those obtained from standardized instruments such as the Diabetes Distress Scale, or medical exams. The Assessment heading includes whether the client meets criteria for a DSM-5 diagnosis as well as the client's personality style. Items in this category should be listed in order of importance. Finally, the Plan heading includes the next steps to be completed in the treatment plan, the plan for the next session, and any referrals, if necessary.

Interventions with Diabetes **269**

Case of James Transcriptions

Case of James: Session 1

Background. James is a 59-year-old Caucasian male who has been diagnosed with Type 2 diabetes. James is married and has grown children. He works as a floor manager in a corporate warehouse. He was referred to counseling by his primary care physician, Dr. Swift. Before meeting with James, the counselor reviewed his electronic health record. James was also administered the Diabetes Distress Scale (DDS-17). His score revealed moderate distress on three scales: Emotional Burden, Physician-related Distress, and Regimen-related Distress.

PROVIDER: Hi James, I am glad to see you since I always enjoy working with Dr. Swift's patients. I am going to start out by asking you a number of questions so I can get a better idea of how you have been doing. Is that ok with you?

JAMES: Sure, that sounds fine.

PROVIDER: Ok, good. Let's start out with some questions about how you manage your diabetes and then we will move on to some questions about how it has been affecting you. In a typical day, how often would you say you measure your blood sugar?

JAMES: Um, maybe twice a day.

PROVIDER: Ok, what usually prompts you to do that? Is there a set time?

JAMES: There's no set time. I usually do it if I'm not feeling so well or if it pops in my head and I remember to do it.

PROVIDER: Ok, how do you help yourself remember to check?

JAMES: Uh, I guess I don't really. It's just if it occurs to me.

PROVIDER: Have you noticed any patterns with your blood sugar during the week?

JAMES: Not really. I guess I should keep track a little more.

PROVIDER: Have you noticed how often your blood sugar levels run too high?

JAMES: Yeah, they tend to run high after I eat. About an hour and a half after I eat.

PROVIDER: What do you do when your blood sugar reading is too high?

JAMES: I take the medication my doctor gave me.

PROVIDER: Ok, how many times in a week do your blood sugar levels get too low?

270 Application of Ultra-Brief Interventions

JAMES: I would say a few times a week.

PROVIDER: Ok, a few times a week.

JAMES: That's correct.

PROVIDER: What do you do when your blood sugar gets too low?

JAMES: I eat something or drink some juice.

PROVIDER: Have you had any serious problems because of your blood sugars?

JAMES: Um, I get light-headed sometimes. Or I just feel generally unwell.

PROVIDER: Have you ever passed out?

JAMES: No.

PROVIDER: What medications are you taking?

JAMES: Just the ones the doctor prescribes me for the diabetes.

PROVIDER: What difficulties are you having taking your medications?

JAMES: Sometimes I forget. Or I feel I don't need it if I feel ok.

PROVIDER: Ok, so you sometimes take your medication as prescribed and sometimes don't. Is that correct?

JAMES: Yes.

PROVIDER: So, you mentioned sometimes you forget or feel like you are well enough not to need the medication. Is there anything else that gets in the way of you taking your medications?

JAMES: No, that's about it.

PROVIDER: What adjunct or alternative treatments do you use?

JAMES: None.

PROVIDER: Ok, thank you for being so cooperative. You have helped me get a better understanding of how you have been managing the diabetes.

JAMES: No problem.

PROVIDER: So, when you came in, you were given an instrument to assess how you have been feeling in regards to dealing with diabetes. I noticed you marked that you have some stress in some areas. Can you tell me more about that?

JAMES: Sure. It's really a lot of pressure to take care of the diabetes. I don't think the doctor understands how hard it is or has given me enough guidance. I'm not sure the doctor really cares that much. People don't realize how hard it is to stick to a routine like that.

PROVIDER: I understand it must be a tough adjustment, particularly if you don't feel heard.

JAMES: Yeah.

PROVIDER: Can you tell me how your mood has been lately?

JAMES: Um it's been ok. Sometimes low.

PROVIDER: Can you tell me more about what you mean by low?

Interventions with Diabetes **271**

JAMES: Sad, I guess. Isolated. I feel like I'm by myself in all this. No one I can really trust to understand what I'm dealing with.

PROVIDER: Are there other times you find it difficult to trust people?

JAMES: Yeah, I think so. A lot of people don't have the best intentions in mind, you know what I mean?

PROVIDER: You mean that some people may be out to hurt you or others?

JAMES: Some people are out to hurt you and some just don't care what happens to you.

PROVIDER: Do you fear people will abandon you?

JAMES: No, it's not that. I just like to know what people's motivations are before I think they're trustworthy.

PROVIDER: Would you say you have a pattern of doubting people's motivations in order to keep yourself safe?

JAMES: Yes, I believe that is accurate.

Background. James' responses indicate a paranoid style with a pattern of not trusting others in order to stay safe.

PROVIDER: I see. Do you think that could be related to how you feel about the doctor?

JAMES: Yeah, I think so. He hasn't shown me what I need to see yet.

PROVIDER: And what is that?

JAMES: That he really cares and is thinking about my best interest.

PROVIDER: I got it. Have you noticed that anything else has changed recently? Say your sleep patterns?

JAMES: No, not really.

PROVIDER: How have you been meeting life's daily demands?

JAMES: It's fine. Not falling behind on anything. Taking care of stuff.

PROVIDER: Ok, good. What about things you enjoy? How much have you been doing those?

JAMES: Um, that's kind of slipped. I just find I'm not that interested in stuff anymore.

PROVIDER: What is something you used to enjoy doing?

JAMES: I like to golf with my wife.

PROVIDER: Ok, that sounds nice. When was the last time you were able to get out and do that?

JAMES: Um, maybe three weeks ago.

PROVIDER: How did you find it?

JAMES: I did enjoy it. But I went back to feeling kind of low afterwards. It was a nice distraction but didn't last.

272 Application of Ultra-Brief Interventions

PROVIDER: Ok, well I'm glad to hear you were able to get at least some enjoyment out of it. Hopefully we can help you start feeling like your old self as we move along. Do you experience any worry or anxiety?

JAMES: Not much. I do worry about how my health is going to turn out. I try not to let myself think about it. Usually when I do, though, I start getting angry at the doctor. You know, if my treatment doesn't work out, that's really on him for not guiding me.

PROVIDER: So, you would like more guidance?

JAMES: Yes.

PROVIDER: How have the symptoms of stress and sadness you described affected your ability to stick with the diet and exercise routine?

JAMES: Well, I have a lot of resentment. So sometimes I say, "screw it, I'm going to eat something I know I shouldn't." I haven't been exercising much at all. Probably because I can't get motivated.

PROVIDER: You said you worry sometimes about your diabetes and the long-term outcome and possible consequences. For some people, that kind of thinking helps them to stay on track. For others, it gets in the way of managing their diabetes. Some people worry so much they avoid checking their blood sugar levels. How do you think it has affected you?

JAMES: Probably that I don't check enough and I'm not following the meal and exercise plan.

PROVIDER: Do you stick to the plan that schedules your eating and controls for things like carbohydrates and cholesterol?

JAMES: Somewhat.

PROVIDER: About what percentage of the time?

JAMES: About 60%.

PROVIDER: Well, that's good because you are more than halfway there. What strategies do you or have you used to manage your weight?

JAMES: Um, I've counted calories. I think if I stuck to the meal plan now, that would help.

PROVIDER: Do you use tobacco products?

JAMES: No.

PROVIDER: What about alcohol?

JAMES: I have a beer once in a while on the weekends. If there's a football game or something I'm watching with my friends or kids.

PROVIDER: Ok, and how good would you say you are about making and keeping your doctor's appointments? That includes things like eye exams.

JAMES: Mostly pretty good. I have to go to the eye doctor, actually. I've been putting that off.

Interventions with Diabetes **273**

PROVIDER: Ok. And when was the last time you checked your feet for any cracks or sores?

JAMES: Just last week. Everything was fine.

PROVIDER: What factors regarding your work, family, or social life interfere with your management of your diabetes?

JAMES: My work can get really busy. Sometimes I forget to check my blood sugar. Or I'll eat pizza or whatever they ordered for lunch if I'm busy and hungry.

PROVIDER: What factors do you find supportive?

JAMES: Well, my wife is pretty supportive. She is very worried about me. She makes sure I have the right food at home and stuff.

PROVIDER: That is very important. How supported do you feel by your wife?

JAMES: Very supported.

PROVIDER: What about the rest of your family?

JAMES: They're pretty good. They want me to be healthy.

PROVIDER: And what about your friends or coworkers?

JAMES: I don't really tell them my business.

PROVIDER: How might it help if you told them what you were dealing with?

JAMES: I don't know. Maybe they would cooperate. Not sure.

PROVIDER: Would you be willing to have your wife join you at some medical appointments as a source of support?

JAMES: Yeah, it might be good to have her there.

PROVIDER: Ok, good. So, your doctor recommended you lose some weight. But I would like to know what it is you would like to change in your life?

JAMES: I would like to weigh less. I'd like to be in a better mood. And it's probably important to stick to the eating routine and the blood sugar checks.

PROVIDER: Ok, so you would like to lose some weight, decrease some of your depression, and stick to your routine more?

JAMES: Yes.

PROVIDER: What about your energy levels?

JAMES: I would like them to be higher.

PROVIDER: So, physical activity is something that can help with the weight, mood, and energy level. What are your thoughts on adding that in?

JAMES: It's ok, I guess.

PROVIDER: How do you think managing your diabetes will improve your life?

274 Application of Ultra-Brief Interventions

JAMES: Well, maybe my mood will be better. My health will be better, obviously.

PROVIDER: Ok, well those sound like some great goals. I have heard you in this session, saying you feel overwhelmed by having to manage your diabetes and maybe even a little worried and depressed about it. I also understand you would like to know the doctor is invested in your treatment and you would like to be more heard.

JAMES: Yes, that is all true.

PROVIDER: Ok, I am glad I was able to understand your concerns because they are valid. I understand it can be challenging, overwhelming, and sometimes even discouraging to manage a chronic illness, especially when the routines can seem complicated at first. Your doctor has told you you should take your medication regularly, check your blood sugar more often, lose weight, increase your physical activity, and manage your stress better. That really is a lot to take on all at once, even though it is necessary.

JAMES: Yes, it's overwhelming.

PROVIDER: It clearly is. I understand how you are overwhelmed by it. Unfortunately, that has been leading you to not do some of the things you need to do in order to prevent any negative future complications. The good thing is, many of those complications can be prevented by sticking to the self-care routine. There are many things you can control that will help you stay healthy.

JAMES: Yeah, it's nice to know there are things I can control.

PROVIDER: Yes, that's sort of a different way of looking at it. Rather than all these rules imposed on you, you can see them as aspects you can control so you can take control of the diabetes. From everything you have told me today, I think I have a better understanding of where you are coming from and what you are dealing with. So, I have a few specific suggestions for you. First, is to increase how often you check your blood sugar. That will help you do what you need to do to keep your blood sugar from getting too high or too low. Keeping the blood sugar in a good range will help stave off some unwanted consequences of diabetes. Another suggestion is to start sticking to the diet and exercise plan the doctor gave you. This will also help you gain control and prevent some negative consequences so you can stay healthy. How do those recommendations sound to you?

JAMES: They sound ok. I'm not really sure I can do all that. Or that I need to do it so strictly.

PROVIDER: What questions do you have for me?

JAMES: None, really.

Interventions with Diabetes **275**

PROVIDER: Ok. On a scale of 0 to 10, where 0 is not at all and 10 is the most, how important is it to you to make these changes to manage your diabetes better?

JAMES: I would say 6.

PROVIDER: Ok so that's pretty important. On the same scale, how confident are you that you can make these changes?

JAMES: Um, probably 5.

PROVIDER: Ok, so halfway there. What do you think it would take to move that to 6 or 7?

JAMES: If I could stick to the diet a little better.

PROVIDER: Ok, and that is very reasonable. I would like to help you reach those goals you have set for yourself. Would you like to continue working with me on this?

JAMES: Sure.

PROVIDER: Ok, I look forward to seeing you again.

Commentary. S – James reports compliance with his diabetes management plan has been poor. He needs to lose weight and take other steps to manage his diabetes.

O – His functional assessment reveals he is not checking his blood sugar regularly enough, and is not maintaining his diet and exercise plan. His scores on the Diabetes Distress Scale (DDS-17) revealed moderate distress on three scales: Emotional Burden, Physician-related Distress, and Regimen-related Distress.

A – James appears to have some mild symptoms of depression as well as some worry. He does not meet any DSM-5 diagnoses. He seems to be in the contemplation stage of change. On a scale from 0–10, his motivation was 6 and his confidence was 5. He seems to find his diabetes diagnosis as emotionally burdensome, and is distressed by having to follow a regimen. He also expresses some skepticism about his doctor's level of care, understanding, and commitment. He displayed a paranoid personality style with a pattern of not trusting others in order to stay safe.

P – Future sessions will focus on increasing his motivation for change, monitoring his progress in meeting his goals, and addressing his pattern's role in his diabetes management. The Diabetes Distress Scale will be administered at each session.

276 Application of Ultra-Brief Interventions

Case of James: Session 2

Background. James was administered the Diabetes Distress Scale (DDS-17). His score revealed moderate distress on three scales: Emotional Burden, Physician-related Distress, and Regimen-related Distress. Because James' assessment revealed he is in the contemplation stage of change, the counselor will focus this session on motivational interviewing, specifying his goals, and introducing self-monitoring.

PROVIDER: Hi James, I am glad you are here. Last time we met, you mentioned you had some concerns about whether you wanted to or could make some of those changes to manage your diabetes. Is that correct?

JAMES: Yes, that's right.

PROVIDER: I would like to begin our session today by discussing some of those concerns so I can help you to get what you need from our sessions, ok?

JAMES: Ok.

PROVIDER: So, can you tell me what you think about some of those suggestions we came up with?

JAMES: Yeah, well the first thing that comes to mind is the physical activity. I'm not sure I need to be as strict about the exercise as the doctor says I need to be.

PROVIDER: Ok, so you are unsure about the doctor's suggestions.

JAMES: Yeah. I know exercise is important but I also have a hard time with it. I don't need to bust my knee or something and then I'll be in worse shape than when I started.

PROVIDER: Oh, ok, would it be alright if we discussed this more?

JAMES: Sure, that's fine.

PROVIDER: Great. How long has it been since you have exercised?

JAMES: Oh, I can't remember. Probably 10–15 years.

PROVIDER: Ok, so you have some concerns about getting started again and potentially injuring yourself.

JAMES: Yes. My wife agrees with me on that, but she still wants me to exercise.

PROVIDER: So, your wife feels you would benefit from exercise?

JAMES: Yeah, and she worries a lot about my health.

PROVIDER: Has she expressed to you why she believes exercise is so valuable for you?

Interventions with Diabetes   **277**

JAMES: Yes, she says I will lose some weight and have more energy.

PROVIDER: Right. Losing weight was one of your goals?

JAMES: Yeah.

PROVIDER: Are there reasons that you believe exercise may be valuable for you?

JAMES: Well, yes. I do agree with my wife it will help me lose weight. I don't know how much energy it's going to give me but I would also like to be in better shape. More muscle.

PROVIDER: Ok, so there are some benefits to exercise that you would really like but you have some worry as to whether you will obtain all those benefits.

JAMES: Yeah. I mean I would hate to put in all that effort and find out it doesn't work.

PROVIDER: You feel uncertain about how well it will work.

JAMES: Yes, just like the eating plan.

PROVIDER: Can you tell me more about that?

JAMES: Like, I don't know if staying on that strict regimen is really going to do anything. I'm worried I won't lose weight or get healthier. My blood sugar seems to do what it wants when it wants to.

PROVIDER: It sounds like you are concerned your efforts won't give you that much control over your diabetes?

JAMES: No, I can stick to the regimen if I wanted to. It's more that I don't know if the regimen will have that much of an effect on the diabetes.

PROVIDER: Ok, and you said your blood sugar seems to do what it wants. Are there any things that have helped with it?

JAMES: Well if I don't eat anything too crazy, and if I make sure to check my blood sugar.

PROVIDER: Ok so checking your blood sugar is important to you?

JAMES: Yes. I want to stick to that goal of checking regularly.

PROVIDER: Ok, that's great. And you said if you don't eat anything too crazy. Can you give me an example of something you might eat that would be bad for your blood sugar?

JAMES: Donuts. I have a weakness for those and I know they aren't good.

PROVIDER: So, you have managed your diet somewhat and you found that it has helped you control your blood sugar?

JAMES: Yes, it has.

PROVIDER: What other factors have helped you control your blood sugar?

JAMES: Um, I guess that's it.

278 Application of Ultra-Brief Interventions

PROVIDER: Do you think that dietary changes similar to the ones you have made will help you to control your diabetes even more effectively?

JAMES: I think they might.

PROVIDER: Where can you get ideas for changes like the one you have already made?

JAMES: I think I can maybe take some suggestions off the diet plan the doctor gave me. I'm just not sure that what the doctor told me to do was prescribed just for me, you know? He seems to just tell everyone with diabetes the same thing. The same diet and exercise. How do I know that's what's going to work for me? What would you think if it was you?

PROVIDER: I understand your concern. It seems to you that the diet and exercise plan prescribed to you by the doctor was sort of generic?

JAMES: Exactly.

PROVIDER: And you would like to be assured that the plan is one that will work for you?

JAMES: Yes.

PROVIDER: Do you think that lack of assurance from the doctor is related to your concerns that the plan will not help?

JAMES: Yes, absolutely. I don't like doctors that want to waste your time making you do something that then doesn't even help. Or it might help but it might not be right for you.

PROVIDER: How might things be different if the doctor explained why he prescribed you that plan?

JAMES: I think I would feel more confident that it would work, and more confident in him and what he tells me.

PROVIDER: That is very important to you?

JAMES: Yes.

PROVIDER: So, if we could set up a meeting with your doctor so he can answer these questions for you, how willing would you be to set some specific goals to work on? Say on a scale from 0 to 10 where 0 is not at all and 10 is the most.

JAMES: Well, if it was a specific plan then probably 8 or 9. I'm not saying I can't do it. I just want to do what's right for me.

PROVIDER: Yes, I believe you can do it as well and I agree it is important to get what you need. I will set up a meeting with the doctor so you can ask any questions you have and I can attend that meeting with you if you like.

JAMES: That would be good.

Interventions with Diabetes **279**

Commentary. James' primary concern was that the doctor was not listening to him and therefore not prescribing a tailored plan for James. The counselor set up a three-way meeting with James, the primary care physician, and the counselor, in which James was able to ask specific questions. He found out that the plan prescribed to him was prescribed with his A1C values, weight, and age in mind. James was satisfied with this and agreed to set specific diabetes goals.

PROVIDER: Ok James. I am giving you this worksheet to specify your diabetes goals. Why don't we fill it out together?

JAMES: Ok.

PROVIDER: Ok, so first we need to schedule your blood sugar checks. Scheduling it will help you do it more often and more regularly. Dr. Swift told you to check your blood sugar three times a day. His suggestion was before breakfast, lunch, and dinner. Do you agree with that recommendation?

JAMES: Yes, I think that's fine.

PROVIDER: What are some ways you can remind yourself?

JAMES: Well, it's good that it's paired with the meals. I can also put a reminder on my phone or a post-it note on my desk at work.

PROVIDER: Ok, good. Next is your physical activity. The suggestion was to start with three times per week. Which days would you prefer to exercise?

JAMES: Monday, Wednesday, and Friday works for me.

PROVIDER: Great. What time of day will you be exercising?

JAMES: I get up early so in the morning. Between 7 and 8 am.

PROVIDER: And have you thought of some exercises you would like to try?

JAMES: I would like to walk and ride my bike. I never do that anymore.

PROVIDER: Where can you complete those activities?

JAMES: In my neighborhood.

PROVIDER: Ok, so you don't have to go very far?

JAMES: No.

PROVIDER: What are some things that can help you meet that goal?

JAMES: If my wife walked with me. Also, I will need a new pair of sneakers.

PROVIDER: Ok so some new sneakers and some company. That sounds good. Moving on to your eating, I know the doctor gave you a routine diet to follow but it's ok to start slowly. What are two changes you can achieve within the next two to four weeks?

JAMES: Um, making sure I eat breakfast, and not eating whatever they have lying around at work.

280 Application of Ultra-Brief Interventions

PROVIDER: Ok, good. What can help you achieve these goals?

JAMES: For the first one, I can have my wife help me with some breakfast ideas. And for the second one, I can bring my own food and snacks to work.

PROVIDER: So, if you get hungry at work you don't have to turn to foods that might not be so healthy for you?

JAMES: Right.

PROVIDER: Are there any additional goals you would like to set to help with your diabetes management?

JAMES: Just taking my medication.

PROVIDER: What can help you with that goal? I agree it is important.

JAMES: I have been thinking about getting one of those pill boxes that lets you sort it out by the day. Because sometimes I can't remember if I took my pills.

PROVIDER: I think that's a great idea. You have set some great goals that are specifically tailored to you and I really believe they will help you manage your diabetes. An important part of this process is monitoring yourself so you know you are sticking to your plan. I am going to give you this form to monitor your eating, activity, medication, and blood sugar readings. Just like the pill box, this can help you remember what you have done and what you still need to do. Eventually many of these things will become habits and easier to complete.

JAMES: Ok, I can do that.

PROVIDER: Good. On a scale of 0 to 10, where 0 is not at all and 10 is the most, how important is it for you to start implementing this specific plan?

JAMES: I would say 8 or 9. I mean the plan might change but with this plan I want to give it a try.

PROVIDER: Alright. On the same scale from 0 to 10, how confident are you that you can start implementing this plan?

JAMES: Probably 9 or 10.

PROVIDER: Ok, great! I'm glad to hear you are confident. Next time we meet, we will review your progress.

Commentary. S – James reports an increased motivation for change.

O – His specific goals include times to check his blood sugar, an exercise plan, and dietary changes. His score on the Diabetes Distress Scale (DDS-17) revealed moderate distress on three scales: Emotional Burden, Physician-related Distress, and Regimen-related Distress.

Interventions with Diabetes **281**

A – He seems skeptical of his doctor's prescription and was able to understand why the doctor made specific recommendations after a meeting with him. He appears to be in the preparation/action stages of change. He was able to increase his motivation and confidence. On a scale from 0–10, his motivation was between 8 and 9 and his confidence was between 9 and 10.

P – Future sessions will focus on monitoring his progress in meeting his goals, and addressing his pattern's role in his diabetes management. The Diabetes Distress Scale will be administered at each session.

Case of James: Session 3

Background. James was administered the Diabetes Distress Scale (DDS-17). His score revealed mild distress on three scales: Emotional Burden, Physician-related Distress, and Regimen-related Distress. This session will focus on teaching James behavioral analysis and stimulus control techniques.

PROVIDER: Hi James. Why don't we start by reviewing your progress with your diabetes goals?

JAMES: Ok.

PROVIDER: Let us start by looking at your goal sheet. Your first goal was to test your blood sugar three times a day. On a scale from 0 to 10, how much would you say you have met that goal?

JAMES: I would say 8.

PROVIDER: Ok, that's good. That is an improvement from last time. How did the log help you stay on track?

JAMES: It mostly helped remind me if I missed one. I would look at it and see I didn't fill it out.

PROVIDER: Ok. Let's go to your dietary goals. How much would you say you completed that goal?

JAMES: Probably 5. I did struggle with that.

PROVIDER: Ok, so reviewing your dietary log I see you ate a number of snacks outside of your meals and some were not part of your plan.

JAMES: Yeah it can be difficult.

PROVIDER: I understand it must be. How have you been coming along with the physical exercise?

JAMES: I definitely did better but I didn't meet the goal.

PROVIDER: Ok, how much would you say you have met that goal? You were going to exercise three times a week.

JAMES: 4.

282 Application of Ultra-Brief Interventions

PROVIDER: That's ok. It's still a change from your previous level of exercise.

JAMES: Yeah hopefully that can get better.

PROVIDER: Ok, and your final goal was to stick to your medication plan. How has that been working out?

JAMES: That's probably an 8. I'm doing better.

PROVIDER: I really think you are doing better overall. The last time we met, you expressed some concerns about your diabetes diagnosis and about your treatment regimen. I would like to address those concerns today since they seem to be quite stressful for you. How does that sound?

JAMES: That sounds good. It is stressful and gets me down sometimes to think about it.

PROVIDER: Can you remind me what were some of the concerns you had about the diabetes diagnosis?

JAMES: Just that it's something I have to live with now. You know? It's not fair. It's just going to compromise my life.

PROVIDER: I understand how thoughts like that can be distressing. What were some of your other concerns?

JAMES: Um, that the treatment stuff wouldn't work and that it's a pain to stick to.

PROVIDER: What do you do to help yourself stick to the treatment regimen?

JAMES: I just try to remind myself that I would get really sick without it.

PROVIDER: What else do you worry about in terms of your treatment?

JAMES: I know I was able to ask the doctor some questions but they never seem to spend that much time with you. I'm never sure if he's really listening to me.

PROVIDER: So, you are not confident that the doctor listens to your concerns?

JAMES: Right.

PROVIDER: Does the doctor ever tell you things that you don't understand?

JAMES: Not really.

PROVIDER: Were you able to get answers to your questions?

JAMES: Yes, I finally did.

PROVIDER: I can imagine it would be quite frustrating to not feel heard by the doctor. I know that this diagnosis has caused you to make a lot of changes in your life and I understand how it must be daunting to stick to a regimen, especially when you have some doubts about whether or not you will get better. Unfortunately, these things, themselves, have become barriers to your treatment. I would like to work with you to make it easier for you to cope and easier to stick to your treatment.

Interventions with Diabetes **283**

JAMES: Ok, I would like to be able to deal with it better.

PROVIDER: Of all the things we discussed about your treatment, are there any that are particularly causing you distress that you would like to work on?

JAMES: Yes. Probably that feeling that my life is over, like I have to deal with this disease for the rest of my life now.

PROVIDER: Yes, ok.

JAMES: And then the worry that no matter what I do, it's probably going to get worse. It's a chronic disease, so what can I really do that matters?

PROVIDER: Ok, I agree those are some difficult thoughts to deal with. Would you like to work together to address those concerns?

JAMES: Yes, sure.

PROVIDER: Ok, what I'm going to introduce you to is called the ABC model. This can help you make some of those behavioral changes in order to maintain a healthier lifestyle. In this model, the A stands for activating event – things that occur before a behavior. The B stands for the belief about the activating event, and the C stands for the consequences.

JAMES: Ok, I think I understand that.

PROVIDER: So, let me give you an example. Is there anything about your treatment that particularly irks you?

JAMES: Yes, I hate that I have to watch everything I eat.

PROVIDER: Ok, good. That is a good example. When would you say you think about that?

JAMES: Um, usually if we are having a big family dinner or something. Then I realize I can't eat something.

PROVIDER: So, realizing you can't eat something would be the "A" in this example. It is the activating event. Realizing there is something you would like to eat that you cannot.

JAMES: Right. That is very upsetting.

PROVIDER: Ok, so when you realize you can't eat something, what are your thoughts on that?

JAMES: I usually think this sucks, why do I have to live with this? I will never be able to enjoy my life again.

PROVIDER: Ok, so thinking "I will never be able to enjoy my life again," how do you feel when you think that?

JAMES: Um, depressed, of course. I feel awful.

PROVIDER: So that thought "I will never be able to enjoy my life again," that is the B, the belief. And the feeling of sadness and depression is the C, the consequence. Can you see how it isn't the A, not being able to

284 Application of Ultra-Brief Interventions

eat something, that causes you to feel depressed, but the B, the belief about what that means about your life, that leads to that?

JAMES: Yes, that makes a lot of sense. I can't believe I did not realize that before.

PROVIDER: Yes, it doesn't always occur to us. I am going to give you this handout where you can track your ABCs. I want you to write the date then the activating event, all your beliefs about it, and then all the consequences.

JAMES: Ok, I will do that.

PROVIDER: I would like to introduce you to another technique that will help you control some of your behaviors. Behaviors like eating unhealthy food are really a culmination of other factors. What I mean is there are specific triggers for your behaviors – a feeling, a smell, a sight, etc. – that usually come before our behaviors. What triggers do you find you have when it comes to eating?

JAMES: Um, feeling stressed. Smelling something like if someone brings in food to work. Sometimes if I'm home alone or if I'm doing something where I'm not thinking like watching TV.

PROVIDER: Ok, so you have some behavior triggers. That includes watching TV. Then there are some environmental triggers like smelling someone's food. You listed an emotional trigger, feeling stressed, and a trigger that involves other people – being home alone. That is a great start. I am glad to hear that you are aware of these triggers. There may be some triggers you are not aware of yet. The more you can become aware of your triggers, the more you can learn to manage them. My suggestion is that you start monitoring what you eat outside of meals. Start out this week by not making any changes. We want to monitor what you are eating so we can get more information about your triggers. I'm going to give you this form for monitoring behavioral triggers. When you eat something outside of regular meals, or get the urge to, log it on the form. How does that sound?

JAMES: Yeah that sounds good. It might be helpful to know what all those triggers are.

PROVIDER: Good, I am glad you agree. You have done a great job. We can also begin helping you control some of those triggers you already listed. Is that something you would like to do?

JAMES: Yes.

PROVIDER: So, which of those triggers do you feel are in your control?

Interventions with Diabetes **285**

JAMES: Um, feeling stressed, watching TV.

PROVIDER: Ok, so feeling stressed and watching TV.

JAMES: Yes.

PROVIDER: Let's come up with a plan to avoid some of those triggers so we can help you control your eating. Let's start with the first one, feeling stressed. What is something you can do about that?

JAMES: Well I get stressed, but I don't have to eat to deal with it.

PROVIDER: What else can you do when you notice yourself getting stressed?

JAMES: I can go for a walk or do something to calm down. Just realize I don't have to eat because I'm stressed.

PROVIDER: Ok, what about the other trigger, watching TV?

JAMES: So, it's really if I get bored, which I do when I'm watching TV sometimes.

PROVIDER: Ok, so boredom is more of the trigger. What can you do about that?

JAMES: I can do something I like. Call someone. Recognize that I can do something other than eat.

PROVIDER: Ok, so substituting some behaviors.

JAMES: Yes.

PROVIDER: Good. You have come up with some great ideas and I think this plan will help you control your triggers and your eating. We can review your progress next time I see you.

Commentary. S – James reports his self-defeating thoughts and low stimulus control contribute to his struggle to maintain the diabetes regimen.

O – His specific goals include times to check his blood sugar, an exercise plan, and dietary changes. His score on the Diabetes Distress Scale (DDS-17) revealed mild distress on three scales: Emotional Burden, Physician-related Distress, and Regimen-related Distress.

A – He appears to have somewhat improved with his diabetes management. His assessment reveals distress about his diagnosis and following his prescribed regimen. He was able to identify some of his triggers to eating and generate realistic alternatives.

P – Future sessions will focus on monitoring James' progress in meeting his goals, and addressing his pattern's role in his diabetes management. The Diabetes Distress Scale will be administered at each session.

286 Application of Ultra-Brief Interventions

Case of James: Session 4

Background. James was administered the Diabetes Distress Scale (DDS-17). His score revealed moderate distress on three scales: Emotional Burden, Physician-related Distress, and Regimen-related Distress. This session will focus on monitoring James' progress and addressing his pattern using Pattern-Focused Therapy.

PROVIDER: Hi James, why don't we start out today by reviewing your diet and exercise logs as well as your diabetes goals.

JAMES: Ok.

PROVIDER: Let us start by looking at your goal sheet. Your first goal was to test your blood sugar three times a day. On a scale from 0 to 10, how much would you say you have met that goal?

JAMES: I would say 10.

PROVIDER: Ok, that's great news. I see your blood sugar chart shows you checked three times a day and were able to stick to the times suggested. How did the log help you stay on track?

JAMES: Well, it reminded me if I did forget and helped me be accountable.

PROVIDER: Good. Now let's move on to your dietary goals. How much would you say you completed that goal?

JAMES: Probably 7. I did struggle with that.

PROVIDER: Ok, so reviewing your dietary log I do see you skipped breakfast a couple of times and you ate some foods that are not recommended for you.

JAMES: Yeah. It's the same with the physical exercise. I did it somewhat but not all the way.

PROVIDER: Ok, how much would you say you have met that goal? You were going to exercise three times a week.

JAMES: Probably 6.

PROVIDER: That's ok. What has been going on in regards to the exercise?

JAMES: Um, it's just hard to get motivated sometimes.

PROVIDER: Ok, and your final goal was to stick to your medication plan. How has that been working out?

JAMES: That's probably an 8. I think the meds aren't very healthy for me. You know how doctors prescribe things that have a million side effects and just make you worse.

PROVIDER: Is that what you feel is happening in your case?

Interventions with Diabetes   **287**

JAMES: Maybe. I don't know.

PROVIDER: Ok, well remember we discussed your pattern of not trusting others in order to stay safe. How do you think that might be related here?

JAMES: Maybe it is. I am skeptical a lot.

PROVIDER: I was hoping we could discuss that pattern in more depth in this session. Did any situation like that come up recently?

JAMES: Um, yeah at work.

PROVIDER: Can you tell me what happened?

JAMES: Sure. My boss offered to send me to a special training program. It's something I actually want to do but I thought it was odd that he was asking me to go out of the blue. He didn't mention a possible promotion or anything. I started to wonder if he was trying to set me up or get me to move to a different division somehow and this was just his ploy. So, I said no and he ended up sending someone else.

PROVIDER: Ok, so your boss offered to send you to a training program that you have wanted to attend but you declined because you were skeptical of his motives and he ended up sending someone else. Is that all of what happened?

JAMES: Yes.

PROVIDER: Ok, what were some of the thoughts going through your head during this situation?

JAMES: I thought this is odd.

PROVIDER: Ok, what else?

JAMES: Um, I thought he must have something he's hiding from me.

PROVIDER: Ok, anything else?

JAMES: I thought he might be trying to get rid of me.

PROVIDER: Ok, so your thoughts were this is odd, he must be hiding something from me, and he might be trying to get rid of me. Is that correct?

JAMES: Yes.

PROVIDER: Ok, then what were some of your behaviors. What did you do?

JAMES: Well first I told him I would think about it and I quickly left his office.

PROVIDER: So, you abruptly left?

JAMES: Yes.

PROVIDER: What else did you do?

JAMES: I looked up all this stuff online like how do you know when your boss has it in for you.

PROVIDER: So, you looked stuff up to try to figure out his motives?

JAMES: Yes, that's correct. Then I told him I couldn't go.

288 Application of Ultra-Brief Interventions

PROVIDER: Ok, so you left abruptly, looked up online if your boss is conspiring against you, and told him you couldn't go. Did I get that right?

JAMES: Yes, that's right.

PROVIDER: What were you hoping to get out of this situation?

JAMES: I wanted to know what my boss was thinking.

PROVIDER: That would be nice. Do you think that is something under your control?

JAMES: No, I can't read minds.

PROVIDER: Then what would have been an outcome that you could control?

JAMES: Honestly, I would have liked to go to the training program. It's a great training to have on your resume no matter what.

PROVIDER: Ok. Then what actually happened?

JAMES: Someone else is going in place of me.

PROVIDER: So, did you get what you wanted?

JAMES: Absolutely not.

PROVIDER: Alright. Then would you like to look at this situation again and see how it may have turned out differently?

JAMES: Sure.

PROVIDER: Ok, so you said your first thought was 'this is odd' when your boss asked you to go to the program. Do you think that thought hurt you or helped you in getting your desired outcome of going to the training?

JAMES: It hurt.

PROVIDER: How so?

JAMES: Well it got me feeling suspicious.

PROVIDER: Ok, what would have been an alternative thought to help you get to the training?

JAMES: Maybe this is a nice surprise.

PROVIDER: Right, since it is something you wanted to do?

JAMES: Yes.

PROVIDER: And how would that thought be helpful?

JAMES: It would have changed my outlook from suspicious to excited.

PROVIDER: Good. Your second thought was he's hiding something from me. Did that thought help you or hurt you in going to the training?

JAMES: It hurt. That's what made me start feeling really nervous.

PROVIDER: Ok, what would have been a more helpful thought?

JAMES: If I thought my boss is trying to help me. It's a good training.

PROVIDER: Ok, so my boss is trying to help me. How would that thought have helped you get what you wanted?

Interventions with Diabetes   **289**

JAMES: I wouldn't have been so fixated on what he was thinking and maybe just let myself go.

PROVIDER: Good. Now, your third thought was he's trying to get rid of me. Did that thought help you or hurt you in getting what you wanted, which was to attend the training?

JAMES: It hurt. It's more of the same, just being suspicious and nervous.

PROVIDER: Ok, what would have been a more helpful thought?

JAMES: If I thought maybe he's trying to do a good thing for me. That would have put me in a good mood and helped me focus on what I wanted.

PROVIDER: So, focus on what you wanted and think he's trying to do a good thing for you.

JAMES: Yes.

PROVIDER: Good. Now moving on to your behaviors. Your first behavior was that you left his office abruptly. Did that behavior help you or hurt you in getting what you wanted, to go to the training?

JAMES: It hurt.

PROVIDER: How so?

JAMES: It's just not the response your boss wants to see. I don't think he liked that. And it didn't convey what I really wanted.

PROVIDER: Right, it might have sent the wrong message.

JAMES: Yes.

PROVIDER: What would have been a more helpful behavior?

JAMES: If I didn't leave. Maybe asked him some more questions about the training and his plans for me.

PROVIDER: Ok, then you could get some more information too.

JAMES: Yes.

PROVIDER: Your second behavior was to look up some stuff online to try to figure out your boss's motives. Did that behavior help you or hurt you in going to the training program?

JAMES: It hurt. By that point, I became totally distracted and absorbed in what I was thinking. It got me totally off track.

PROVIDER: I can understand that. What would have been a more helpful behavior?

JAMES: If I just didn't do that. Didn't get myself all worked up.

PROVIDER: Alright. Now how did your third behavior, turning down the training, help you or hurt you?

JAMES: Obviously, it hurt me because I said no to the thing I wanted to do.

PROVIDER: Yes, then what would have been more helpful?

JAMES: If I had said yes.

290 Application of Ultra-Brief Interventions

PROVIDER: Right. Well, you have generated some excellent alternatives today. Do these seem like realistic changes you can make in your daily life?

JAMES: Yes, I think so.

PROVIDER: Ok, so on a scale from 0 to 10, where 0 is not at all and 10 is the most, how important is it for you to change this pattern of not trusting others in order to stay safe?

JAMES: I would say 10 because it's not actually helping me.

PROVIDER: Right. I am glad it is that important to you. On the same 0 to 10 scale, how confident are you that you can change this pattern?

JAMES: Probably 7.

PROVIDER: Good, that is pretty confident. What would it take to move that to an 8 or a 9?

JAMES: I think if I can practice some of those self-analysis things we learned in the last session.

PROVIDER: I agree with that.

Commentary. S – James reports his pattern of not trusting others impedes his diabetes management as his skepticism of the doctor's prescription keeps him from following his plan.

O – His specific goals include times to check his blood sugar, an exercise plan, and dietary changes. His score on the Diabetes Distress Scale (DDS-17) revealed moderate distress on three scales: Emotional Burden, Physician-related Distress, and Regimen-related Distress.

A – He appears to have improved with his diabetes management. He has made the most progress with his goal of checking his blood sugar regularly but he still lags behind in diet, exercise, and medication management, despite improvements in these areas. His assessment reveals distress about his diagnosis and following his prescribed regimen. He has some mild symptoms of depression and displays a paranoid personality style.

P – Future sessions will focus on monitoring James' progress in meeting his goals, and addressing his pattern's role in his diabetes management. The Diabetes Distress Scale will be administered at each session.

Concluding Note

Diabetes is a prevalent problem in integrated care settings, and can lead to a number of related medical and psychological issues. Because of the number of potentially fatal consequences of this diagnosis, treating it effectively requires client motivation and compliance with treatment plans. Unfortunately, many clients are resistant because of environmental factors or cognitions about their diagnosis or treatment. The behavioral health provider should assess the client's symptoms, compliance with treatment plans, and related emotions, cognitions, and behaviors. Interventions include goal setting, motivational interviewing, self-monitoring, stimulus control, and the ABC model.

References

Golden, S.H., Lazo, M., Carnethon, M., Bertoni, A.G., Schreiner, P.J., Diez Roux, A.V., Lee, H.B., & Lyketsos, C. (2008, June). Examining a bidirectional association between depressive symptoms and diabetes. *Journal of American Medical Association.* 299(23), 2751-2759.

Lew, V., & Ghassemzadeh, S. (2018). SOAP Notes. Retrieved from www.ncbi.nlm.nih.gov/books/NBK482263/

Miller, W.R., & Rollnick, S. (2002). *Motivational interviewing: Preparing people for change* (2nd ed.). New York, NY: Guilford Press.

National Center for Chronic Disease Prevention and Health Promotion. (2017). National diabetes statistics report, 2017: Estimates of diabetes and its burden in the United States. Retrieved from www.cdc.gov/diabetes/pdfs/data/statistics/national-diabetes-statistics-report.pdf

National Institute of Diabetes and Digestive and Kidney Diseases. (n.d.). www.niddk.nih.gov

Appendix A
Screening Instruments

The following is a list of screening instruments referenced in this text. All instruments can be accessed from the URL links provided below. Copies of some instruments are also included here. These have the notation: [**FULL COPY**].

294 Appendix A

Columbia Suicide Severity Rating Scale (C-SSRS) [FULL COPY]

COLUMBIA-SUICIDE SEVERITY RATING SCALE (C-SSRS)

Risk Assessment (Lifeline crisis center version)

NATIONAL SUICIDE PREVENTION LIFELINE

Columbia-Suicide Severity Rating Scale (C-SSRS)

The **Columbia-Suicide Severity Rating Scale (C-SSRS)** is a questionnaire used for suicide assessment developed by multiple institutions, including Columbia University, with NIMH support. The scale is evidence-supported and is part of a national and international public health initiative involving the assessment of suicidality. Available in 103 different languages, the scale has been successfully implemented across many settings, including schools, college campuses, military, fire departments, the justice system, primary care and for scientific research.

Several versions of the C-CCRS have been developed for clinical practice. The **Risk Assessment** version is three pages long, with the initial page focusing on a checklist of all risk and protective factors that may apply. This page is designed to be completed following the client (caller) interview. The next two pages make up the formal assessment. The C-SSRS Risk Assessment is intended to help establish a person's immediate risk of suicide and is used in acute care settings.

In order to make the C-SSRS Risk Assessment available to all Lifeline centers, the Lifeline collaborated with Kelly Posner, Ph.D., Director at the Center for Suicide Risk Assessment at Columbia University/New York State Psychiatric Institute to slightly adjust the first checklist page to meet the Lifeline's Risk Assessment Standards. The following components were added: helplessness, feeling trapped, and engaged with phone worker.

The approved version of the C-SSRS Risk Assessment follows. This is one recommended option to consider as a risk assessment tool for your center. If applied, it is intended to be followed exactly according to the instructions and cannot be altered.

Training is available and recommended (though not required for clinical or center practice) before administering the C-SSRS. Training can be administered through a 30-minute interactive slide presentation followed by a question-answer session or using a DVD of the presentation. Those completing the training are then certified to administer the C-SSRS and can receive a certificate, which is valid for two years.

To complete the C-SSRS Training for Clinical Practice, visit http://c-ssrs.trainingcampus.net/

For more general information, go to http://cssrs.columbia.edu/

Any other related questions, contact Gillian Murphy at gmurphy@mhaofnyc.org.

296 Appendix A

COLUMBIA-SUICIDE SEVERITY RATING SCALE
(C-SSRS)

Posner, Brent, Lucas, Gould, Stanley, Brown, Fisher, Zelazny, Burke, Oquendo, & Mann
© 2008 The Research Foundation for Mental Hygiene, Inc.

RISK ASSESSMENT VERSION
(* elements added with permission for Lifeline centers)

Instructions: Check all risk and protective factors that apply. To be completed following the patient interview, review of medical record(s) and/or consultation with family members and/or other professionals.

Suicidal and Self-Injury Behavior (Past week)		Clinical Status (Recent)	
☐ Actual suicide attempt	☐ Lifetime	☐	Hopelessness
☐ Interrupted attempt	☐ Lifetime	☐	Helplessness*
☐ Aborted attempt	☐ Lifetime	☐	Feeling Trapped*
☐ Other preparatory acts to kill self	☐ Lifetime	☐	Major depressive episode
☐ Self-injury behavior w/o suicide intent	☐ Lifetime	☐	Mixed affective episode
Suicide Ideation (Most Severe in Past Week)		☐	Command hallucinations to hurt self
☐ Wish to be dead		☐	Highly impulsive behavior
☐ Suicidal thoughts		☐	Substance abuse or dependence
☐ Suicidal thoughts with method (but without specific plan or intent to act)		☐	Agitation or severe anxiety
☐ Suicidal intent (without specific plan)		☐	Perceived burden on family or others
☐ Suicidal intent with specific plan		☐	Chronic physical pain or other acute medical problem (AIDS, COPD, cancer, etc.)
Activating Events (Recent)		☐	Homicidal ideation
☐ Recent loss or other significant negative event		☐	Aggressive behavior towards others
Describe:		☐	Method for suicide available (gun, pills, etc.)
		☐	Refuses or feels unable to agree to safety plan
☐ Pending incarceration or homelessness		☐	Sexual abuse (lifetime)
☐ Current or pending isolation or feeling alone		☐	Family history of suicide (lifetime)
Treatment History		**Protective Factors (Recent)**	
☐ Previous psychiatric diagnoses and treatments		☐	Identifies reasons for living
☐ Hopeless or dissatisfied with treatment		☐	Responsibility to family or others; living with family
☐ Noncompliant with treatment		☐	Supportive social network or family
☐ Not receiving treatment		☐	Fear of death or dying due to pain and suffering
Other Risk Factors		☐	Belief that suicide is immoral, high spirituality
☐		☐	Engaged in work or school
		☐	Engaged with Phone Worker *
		Other Protective Factors	
		☐	

Describe any suicidal, self-injury or aggressive behavior (include dates):

Lifeline Version 1/2014

Screening Instruments 297

SUICIDAL IDEATION				
Ask questions 1 and 2. If both are negative, proceed to "Suicidal Behavior" section. If the answer to question 2 is "yes", ask questions 3, 4 and 5. If the answer to question 1 and/or 2 is "yes", complete "Intensity of Ideation" section below.			**Lifetime: Time He/She Felt Most Suicidal**	**Past 1 month**
1. Wish to be Dead Subject endorses thoughts about a wish to be dead or not alive anymore, or wish to fall asleep and not wake up. *Have you wished you were dead or wished you could go to sleep and not wake up?* If yes, describe:			Yes ☐ No ☐	Yes ☐ No ☐
2. Non-Specific Active Suicidal Thoughts General non-specific thoughts of wanting to end one's life/commit suicide (e.g., "I've thought about killing myself") without thoughts of ways to kill oneself/associated methods, intent, or plan during the assessment period. *Have you actually had any thoughts of killing yourself?* If yes, describe:			Yes ☐ No ☐	Yes ☐ No ☐
3. Active Suicidal Ideation with Any Methods (Not Plan) without Intent to Act Subject endorses thoughts of suicide and has thought of at least one method during the assessment period. This is different than a specific plan with time, place or method details worked out (e.g., thought of method to kill self but not a specific plan). Includes person who would say, "I thought about taking an overdose but I never made a specific plan as to when, where or how I would actually do it...and I would never go through with it." *Have you been thinking about how you might do this?* If yes, describe:			Yes ☐ No ☐	Yes ☐ No ☐
4. Active Suicidal Ideation with Some Intent to Act, without Specific Plan Active suicidal thoughts of killing oneself and subject reports having some intent to act on such thoughts, as opposed to "I have the thoughts but I definitely will not do anything about them." *Have you had these thoughts and had some intention of acting on them?* If yes, describe:			Yes ☐ No ☐	Yes ☐ No ☐
5. Active Suicidal Ideation with Specific Plan and Intent Thoughts of killing oneself with details of plan fully or partially worked out and subject has some intent to carry it out. *Have you started to work out or worked out the details of how to kill yourself? Do you intend to carry out this plan?* If yes, describe:			Yes ☐ No ☐	Yes ☐ No ☐

INTENSITY OF IDEATION		
The following features should be rated with respect to the most severe type of ideation (I.e., 1-5 from above, with 1 being the least severe and 5 being the most severe). Ask about time he/she was feeling the most suicidal.		

Lifetime - *Most Severe Ideation:* _____ _____
                     Type # (1-5)   *Description of Ideation*
 Recent - *Most Severe Ideation:* _____ _____
                     Type # (1-5)   *Description of Ideation*
	Most Severe	Most Severe

Frequency *How many times have you had these thoughts?* (1) Less than once a week (2) Once a week (3) 2-5 times in week (4) Daily or almost daily (5) Many times each day	——	——
Duration *When you have the thoughts how long do they last?* (1) Fleeting - few seconds or minutes (4) 4-8 hours/most of day (2) Less than 1 hour/some of the time (5) More than 8 hours/persistent or continuous (3) 1-4 hours/a lot of time	——	——
Controllability *Could/can you stop thinking about killing yourself or wanting to die if you want to?* (1) Easily able to control thoughts (4) Can control thoughts with a lot of difficulty (2) Can control thoughts with little difficulty (5) Unable to control thoughts (3) Can control thoughts with some difficulty (0) Does not attempt to control thoughts	——	——
Deterrents *Are there things - anyone or anything (e.g., family, religion, pain of death) - that stopped you from wanting to die or acting on thoughts of committing suicide?* (1) Deterrents definitely stopped you from attempting suicide (4) Deterrents most likely did not stop you (2) Deterrents probably stopped you (5) Deterrents definitely did not stop you (3) Uncertain that deterrents stopped you (0) Does not apply	——	——

Reasons for Ideation *What sort of reasons did you have for thinking about wanting to die or killing yourself? Was it to end the pain or stop the way you were feeling (in other words you couldn't go on living with this pain or how you were feeling) or was it to get attention, revenge or a reaction from others? Or both?*
 (1) Completely to get attention, revenge or a reaction from others   (4) Mostly to end or stop the pain (you couldn't go on
 (2) Mostly to get attention, revenge or a reaction from others   living with the pain or how you were feeling)
 (3) Equally to get attention, revenge or a reaction from others   (5) Completely to end or stop the pain (you couldn't go on
      and to end/stop the pain   living with the pain or how you were feeling)
                (0) Does not apply
	——	——

© 2008 Research Foundation for Mental Hygiene, Inc.   C-SSRS—Lifetime Recent - Clinical (Version 1/14/09)   Page 1 of 2

298 Appendix A

SUICIDAL BEHAVIOR (Check all that apply, so long as these are separate events; must ask about all types)	Lifetime	Past 3 months

Actual Attempt:
A potentially self-injurious act committed with at least some wish to die, *as a result of act.* Behavior was in part thought of as method to kill oneself. Intent does not have to be 100%. If there is *any* intent/desire to die associated with the act, then it can be considered an actual suicide attempt. *There does not have to be any injury or harm,* just the potential for injury or harm. If person pulls trigger while gun is in mouth but gun is broken so no injury results, this is considered an attempt.
Inferring Intent: Even if an individual denies intent/wish to die, it may be inferred clinically from the behavior or circumstances. For example, a highly lethal act that is clearly not an accident so no other intent but suicide can be inferred (e.g., gunshot to head, jumping from window of a high floor/story). Also, if someone denies intent to die, but they thought that what they did could be lethal, intent may be inferred.
Have you made a suicide attempt?
Have you done anything to harm yourself?
Have you done anything dangerous where you could have died?
   What did you do?
   Did you_____ as a way to end your life?
   Did you want to die (even a little) when you_____?
   Were you trying to end your life when you _____?
   Or Did you think it was possible you could have died from_____?
Or did you do it purely for other reasons / without ANY intention of killing yourself (like to relieve stress, feel better, get sympathy, or get something else to happen)? (Self-Injurious Behavior without suicidal intent)
If yes, describe:
Has subject engaged in Non-Suicidal Self-Injurious Behavior?
	Yes No
	☐ ☐
	
	Total # of
	Attempts
	_____
	
	Yes No
	☐ ☐
		Yes No
		☐ ☐
		
		Total # of
		Attempts
		
		Yes No
		☐ ☐

Interrupted Attempt: When the person is interrupted (by an outside circumstance) from starting the potentially self-injurious act *(if not for that, actual attempt would have occurred).* Overdose: Person has pills in hand but is stopped from ingesting. Once they ingest any pills, this becomes an attempt rather than an interrupted attempt. Shooting: Person has gun pointed toward self, gun is taken away by someone else, or is somehow prevented from pulling trigger. Once they pull the trigger, even if the gun fails to fire, it is an attempt. Jumping: Person is poised to jump, is grabbed and taken down from ledge. Hanging: Person has noose around neck but has not yet started to hang - is stopped from doing so. *Has there been a time when you started to do something to end your life but someone or something stopped you before you actually did anything?* If yes, describe:	Yes No ☐ ☐ Total # of interrupted _____	Yes No ☐ ☐ Total # of interrupted _____
Aborted or Self-Interrupted Attempt: When person begins to take steps toward making a suicide attempt, but stops themselves before they actually have engaged in any self-destructive behavior. Examples are similar to interrupted attempts, except that the individual stops him/herself, instead of being stopped by something else. *Has there been a time when you started to do something to try to end your life but you stopped yourself before you actually did anything?* If yes, describe:	Yes No ☐ ☐ Total # of aborted or self- interrupted	Yes No ☐ ☐ Total # of aborted or self- interrupted
Preparatory Acts or Behavior: Acts or preparation towards imminently making a suicide attempt. This can include anything beyond a verbalization or thought, such as assembling a specific method (e.g., buying pills, purchasing a gun) or preparing for one's death by suicide (e.g., giving things away, writing a suicide note). *Have you taken any steps towards making a suicide attempt or preparing to kill yourself (such as collecting pills, getting a gun, giving valuables away or writing a suicide note)?* If yes, describe:	Yes No ☐ ☐ Total # of preparatory acts	Yes No ☐ ☐ Total # of preparatory acts

	Most Recent Attempt Date:	Most Lethal Attempt Date:	Initial/First Attempt Date:
Actual Lethality/Medical Damage: 0. No physical damage or very minor physical damage (e.g., surface scratches). 1. Minor physical damage (e.g., lethargic speech; first-degree burns; mild bleeding; sprains). 2. Moderate physical damage; medical attention needed (e.g., conscious but sleepy, somewhat responsive; second-degree burns; bleeding of major vessel). 3. Moderately severe physical damage; *medical* hospitalization and likely intensive care required (e.g., comatose with reflexes intact; third-degree burns less than 20% of body; extensive blood loss but can recover; major fractures). 4. Severe physical damage; *medical* hospitalization with intensive care required (e.g., comatose without reflexes; third-degree burns over 20% of body; extensive blood loss with unstable vital signs; major damage to a vital area). 5. Death	Enter Code _____	Enter Code _____	Enter Code _____
Potential Lethality: Only Answer if Actual Lethality=0 Likely lethality of actual attempt if no medical damage (the following examples, while having no actual medical damage, had potential for very serious lethality: put gun in mouth and pulled the trigger but gun fails to fire so no medical damage; laying on train tracks with oncoming train but pulled away before run over). 0 = Behavior not likely to result in injury 1 = Behavior likely to result in injury but not likely to cause death 2 = Behavior likely to result in death despite available medical care	Enter Code _____	Enter Code _____	Enter Code _____

© 2008 Research Foundation for Mental Hygiene, Inc.   C-SSRS—Lifetime Recent - Clinical (Version 1/14/09)

This instrument assesses suicide intent and risk.

http://cssrs.columbia.edu/the-columbia-scale-c-ssrs/cssrs-for-communities-and-healthcare/#filter=.general-use.english

Current Opioid Misuse Measure (COMM)

This instrument measures misuse of prescribed opioid medications and effects on daily functioning and social relationships.
   http://mytopcare.org/wp-content/uploads/2013/05/COMM.pdf

Drug Abuse Screening Tool (DAST)

This instrument assesses abuse of illegal and prescription drugs.
   www.integration.samhsa.gov/clinical-practice/screening-tools

The Diabetes Distress Scale (DDS)[FULL COPY]

This instrument assesses distress associated with diabetes diagnosis and treatment plans.
   https://behavioraldiabetes.org/scales-and-measures/

DDS

DIRECTIONS: Living with diabetes can sometimes be tough. There may be many problems and hassles concerning diabetes and they can vary greatly in severity. Problems may range from minor hassles to major life difficulties. Listed below are 17 potential problem areas that people with diabetes may experience. Consider the degree to which each of the 17 items may have distressed or bothered you DURING THE PAST MONTH and circle the appropriate number.

Please note that we are asking you to indicate the degree to which each item may be bothering you in your life, NOT whether the item is merely true for you. If you feel that a particular item is not a bother or a problem for you, you would circle "1". If it is very bothersome to you, you might circle "6".

	Not A Problem	A Slight Problem	A Moderate Problem	Somewhat Serious Problem	A Serious Problem	A Very Serious Problem
1. Feeling that diabetes is taking up too much of my mental and physical energy every day.	1	2	3	4	5	6
2. Feeling that my doctor doesn't know enough about diabetes and diabetes care.	1	2	3	4	5	6
3. Not feeling confident in my day-to-day ability to manage diabetes.	1	2	3	4	5	6
4. Feeling angry, scared and/or depressed when I think about living with diabetes.	1	2	3	4	5	6
5. Feeling that my doctor doesn't give me clear enough directions on how to manage my diabetes.	1	2	3	4	5	6
6. Feeling that I am not testing my blood sugars frequently enough.	1	2	3	4	5	6
7. Feeling that I will end up with serious long-term complications, no matter what I do.	1	2	3	4	5	6
8. Feeling that I am often failing with my diabetes routine.	1	2	3	4	5	6

	Not A Problem	A Slight Problem	A Moderate Problem	Somewhat Serious Problem	A Serious Problem	A Very Serious Problem
9. Feeling that friends or family are not supportive enough of self-care efforts (e.g., planning activities that conflict with my schedule, encouraging me to eat the "wrong" foods).	1	2	3	4	5	6
10. Feeling that diabetes controls my life.	1	2	3	4	5	6
11. Feeling that my doctor doesn't take my concerns seriously enough.	1	2	3	4	5	6
12. Feeling that I am not sticking closely enough to a good meal plan.	1	2	3	4	5	6
13. Feeling that friends or family don't appreciate how difficult living with diabetes can be.	1	2	3	4	5	6
14. Feeling overwhelmed by the demands of living with diabetes.	1	2	3	4	5	6
15. Feeling that I don't have a doctor who I can see regularly enough about my diabetes.	1	2	3	4	5	6
16. Not feeling motivated to keep up my diabetes self-management.	1	2	3	4	5	6
17. Feeling that friends or family don't give me the emotional support that I would like.	1	2	3	4	5	6

302 Appendix A

Generalized Anxiety-7 (GAD-7)[FULL COPY]

This instrument assesses symptoms of Generalized Anxiety Disorder.
www.phqscreeners.com/sites/g/files/g10016261/f/201412/GAD-7_
English.pdf

GAD-7

Over the <u>last 2 weeks</u>, how often have you been bothered by the following problems? *(Use "✔" to indicate your answer)*	Not at all	Several days	More than half the days	Nearly every day
1. Feeling nervous, anxious or on edge	0	1	2	3
2. Not being able to stop or control worrying	0	1	2	3
3. Worrying too much about different things	0	1	2	3
4. Trouble relaxing	0	1	2	3
5. Being so restless that it is hard to sit still	0	1	2	3
6. Becoming easily annoyed or irritable	0	1	2	3
7. Feeling afraid as if something awful might happen	0	1	2	3

(For office coding: Total Score T____ = ____ + ____ + ____)

Developed by Drs. Robert L. Spitzer, Janet B.W. Williams, Kurt Kroenke and colleagues, with an educational grant from Pfizer Inc. No permission required to reproduce, translate, display or distribute.

Insomnia Severity Index (ISI)

This instrument assesses severity of insomnia and effects on functioning.
www.ons.org/sites/default/files/InsomniaSeverityIndex_ISI.pdf

PCL-5 PTSD Checklist

This instrument assesses symptoms of Posttraumatic Stress Disorder.
www.ptsd.va.gov/professional/assessment/documents/PCL-5_Standard.
pdf

PEG Pain Scale

This instrument assesses levels of physical pain.
http://mytopcare.org/wp-content/uploads/2013/06/PEG-pain-screening-tool.pdf

Patient Health Questionnaire-9 (PHQ-9)[FULL COPY]

This instrument assesses symptoms of Major Depressive Disorder.
www.phqscreeners.com/sites/g/files/g10049256/f/201412/PHQ-9_
English.pdf

304 Appendix A

PATIENT HEALTH QUESTIONNAIRE-9 (PHQ-9)

Over the <u>last 2 weeks</u>, how often have you been bothered by any of the following problems? *(Use "✔" to indicate your answer)*	Not at all	Several days	More than half the days	Nearly every day
1. Little interest or pleasure in doing things	0	1	2	3
2. Feeling down, depressed, or hopeless	0	1	2	3
3. Trouble falling or staying asleep, or sleeping too much	0	1	2	3
4. Feeling tired or having little energy	0	1	2	3
5. Poor appetite or overeating	0	1	2	3
6. Feeling bad about yourself — or that you are a failure or have let yourself or your family down	0	1	2	3
7. Trouble concentrating on things, such as reading the newspaper or watching television	0	1	2	3
8. Moving or speaking so slowly that other people could have noticed? Or the opposite — being so fidgety or restless that you have been moving around a lot more than usual	0	1	2	3
9. Thoughts that you would be better off dead or of hurting yourself in some way	0	1	2	3

FOR OFFICE CODING __0__ + _____ + _____ + _____

=Total Score: _____

If you checked off <u>any</u> problems, how <u>difficult</u> have these problems made it for you to do your work, take care of things at home, or get along with other people?

Not difficult at all	Somewhat difficult	Very difficult	Extremely difficult
☐	☐	☐	☐

Developed by Drs. Robert L. Spitzer, Janet B.W. Williams, Kurt Kroenke and colleagues, with an educational grant from Pfizer Inc. No permission required to reproduce, translate, display or distribute.

Screening Instruments **305**

Weight-Related Eating Questionnaire

This instrument assesses eating habits associated with being overweight.
www.ncbi.nlm.nih.gov/pubmed/19447354

DDS1.1 SCORING SHEET

INSTRUCTIONS FOR SCORING:

The DDS17 yields a total diabetes distress score plus four subscale scores, each addressing a different kind of distress.[1] To score, simply sum the patient's responses to the appropriate items and divide by the number of items in that scale.

Current research[2] suggests that a mean item score 2.0–2.9 should be considered 'moderate distress,' and a mean item score $\geq$ 3.0 should be considered 'high distress.' Current research also indicates that associations between DDS scores and behavioral management and biological variables (e.g., A1C) occur with DDS scores of $\geq$ 2.0. Clinicians may consider moderate or high distress worthy of clinical attention, depending on the clinical context.

We also suggest reviewing the patient's responses across all items, regardless of mean item scores. It may be helpful to inquire further or to begin a conversation about any single item scored $\geq$ 3.

306 Appendix A

Total DDS Score:	a. Sum of 17 item scores.	_____
	b. Divide by:	____17_____
	c. Mean item score:	_____
	Moderate distress or greater? (mean item score > 2)	yes__ no__
A. Emotional Burden:	a. Sum of 5 items (1, 4, 7, 10, 14)	_____
	b. Divide by:	_____5_____
	c. Mean item score:	_____
	Moderate distress or greater? (mean item score > 2)	yes__ no__
B. Physician Distress:	a. Sum of 4 items (2, 5, 11, 15)	_____
	b. Divide by:	_____4_____
	c. Mean item score:	_____
	Moderate distress or greater? (mean item score > 2)	yes__ no__
C. Regimen Distress:	a. Sum of 5 items (6, 8, 3, 12, 16)	_____
	b. Divide by:	_____5_____
	c. Mean item score:	_____
	Moderate distress or greater? (mean item score > 2)	yes__ no__
D. Interpersonal Distress:	a. Sum of 3 items (9, 13, 17)	_____
	b. Divide by:	_____3_____
	c. Mean item score:	_____
	Moderate distress or greater? (mean item score $\geq$ 2)	yes__ no__

1. Polonsky, W.H., Fisher, L., Earles, J., Dudl, R.J., Lees, J., Mullan, J.T., & Jackson, R. (2005). Assessing psychosocial distress in diabetes: Development of the Diabetes Distress Scale. *Diabetes Care*, 28, 626–631.

2. Fisher, L., Hessler, D.M., Polonsky, W.H., & Mullan, J. (2012). When is diabetes distress clinically meaningful? Establishing cut-points for the Diabetes Distress Scale. *Diabetes Care*, 35, 259–264.

References

Bardhoshi, G., Erford, B.T., Duncan, K., Dummett, B., Falco, M., Deferio, K., & Kraft, J. (2016, April). Choosing assessment instruments for posttraumatic stress disorder screening and outcome research. *Journal of Counseling and Development*, 94, 184–194.

James, B.L., Loken, E., Roe, L.S., & Rolls, B.J. (2017). The Weight-Related Eating Questionnaire offers a concise alternative to the Three-Factor Eating Questionnaire for measuring eating behaviors related to weight loss. *Appetite*, 116, 108–114.

Krebs, E.E., Lorenz, K.A., Bair, M.J., Damush, T.M., Wu, J., Sutherland, J.M., ... Kroenke, K. (2009). Development and initial validation of the PEG, a three-item scale assessing pain intensity and interference. *Journal of General Internal Medicine*, 26(6), 733–738.

McKnight, T.L. (2006). *Obesity management in family practice*. New York, NY: Springer.

Na, P.J., Yaramala, S.R., Kim, J.A., Kim, H., Goes, F., Zandi, P.P., ... Bobo, W.V. (2018, May). The PHQ-9 Item 9 based screening for suicide risk: A validation study of the Patient Health Questionnaire (PHQ-9) Item 9 with the Columbia Suicide Severity Rating Scale (C-SSRS). *Journal of Affective Disorders*, 232, 34–40.

National Heart, Lung, and Blood Institute. (n.d.). Body Mass Index Table. Retrieved from www.nhlbi.nih.gov/health/educational/lose_wt/BMI/bmi_tbl.pdf

Rutter, L.A., & Brown, T.A. (2017). Psychometric properties of the Generalized Anxiety Disorder Scale-7 (GAD-7) in outpatients with anxiety and mood disorders. *Journal of Psychopathology and Behavioral Assessment*, 39, 140–146.

Schembre, S., Greene, G., & Melanson, K. (2009). Development and validation of a weight-related eating questionnaire. *Eating Behaviors*, 10, 119–124.

Smith, S.M., Paillard, F., McKeown, A., Burke, L.B., Edwards, R.R., Katz, N.P., ... Dworkin, R.H. (2015, May). Instruments to identify prescription medication misuse, abuse, and related events in clinical trials: An ACTTION systematic review. *The Journal of Pain*, 16(5), 389–411.

Wong, M.L., Lau, K.N.T., Espie, C.A., Luik, A.I., Kyle, S.D., & Lau, E.Y.Y. (2017). Psychometric properties of the Sleep Condition Indicator and Insomnia Severity Index in the evaluation of insomnia disorder. *Sleep Medicine*, 33, 76–81.

Appendix B
Treatment Handouts

The 22 treatment handouts that follow are commonly used in integrated care settings and increasingly in mental health settings to provide patients/clients with additional information about their condition and its treatment.

1. ABC Worksheet
2. Adjectives for Describing Pain
3. Behavioral Health Triggers Worksheet
4. Common Pain Myths
5. Controlled Breathing Log
6. Daily Food Journal
7. Daily Mood Journal
8. Decrease-Increase-Modify-Exclude-Swap (DIMES)
9. Eating Habits and Portion Control
10. Gate Control Theory
11. My Goals
12. Pain Incidences Log
13. Pain Thoughts
14. Physical Activity Log
15. PMR Log
16. Sample Medication Treatment Agreement
17. Scheduled Activities Log
18. Short-Term Behavioral Goals
19. Understanding Pain Management
20. Pleasant Activities List
21. Ways to Increase Physical Activity
22. Worry Time Log

ABC Worksheet

In the ABC model, A stands for activating event. Activating events are things that happen to us or between us and other people. We may find them pleasant or stressful. B stands for beliefs about the event. Our beliefs affect how we feel and react in relation to an activating event. Finally, C stands for consequences. We experience emotional and behavioral consequences as a result of what we believe about activating events. Use this worksheet to document your activating events, your beliefs about them, and the resulting consequences.

Activating Event (A)	Beliefs (B)	Consequences (C)
		Emotional: Behavioral:
		Emotional: Behavioral:
		Emotional: Behavioral:
		Emotional: Behavioral:

Adapted from Otis, J.D. (2007). *Managing chronic pain: A cognitive-behavioral therapy approach workbook*. New York, NY: Oxford University Press.

310 Appendix B

Adjectives for Describing Pain

Throbbing	Knot-like	Squeezing
Burning	Tender	Pinching
Stinging	Raw	Pulsating
Intense	Radiating	Sore
Blinding	Waves	Drilling
Scalding	Quivering	Constant
Heavy	Dull	Tugging
Exhausting	Aching	Unbearable
Miserable	Tingling	Jolts
Piercing	Tight	Pulling
Tearing	Cold	Pressing
Electrical	Hot	Crushing
Pounding	Agonizing	Shooting
Pins & Needles	Cramping	Prickly
Penetrating	Intermittent	Cutting
Nagging	Itchy	Trigger-point
Nauseating	Excruciating	Widespread
Superficial	Deep	Gouging

Behavioral Triggers Worksheet

Behavior	Context (day, time, location, others, etc.)	I was doing:	I was thinking:	Others were doing:	My emotions:	My physical sensations:

Common Pain Myths

Many people believe the following myths about pain. Check off the beliefs you have about pain:

Myth	My Beliefs
The best treatment for pain is rest.	
Having pain means there is something wrong with me.	
Pain must be a sign of a serious illness or injury.	
I can only go on with my life if I am completely pain-free.	
My life is ruined because of pain.	
Pain makes it so that I cannot enjoy anything in life.	
Suggesting behavioral interventions means my doctor believes the pain is all in my head.	
My loved ones should understand how much pain I am in.	
As long as I have pain, I will be miserable.	
Only painkillers can decrease pain.	
Other:	
Other:	
Other:	
Other:	

Adapted from Hunter, C.L., Goodie, J.L., Oordt, M.S., & Dobmeyer, A.C. (2017). *Integrated behavioral health in primary care: Step-by-step guidance for assessment and intervention* (2nd ed.). Washington, DC.: American Psychological Association.

Controlled Breathing Log

Date	Time Spent in Controlled Breathing Practice	Distress Before (0–10)	Distress After (0–10)

Daily Food Journal

Date:_____

Meal	Food Eaten	Calories
Breakfast		
Mid-morning snack		
Lunch		
Mid-afternoon snack		
Dinner		
Other		

Total Calories:_____

314 Appendix B

Daily Mood Journal

Date:_____

Time	Mood Rating (0–10)	Comments
6 a.m.–8 a.m.		
8 a.m.–10 a.m.		
10 a.m.–12 p.m.		
12 p.m.–2 p.m.		
2 p.m.–4 p.m.		
4 p.m.–6 p.m.		
6 p.m.–8 p.m.		
8 p.m.–10 p.m.		
10 p.m.–12 a.m.		
12 a.m.–2 a.m.		
2 a.m.–4 a.m.		
4 a.m.–6 a.m.		

DIMES: Decrease – Increase – Modify – Exclude – Swap

Decrease: foods to decrease include foods that are less healthy but enjoyable as an occasional treat.

Increase: foods to increase are parts of a healthy diet like fruits and vegetables.

Modify: foods to modify are those you enjoy but could cut calories, e.g., still drinking coffee with cream but modifying by removing sugar.

Exclude: foods to exclude are those that are counter to your eating plan, like foods high in sugar and calories.

Swap: foods to swap are those that contribute too many calories, or little nutritional value, and can be swapped with better foods, e.g., swapping plain popcorn for potato chips as a snack.

Decrease:	Increase:
1.	1.
2.	2.
3.	3.
4.	4.
Modify:	Exclude:
1.	1.
2.	2.
3.	3.
4.	4.
Swap:	Notes:
1.	
2.	
3.	
4.	

Eating Habits and Portion Control

These are ways you can maintain eating habits to support your weight loss:

1. Concentrate on your food while eating. Do not eat while you are distracted, e.g., while watching television.
2. Schedule your meals.
3. Eat more slowly. Focus on savoring your food.
4. Do not eat foods directly from a container. Pour out a measured portion.
5. Read food labels and pay attention to calories, sugar, and serving sizes.
6. Do not keep snacks and tempting, unhealthy foods in your home.
7. Bring your own lunch to work to avoid eating out.
8. Eat light, healthy snacks between meals to avoid hunger and temptations.
9. Be aware of triggers that lead you to eat.
10. Avoid shopping for food when you are hungry.
11. When eating out, only eat half of your meal and take the rest home, or split a meal.

316 Appendix B

12. Be careful of foods and beverages with hidden calories and sugar, like soda, coffee drinks, energy drinks, alcoholic beverages, juice, salad dressings, and sauces.
13. Avoid foods with simple carbohydrates and empty calories, like bread, pretzels, etc.
14. Avoid diet foods and beverages.
15. Be careful with foods and beverages that seem healthy but are high in sugar and calories, like granola, protein shakes, granola and fitness bars, dried fruit, etc.
16. Measure foods by calorie content. For example, nuts are a healthy part of a diet but can quickly add calories.
17. Add healthy, low-calorie foods to your diet. For example, structuring your dinner so you are eating a large portion of vegetables, medium portion of protein, and small portion of complex carbohydrates.
18. Find substitutes for your favorite snacks. For example, salted popcorn with no butter can be a good alternative to potato chips.
19. Involve your family in preparing healthy meals.
20. Prepare all your meals at the beginning of the week to eat healthy on a busy schedule.

Medication Treatment Agreement (Sample)

Patient Name:_____   Date: _____

You are being given this agreement for your safety while you are prescribed opiate medications for treatment of pain. Opiates are narcotic medications that are meant to reduce pain. Unfortunately, these medications can be highly addictive and can lead to serious side effects during use, and when the patient ceases use. While opiate medications can be useful for reducing pain, their use must be carefully monitored to ensure patient safety. This document is an agreement between you and your medication provider, outlining your responsibilities as a patient. This document may be revisited or updated when need be.

I, _____, understand the following guidelines and that failure to adhere to them may result in termination of pain treatment by Dr. _____.

1. I understand that my responsibilities as a patient are the following:
   a. I will take my medications exactly as prescribed, both dose and frequency.

Treatment Handouts **317**

    b. I will not increase my dose, or take different medications, unless prescribed by my doctor.

    c. I will not request opiates or other medications from other doctors without informing my opiate-prescribing doctor.

    d. I will inform the doctor of all medications I take, including supplements.

    e. I will refrain from combining medications and alcohol with my opiate pain medication.

    f. I will disclose my use of other medications, alcohol, and other drugs to my doctor.

    g. I will fill all my prescriptions at one pharmacy, and understand that the doctor may consult with the pharmacy at any time.

    h. I will keep my prescriptions in a safe place where children cannot accidentally reach it and others cannot take it. If I lose my medication, I understand I will only receive one replacement prescription per year.

    i. I will not share my medication with anyone or take any medication that is not prescribed to me.

    j. I will not hoard my medications. If I do not finish a prescription, I will inform my doctor that I have extra medication left.

    k. I will take my medication exactly as prescribed. If I find I need more or less medication, or a different medication schedule, I will discuss this with my prescribing physician first.

    l. I will disclose any current or history of substance abuse or addiction.

    m. I agree to participating in psychological or psychiatric assessments if indicated by my doctor.

    n. I understand my doctor may ask for a random drug screen, if necessary. A drug screen tests urine or blood to determine which drugs and how much a person has been taking.

    o. I will keep all of my scheduled appointments. If I must cancel an appointment, I will do so with a minimum of 24 hours' notice and reschedule in a timely manner.

    p. If I want to stop taking my medication, I will do so with the help of my prescribing doctor, as withdrawal from these medications can be dangerous.

2. Emergency Policy – I understand that should I encounter an emergency regarding my medication, I will call my prescribing physician. If I visit another doctor, urgent care, or an emergency room, only three days of medications may be prescribed and I will sign a consent to release information from the facility to my prescribing physician. If I am experiencing an emergency and my prescribing doctor is not available, I will call 911.

318 Appendix B

3. I understand my doctor may stop prescribing me opiate medications in the case of the following:
   a. I do not show improvement from my pain medication.
   b. I do not use alternative strategies like exercise, etc.
   c. I do not comply with other orders, like seeing a counselor, etc.
   d. I share or sell my medication.
   e. I see multiple doctors, or visit emergency rooms, to obtain more medication.
   f. I refuse a drug screen, if one is prescribed.
   g. I do not comply with my follow-up appointments.
   h. My doctor suspects I am using other medications or substances that can be potentially harmful.
   i. My doctor suspects I am overusing or addicted to the medication.
   j. I am pregnant or breastfeeding.
4. If I have a substance use or addiction problem, I will not use any alcohol, illegal drugs, or drugs that are not prescribed for me. I understand I may be required to participate in certain programs to continue my pain medication prescription. These may include 12-step meetings, meeting with a sponsor, individual and/or group counseling, inpatient or outpatient treatment, an education session on safe use of opiate medication, and/or regular drug screening.
5. I have been provided with information about opiate medications and understand the following risks of these medications:
   a. Side effects while taking medication: drowsiness, nausea, confusion, fatigue, poor judgment, problems with balance or coordination, slowed reflexes, excessive sleeping, irritability, anger, depression, constipation. Constipation may become chronic and require other medications.
   b. You may develop tolerance, meaning you need higher doses to achieve the same effect. Tolerance is a risk factor for addiction.
   c. You may begin to feel dependent on your medication. For example, worrying about not taking medication can cause tension, increasing your pain, making you believe that you need the medication.
   d. You, or loved ones, may notice a change in your mood. You may experience more difficulty communicating with others.
   e. Side effects when stopping medication: especially if stopping abruptly, you will experience unpleasant withdrawal side effects when stopping opiate medication. These include, diarrhea, sweating, nausea and vomiting, difficulty sleeping, temporary increase in dreams or

nightmares, goosebumps or chills, shaking, nervousness, rapid heart rate. In some cases, especially with underlying medical conditions, withdrawal from opiate medications can be dangerous or deadly. This should only be done with the help of the prescribing doctor.

    f.   Side effects of opiate medications are increased when these medications are combined with alcohol, illegal drugs, other opiates, or certain prescriptions. Because opiates slow breathing, combination with these other substances can be deadly.

6. Recommendations:

    a.   Keep a structured schedule of your medications, time of administration, and dosages. This may be done in a journal so you can reference it.

    b.   Use a medication box that lets you divide medication into the days you will take it. This will help you remember if you have taken your medication for that day.

    c.   Keep your medication safe. If you must take some with you, take only what you need to avoid losing medication. Keep medication out of reach of children and anyone that may take it. Do not offer to share your medication, even if someone you love is in extreme pain. Taking medications not prescribed for you can be dangerous. If someone needs pain medication, they must visit a doctor, urgent care center, or emergency room.

7. Your rights: as a patient you have several rights:

    a.   You may request counseling for you or your loved ones. Your doctor will provide a referral.

    b.   You have the right to ask questions about your medication in order to know how your doctor makes decisions about your prescription and why.

    c.   You have the right to terminate treatment with this doctor and switch to a new prescribing physician, at which point your prescriptions from this doctor will end and you will be asked to sign a release of information so records can be sent to the new doctor.

    d.   You have the right to refuse prescription opiate medication and discuss alternate pain management methods with your doctor.

    e.   You have right to information about opiate medications, how they work, and the pros and cons of using them.

    f.   You have the right to voice your concerns to your prescribing doctor.

320 Appendix B

I have read this document and fully understand the risks of opiate medications, as well as my rights and responsibilities as a patient. I have had all of my questions answered and understand the rules for my treatment, as outlined. I understand that I may be asked to sign this document again, in the future, and that recommendations can be modified based on my compliance as a patient. By signing this document, I affirm I understand what the document states and agree to the terms and conditions of treatment with opiate medications. This document will be kept in my confidential patient file.

Patient signature	Date	Physician signature	Date

My Goals

My Goal	Steps to Take to Achieve My Goal	How I Will Know I Achieved My Goal
	1. 2. 3.	1. 2. 3.
	1. 2. 3.	1. 2. 3.

Treatment Handouts   **321**

Pain Incidences Log

Date	Time of Day	Location of Pain	Pain Quality (e.g., throbbing, stabbing, burning)	Pain Intensity (0–10)	Duration of Pain Episode	Triggering Event

Managing Your Thoughts About Pain

Many people have negative thoughts about pain that make pain more difficult to manage. It is helpful to replace these statements with ones that are more accurate and positive. What are some of your negative thoughts about pain?

Negative Thought	Replacement Thought
I can't stand this pain; it's unbearable.	I can stand it. I can get through this.
My life is ruined because of this pain.	I can still enjoy many things in my life, even with pain.
There's nothing I can do about this pain.	There are things I can do to manage my pain.

322 Appendix B

Negative Thought	Replacement Thought

Physical Activity Log

Date	Activities	Duration	Intensity (low, medium, high)	Total Steps Taken

Pleasant Activities List

- Reading
- Taking a walk
- Taking a bath
- Watching the clouds
- Calling a friend
- Enjoying a coffee or tea
- Painting
- Coloring book
- Breathing exercise
- Riding a bicycle
- Tidying a space
- Hobbies
- Listening to music
- Volunteering
- Entertaining
- Planning a vacation or date
- Arranging flowers
- Going camping
- Going somewhere new
- Window shopping
- Going to a museum
- Sightseeing
- Singing
- Cooking
- Photography
- Playing with a pet
- Journaling
- Going to an aquarium
- Playing cards
- Playing sports
- Watching sports
- Watching live music
- Rearranging a room
- Making crafts
- Completing a puzzle
- Gardening
- Taking a shower

324 Appendix B

- Exploring the outdoors
- Going boating
- Listening to a friend
- Throwing a party
- Getting hair or nails done
- Getting a massage
- Learning a new skill
- Visiting friends
- Birdwatching
- Smelling flowers
- Trying a new recipe
- Going to a garage sale
- Going to the beach
- Looking at the stars
- Taking an exercise class
- Yoga
- Meditation
- Taking a meditation class
- At-home spa day
- Going out to eat
- Shopping for gifts
- Crafting
- Collecting
- People watching
- Taking a walk with a friend
- Going skiing or sledding
- Baking something
- Hiking
- Going kayaking or canoeing
- Taking an art class
- Playing games
- Watching a movie or show
- Playing video games
- Going to the library
- Having a quiet morning
- Going to a comedy show
- Writing a card to a loved one
- Going to an amusement park
- Having a lunch date
- Taking pictures

- Making videos
- Going to church, temple, etc.
- Praying
- Doing crossword puzzles, sudoku
- Playing a musical instrument

Progressive Muscle Relaxation Log

Date	Time	Distress Before (0–10)	Distress After (0–10)	Comments

326 Appendix B

Date	Time	Distress Before (0–10)	Distress After (0–10)	Comments

Scheduled Activities Log

Date	Activity	Duration	Level of Completion (0–10)	Level of Enjoyment (0–10)

Short-Term Behavioral Goals

Week: __ / __ / ____ – __ / __ / ___

My Behavioral Goals This Week :

Understanding Pain Management

Factors can help you reduce and manage your pain

Stay physically active.
Keep muscles toned.
Use stress management techniques.
Schedule time to relax.
Practice mindfulness.
Manage negative and stressful thoughts about pain.
Participate in enjoyable activities.
Do not neglect chores and important activities.
Stay active without overexerting yourself.
Take medications as prescribed.
Communicate your needs to loved ones.
Maintain an active social life.
Build a social support system.

Adapted from Hunter, C.L., Goodie, J.L., Oordt, M.S., & Dobmeyer, A.C. (2017). *Integrated behavioral health in primary care: Step-by-step guidance for assessment and intervention* (2nd ed.). Washington, DC: American Psychological Association.

328 Appendix B

Ways to Increase Physical Activity

1. Walking around your neighborhood or walking your dog.
2. Exercise like running, jogging, lifting weights, aerobic exercises.
3. Going to a yoga class.
4. Taking the stairs instead of the elevator or escalator.
5. Parking far away from where you are going.
6. Walking quickly around the mall.
7. Taking a fitness class.
8. Signing up for a specialized fitness program.
9. Joining a fitness group, like a running club or 5k training group.
10. Signing up for a fitness challenge with a friend.

Worry Time Log

Date	Time	Time Spent Worrying	Comments

Date	Time	Time Spent Worrying	Comments

Index

Note: Page numbers in **bold** denote tables.

ABC model, 36, 37; for diabetes, 267; worksheet, 309; *see also* behavioral self-analysis

activity log, 30, 255; for depression, 137–138, 140, 143; physical activity log, 322

acute emotional distress, 154–155; *see also* anxiety

adaptive patterns, 79, 101, 103–104, 105, 107, 115, 121, 160, 242, 268; *see also* pattern-focused therapy

addictions, 54, 55, 80, 191, 208, 232, 317, 318; *see also* medication misuse

adherence to treatment plans, and goal setting, 50

adolescents, 39, 52, 60, 86

African Americans, 86–87

aggression, problem-solving training for, 60

alcohol, 186, 216, 263; medication with, 82, 97, 186, 216

alcohol use disorder, 46, 55–56, 65

American Psychological Association, 17, 101

anger, problem-solving training for, 60

antisocial behaviors, problem-solving training for, 60

anxiety, 115, 118; assertive communication, 26; behavioral rehearsal, 180; behavioral

self-analysis, 37; case example, 162–182; cognitive defusion, 44; cognitive disputation, 41; combined medication treatment, 160–161, 175; controlled breathing, 39, 159, 165, 173; diagnostic assessment, 155; distress tolerance, 46, 159; functional assessment, 155–157, **156–157**, 162–163; generalized anxiety disorder (GAD) (*see* generalized anxiety disorder (GAD)); and mindfulness, 57; and obesity, 236; overview, 152–153; panic disorder, 153–154; pattern-focused therapy, 160, 176–182; problem-solving training, 60; progress monitoring, 161; psychoeducation about, 160, 166; record keeping, 161, 168, 173, 175, 181–182; relaxation training, 66; risk assessment, 158; screening instruments, 158; thought stopping, 159, 165, 173

assertive communication, 14; for anxiety, 160; application method, 27–28; definition, **23**, 26; example, 28; indications, **25**, 26; objectives, 26

assessment, 73; and case conceptualization, 93; case example, 95–97; compliance, 79–80, **81–82**; cultural assessment, 84, 86–88, 94;

diagnostic evaluation, 76; functional assessment (*see* functional assessment); of goals, 88–89, 94; information gathering, 90–91; of medication misuse, 80–84; medication misuse assessment, **83**; noncompliance, 94; pattern identification, 79, 93–94; and progress monitoring, 89, **90**, 94, 102; provider demeanor and interview qualities, 91; risk assessment, **85–86**, 94; screening instruments, 91, **92**, 94; and treatment planning, 92

asthma attacks, relaxation training for, 66

autism spectrum disorders, assertive communication for, 26

avoidant pattern, 29–30, 79; behavioral activity, 29; in depression, 140, 146, 150

avoidant personality style, 109; in depression, 134–135, 136, 143

backup activity, 30, 31, 110, 114, 128

behavioral activation, 14, 109–110, 113, 121; application method, 30–31; definition, **23**, 29; for depression, 128, 136, 138, 143; example, 31; indications, **25**, 29; objectives, 29

behavioral experiments: application method, 32–34; definition, **23**, 32; indications, **25**, 32; objectives, 32

behavioral health clinicians, 12

behavioral health consultant (BHC), 12, 13; a day in integrated care setting, 15–16; job description and intervention competencies, 13–14

behavioral rehearsal, 27; for anxiety and trauma, 180; application method, 35–36; definition, **23**, 34; example, 35–36; indications, **25**, 34–35; objectives, 34

behavioral self-analysis, 14; application method, 37–38; definition, **23**, 36; example, 38; indications, **25**, 37; objectives, 36

behavioral triggers worksheet, 310

beliefs, 32; collectivistic belief systems, 126; maladaptive and irrational, 40–41, 64; negative beliefs, 32

benzodiazepines, 86, 186

billing codes, 1, 9–10

binge eating disorder, 236, 238, 259; *see also* weight management issues

biopsychosocial therapy, 102, 103

body dysmorphic disorder, thought stopping for, 71

Body Mass Index (BMI), 235, 236, 239

borderline intellectual functioning: cognitive disputation, 41; habit reversal, 52

breathing *see* controlled breathing

bulimia, 238; *see also* weight management issues

bullying, assertive communication for, 26

caffeine, 216, 217

case conceptualization, and assessment, 93

Centers for Disease Control and Prevention (CDC), 235–236, 261–262

Centers for Medicare and Medicaid Services, 9

challenges, for mental health professionals, 1, 7

chronic pain: adjectives for describing pain, 310; case example, 193–209; controlled breathing, 39; environmental factors, 185; functional assessment of, 186, **187–189**; and medical misuse, 80, 82; medication contract, 191–192; medication misuse assessment, 186; mindfulness, 57; myths, 311; overview, 184–185; pattern-focused therapy, 191, 202–206; psychoeducation about, 190–191, 198; psychological factors, 184–185; record keeping, 192, 198, 201–202, 206, 209; relaxation training, 66; risk assessment, 187; screening instrument, 189

client strengths, 74–75

clinical outcomes measurement, 102

closed-ended questions, 90, 186

Cognitive Behavioral Analysis System of Psychotherapy (CBASP), 101, 102, 104

cognitive behavioral approaches, 8

cognitive behavioral therapy (CBT), 19, 101, 218

332 Index

cognitive defusion: application method, 44–45; definition, **23**, 43; example, 44–45; indications, **25**, 44; objectives, 43

cognitive disputation: application method, 41–43; definition, **23**, 40; example, 42–43; indications, **25**, 41; objectives, 40–41

cognitive restructuring, 39

collectivistic belief systems, 126

co-located model, 13

Columbia Suicide Severity Rating Scale (C-SSRS), 84, 127, 294–298; and depression, 128

communication: types of, 26; *see also* assertive communication

competence, 2; personal and interpersonal, 101; in providing evidence-based interventions, 1

competing behavior, 52

compliance, 79–80

compulsive behaviors, 51–52

controlled breathing, 14; for anxiety and trauma, 159, 165, 173; application method, 39–40; definition, **23**, 38; example, 39–40; indications, **25**, 39; log, 312; objectives, 38–39

coordinated model, 13

critical thinking, 16

cultural assessment, 84, 86–88, 94

current opioid misuse measure (COMM), 84, 189, 299

Current Procedural Terminology (CPT) codes for billing, 1, 9–10

daily food journal, 313

daily mood journal, 314

deep breathing techniques, 66

dementia, cognitive disputation for, 41

dependent personality style, 165, 246

depression, 61–62; assertive communication, 26; behavioral activation, 128; behavioral self-analysis, 37; behavioral activity, 29; case example, 132–150; cognitive defusion, 44; cognitive disputation, 41; diagnostic evaluation, 126–127; distress tolerance, 46; functional assessment, 127, **129–130**; and obesity, 236; pattern-focused

therapy, 131, 140–141, 146–150; problem-solving training, 60; progress monitoring, 131–132; psychoeducation about, 130–131, 136; push-button technique, 62; record keeping, 132, 139, 143, 146, 150; referral for medication evaluation, 131; risk assessment, 127; screening instruments, 127–128, 132; symptoms, 125–126; thought stopping, 71

diabetes, 269–290; ABC model, 267; behavioral factors, 263; cognitive factors, 263; emotional factors, 263; environmental factors, 263; functional assessment, 263, **264–265**; goal setting, 266, 279; motivational interviewing, 266; overview, 261–262; pattern-focused therapy, 267–268, 286–290; psychoeducation about, 266; record keeping, 268, 275, 280–281, 285, 290; screening instruments, 263–265; self-monitoring, 267; stimulus control, 267

Diabetes Distress Scale (DDS), 263, 265, 266, 299–301, 305–306

Diagnostic and Statistical Manual (DSM-5), 127

diagnostic evaluation, 13, 15, 74, 76, 93–94

diaphragmatic breathing, 38, 166

dietician/nutritionist, 13

DIMES (decrease, increase, modify, exclude, swap) handouts, 214–215, 241

distraction techniques, 45, 47

distress tolerance training: for anxiety and trauma, 159; application method, 46; definition, **23**, 45; example, 46; indications, **25**, 46; objectives, 45

distressing thoughts, acceptance of, 43

drug abuse screening test (DAST), 215, 299

eating behavior, 236, 238–239, 240, 252

eating disorders: assertive communication, 26; cognitive defusion, 44; cognitive disputation, 41; distress tolerance, 46; mindfulness, 57; relapse prevention, 64

eating habits and portion control, 315–316

economy, 8

emotional factors, 75

Index **333**

emotional first aid, 14; application method, 48–49; definition, **23**, 47; example, 48–49; indications, **25**, 47; objectives, 47

emotive imagery, 67

employment, 2, 7

evidence-based practice (EBP), 8; anti-empirical research bias and antipathy towards, 18; elements, 17; and ethics, 17; implications, 18; in integrated care, 16–17; origin of, 17; process of, 18

evidence-based psychotherapy, 9

evidence-based treatment, 8

exercise, goal setting for, 50

external evidence, 17

eye contact, 111–112, 115, 116–117, 121

failure, emotional first aid for, 47

family(ies), 87, 94; and compliance, 80

fear, definition of, 153; *see also* anxiety

feelings chart, 27

forecast scenarios, predictions on, 8

fully integrated model, 13

functional assessment, 74–76, **77**, 93; of anxiety, 155–157, **156–157**, 162–163; of chronic pain, 186, **187–189**; of depression, 127, **129–130**; of diabetes, 263, **264–265**; of insomnia, 212, **213–214**; of medication misuse, **187–189**; of weight management issues, 236, **237–238**

gate control theory of pain, 184–185, 190–191, 196

generalized anxiety disorder (GAD), 153, 165; functional assessment, 156; screening instruments, 155; thought stopping for, 71; *see also* anxiety

Generalized Anxiety Disorder-7 (CAD-7), 156, 158, 302

goal setting: application method, 50–51; definition, **24**, 49; for diabetes, 266, 279; example, 50–51; indications, **25**, 50; objectives, 49–50; for weight management issues, 240–241

goals, 320; assessment of, 88–89, 94; collaborative, 88; long-and short-term,

88; mental health services in primary care settings, 13; response to, 88–89; specific *versus* vague, 88

guided imagery, 39, 67

guilt, emotional first aid for, 47

habit reversal, 14; application method, 52–54; awareness stage, 52; competing response stage, 52; definition, **24**, 51; example, 53–54; indications, **25**, 52; motivation stage, 52; objectives, 51–52; skill generalization stage, 52

hair-pulling disorder, habit reversal for, 52

harm reduction: application method, 55–56; definition, **24**, 54; example, 55–56; indications, **25**, 55; objectives, 54–55

headaches, controlled breathing for, 39

homework assignment, for clients, 27, 42, 58, 109

hydrocodone, 185

hyperactivity, relaxation training for, 66

illicit drugs, 186; *see also* medication misuse

imagery-based relaxation, 66, 67

impulse control disorders, cognitive defusion for, 44

impulsivity, problem-solving training for, 60

innovation, 8

insomnia: case example, 219–233; combined medication treatment, 218; controlled breathing, 39; medication misuse assessment, 215; overview, 211–212; pattern-focused therapy, 217–218, 226–230; progress monitoring, 218; progressive muscle relaxation, 216; psychoeducation about, 216; record keeping, 218–219, 224, 226, 230, 232–233; relaxation training, 66; screening instruments, 215; types, 211–212

Insomnia Severity Index (ISI), 215, 218, 303

integrated care, 8, 11–12, 13; continuum of services, 13; a day of a mental health clinician, 15–16; evidence-based practice, 16–18; need for, 12; team, 13; ultra-brief interventions, 18–19

334 Index

intellectual disability: cognitive disputation, 41; habit reversal, 52
internal evidence, 17
internet programs, 8
interpersonal skills development, assertive communication for, 26
irrational beliefs, 40–41, 64

Jungian therapy, 8

language, 43, 44
limited cognitive capacity, cognitive disputation for, 41
loneliness, emotional first aid for, 47
loss, emotional first aid for, 47

major depressive disorder, 136, 143; symptoms, 125–126; *see also* depression
maladaptive patterns, 79, 100–101, 103–105, 107, 110, 115, 121, 140, 150, 241, 267; *see also* pattern-focused therapy
marital distress, cognitive disputation for, 41
MAs, 13
master's degree practitioners, 8
Medicaid, 9
medical conditions, behavioral self-analysis, 37
Medicare, 9
medication evaluation: for depression, 145–146
medication management, goal setting for, 50
medication misuse, 86, 94, 185–186; chronic pain assessment, 186; high-risk behaviors, 82; improper handling, 82; improper use, 82; medication-seeking behaviors, 82; screening instruments, 189
medication misuse assessment, 80–84, **83**; insomnia, 215
medication treatment agreement, 316–320
mental health services: in integrated settings, benefits of, 13; need in primary care settings, **12**
migraine headaches, relaxation training for, 66

mindfulness, 8, 14; application method, 57–58; definition, **24**, 56; example, 58; indications, **25**, 57; objectives, 57
mood disorders, mindfulness for, 57
mood scale, 89; for depression, 128, 138, 141, 143
mood state, assertive communication for, 26
morphine, 80
motivation, and goals, 89
motivational interviewing (MI), 14, 91, 92, 102; for diabetes, 266; for weight management issues, 236, 240
multicultural approach, 8
muscle relaxation exercise, for insomnia, 216, 225–226

nail biting, habit reversal for, 52
narcotics, 185
negative beliefs, behavioral experiments for, 32
negative cognitions, and diabetes, 266
negative emotional states, emotional first aid for, 47
new diversity, 9
new model of mental health practice, 8
nicotine, 216
noncompliance assessment, 79–80, **81**, 94
nonverbal communication strategies, 27

OARS skill, motivational interviewing, 240, 266
obesity *see* weight management issues
observation, 103
obsessive thoughts, 70
obsessive-compulsive personality style, 194, 222
open-ended questions, 90
opioids, 80, 86, 94, 185–186; COMM (*see* Current Opioid Misuse Measure (COMM))
oral-digital habits, habit reversal for, 52
outcomes assessment, 10–11, 102
overeating, relapse prevention, 64
oxycodone, 185

paced respiration, 38–39
pain: gate control theory, 184–185, 190–191, 196; management, 327;

Index **335**

managing thoughts about, 321–322; misconceptions about, 191; pain incidences log, 321; and suffering, difference between, 190; *see also* chronic pain

panic disorder, 153–154, 165; controlled breathing, 39; functional assessment, 156; thought stopping, 71

Patient Health Questionnaire-9 (PHQ-9), 126, 303–304; for depression, 127–128, 132

pattern-focused therapy: adaptive patterns (*see* adaptive patterns); anxiety and trauma, 160, 176–182; case example, 108–121; chronic pain, 191, 202–206; clinical value, 101; for depression, 131, 140–141, 146–150; diabetes, 267–268, 286–290; for insomnia, 217–218, 226–230; maladaptive patterns (*see* maladaptive patterns); origins, 101–102; overview, 100–101; pattern identification, 79, 93–94, 103–104; pattern shifting, 104, 115; patterns, 103, 105; premises, 104; query sequence, 106; therapeutic relationship, 105–106; therapeutic strategy, 105, 107; treatment process, 106; weight management issues, 241–243, 254–259

PCL-5 PTSD checklist, 158, 303

PEG Pain Scale, 95, 186, 189, 192, 303

persistent depressive disorder, 126; *see also* depression

personality disorders, 101; distress tolerance, 46; mindfulness, 57

personality style, 103–104, 243; and obesity, 238, 241

phobias, relaxation training for, 66

physical activity, 241; log, 322; suggestions for, 328

physical factors, 75

pleasant activities list, 323–325

posttraumatic stress disorder (PTSD), 154, 155; risk assessment, 158; screening instrument, 158; *see also* anxiety

prediction for mental health practice, 8–9, 11

primary care providers (PCP), 13

problem-solving training: application method, 60–61; definition, **24**, 59; example, 60–61; indications, **25**, 60; objectives, 59

prognostications, 8

progress monitoring, 89, 94, 102; for anxiety and trauma, 161; for chronic pain, 192; for depression, 131–132, 143–145; for diabetes, 268; tools for, **90**; for weight loss, 243

progressive muscle relaxation, 39, 66, 67; for insomnia, 216, 225–226; log, 325–326

psychoanalysis, classical, 8

psychoeducation: about anxiety, 160, 166; about chronic pain, 190–191, 198; about depression, 130–131, 136; about diabetes, 266; about insomnia, 216; about weight management, 241, **242**

psychological assessment, 1–2, 7, 103

psychopharmacotherapy, 8

psychosis, cognitive disputation for, 41

psychotherapist background, predictions on, 8

psychotherapy practice, shifts in, 1, 7

push-button technique: application method, 62–63; definition, **24**, 61; example, 62–63; indications, **25**, 62; objectives, 61–62

radical acceptance skills, 45

rapid breathing, 38

rational emotive behavior therapy (REBT), 41

record keeping: for anxiety and trauma, 161, 168, 173, 175, 181–182; for depression, 132, 139, 143, 146, 150; for diabetes, 268, 275, 280–281, 285, 290; for insomnia, 218–219, 224, 226, 230, 232–233; for weight management, 243, 249, 252, 254, 259

reform in health and mental health care, need for, 2

reimbursement, 2, 7

rejection, emotional first aid for, 47

relapse prevention: application method, 64–65; definition, **24**, 63; example, 65; indications, **25**, 64; objectives, 63–64

336 Index

relational problems, problem-solving training for, 60
relationship-fostering intervention, 8
relationships, goal setting for, 50
relaxation training: application method, 66–67; definition, **24**, 65; example, 67; indications, **25**, 66; objectives, 66
research-based policy, 2
risk assessment, 84, **85–86**, 94; chronic pain, 187
RNs, 13
role-plays, 27, 34, 35, 120
rumination, emotional first aid for, 47

scheduled activities log, 326
scratching, habit reversal, 52
screening instruments, 91, **92**, 94, 293–306; Body Mass Index (BMI), 235, 236, 239; Columbia Suicide Severity Rating Scale (C-SSRS), 84, 127, 128, 294–298; current opioid misuse measure (COMM), 84, 189, 299; Diabetes Distress Scale (DDS), 263, 265, 266, 299–301, 305–306; drug abuse screening test (DAST), 215, 299; Generalized Anxiety Disorder-7 (CAD-7), 156, 158, 302; Insomnia Severity Index (ISI), 215, 218, 303; mood scale, 89, 128, 138, 141, 143; Patient Health Questionnaire-9 (PHQ-9), 126, 127–128, 132, 303–304; PCL-5 PTSD checklist, 158, 303; PEG Pain Scale, 95, 186, 189, 192, 303; Weight-Related Eating Questionnaire (WREQ), 236, 239, 243, 305
self-change interventions, 8
self-compassion, 47
self-defeating behaviors, 48
self-efficacy, 266
self-esteem, assertive communication for, 26
self-harm, 84; relapse prevention, 64; through drug overdose, 186; *see also* suicidal ideation
self-monitoring, 14; diabetes, 267
self-reports, 89, 218
self-soothing skills, 45; for anxiety and trauma, 159

self-talk management, 47, 201
session duration, 9–10
shallow breathing, 38, 166
short-term behavioral goals, 327
short-term therapy, 7
skill-building interventions, 8
skin-picking disorder, habit reversal for, 52
sleep apnea, 211
sleep hygiene, 216, **217**
sleep problems *see* insomnia
smoking: cessation, goal setting for, 50; relapse prevention, 64
SOAP note: anxiety and trauma, 161, 168, 173, 175, 181–182; chronic pain, 192, 198, 201–202, 206, 209; depression, 132, 139, 143, 146, 150; diabetes, 268, 275, 280–281, 285, 290; insomnia, 218–219, 224, 226, 230, 232–233; weight management issues, 243, 249, 252, 254, 259
sobriety, 63
social anxiety disorder, 109; problem-solving training, 60
social factors, 75
social skill deficits, 34–35; behavioral rehearsal, 34
Socratic questioning, 41
somatic symptoms, 87, **88**, 94
specialized mental health settings, 1, 2, 18
statistics and research method courses, 16
stimulus control, 14, **217**; application method, 69–70; definition, **24**, 68; for diabetes, 267; example, 69–70; indications, **25**, 69; for insomnia, 216; objectives, 68
stress: assertive communication, 26; controlled breathing, 39
stuttering, habit reversal for, 52
Subjective Units of Distress Scale (SUDS), 89, 157, 160
substance abuse: assertive communication, 26; cognitive defusion, 44; cognitive disputation, 41; mindfulness, 57; relapse prevention, 64
substance misuse, 215; *see also* medication misuse

Index 337

substance use disorders, 54; distress tolerance, 46; impacts of, 2
suicidal ideation, 94; active ideation, 84; and chronic pain, 187; and depression, 127; passive ideation, 84; risk assessment, 84

technology, 8, 9; and interventions, 8; and outcome measures, 10–11
teeth grinding, habit reversal, 52
telephone therapy, 8
telepsychology, 8
theoretical orientations, predictions on, 8
therapeutic interventions, predictions on, 8
therapeutic relationship, in pattern-focused therapy, 105–106
therapy formats, predictions on, 8
thought stopping, 15; for anxiety and trauma, 159, 165, 171, 173; application method, 71–72; definition, **24**, 70; example, 71–72; indications, **25**, 71; objectives, 70–71
tic disorders, habit reversal, 52
tobacco use, thought stopping for, 71
transactional analysis, 8
treatment adherence, strategies for improvement of, 15

treatment duration, 9–10
treatment instruments, 308–329
treatment nonadherence, 12
treatment planning, and assessment, 92

ultra-brief interventions, 2, 7, 14, 18–19; definitions, **23–24**; protocols, 19; *see also specific interventions*
US Department of Defense, 185

verbal and nonverbal behaviors, 34

weight management issues, 259–260; case example, 244–259; contributing factors assessment, 238–239; diagnostic assessment, 238; functional assessment, 236, **237–238**; goal setting, 50, 240–245; motivational interviewing (MI), 240; overview, 235–236; pattern-focused therapy, 241–243, 254–259; personality factors, 241; progress monitoring for weight loss, 243; psychoeducation about, 241, **242**; record keeping, 243, 249, 252, 254, 259; screening instruments, 239
Weight-Related Eating Questionnaire (WREQ), 236, 239, 243, 305
worry time log, 328–329

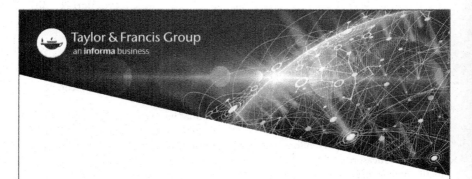